The Pudding Book

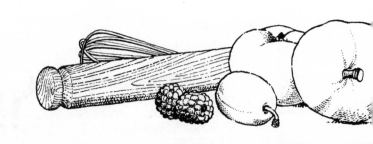

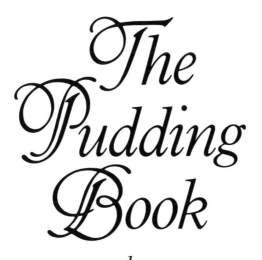

The Pudding Book

by

Helen Thomas

Decorations by Kate Simunek

Hutchinson

London Melbourne Sydney Auckland Johannesburg

Hutchinson & Co. (Publishers) Ltd

An imprint of the Hutchinson Publishing Group

3 Fitzroy Square, London W1P 6JD

Hutchinson Group (Australia) Pty Ltd
30–32 Cremorne Street, Richmond South, Victoria 3121
PO Box 151, Broadway, New South Wales 2007

Hutchinson Group (NZ) Ltd
32–34 View Road, PO Box 40–086, Glenfield, Auckland 10

Hutchinson Group (SA) (Pty) Ltd
PO Box 337, Bergvlei 2012, South Africa

First published 1980

Set in VIP Plantin

Set, printed and bound in Great Britain by
Fakenham Press Limited, Fakenham, Norfolk

ISBN 09 140760 5

Contents

Acknowledgements

I am indebted to the following:

Barbara O'Neill
Claire Holleley
Philippa Thomas
Sue Krisman
Angela and Peter Sealey
Antonia Bifulco
Angela Bifulco
Halina Oltarzewska
Margot Holleley
Barbara Vowles
Deirdre Burrell
Pam Wentworth
Gillian van der Meer
Pam Bagnall

Introduction

The first pudding I ever made was a mixture of powdered milk, dried egg, water, cornflour, cocoa and saccharin. This required beating with a wire whisk until my ten-year-old arms ached, when it would grudgingly congeal into a spongy mass. Gleefully I would spoon into dishes what little I had not spun high on to the kitchen walls and felt a blow had been struck for gastronomy, for there was a war on and a pudding course was a challenge.

A lot of water has passed under the bridge since then. I have weaned my own children on to apple purée, steered them away from iced lollies and introduced them to Tipsy Cake and Crème Brûlée. Now I get frantic phone calls as they prepare to entertain their own friends saying, 'How did you used to make that Convent Cream?', 'Why does my meringue go all sticky?' I am convinced that the tradition of adventurous cooking runs right from one generation to the next. My paternal grandmother had seven children, so her meals were always on a memorably epic scale and my maternal grandmother was a cook of rare finesse. I remember vividly the little copper pan in which she made bread sauce and the way the clovey-onion smell of it would pervade her house. My own mother fed five hungry children all through the war and later showed herself capable of staging elegant dinner parties as well as producing delicious nursery food for an ever growing number of grandchildren.

So – my appetite was already whetted by the time I went off to spend a year in France as a student. There I discovered that food does not have to be elaborate to be excellent. I lodged in a state-run boarding school for country children from a large area. The catering for the 200 of us who lived there was done by one French cook assisted by a hard-working Spanish couple. She was a formidable figure, built for comfort, not for speed, dressed unfailingly in black, who would come into the teachers' dining room at the end of each meal, remove her steel spectacles, mop her face with a tea towel and ask, hands on hips, '*Alors, m'sieurs, dames, – ça va?*' I was left quite speechless by the variety of her menus but it is the simplest things which stick in my mind – the noodles turned in garlicky beef juices, the radishes with butter, olives and fresh bread, the branch of ripe peaches she laid across the table for dessert.

I am cheered by the amount of really good cooking that is going on in this country especially among the much-travelled young. There is a nostalgic return to handsome and functional kitchen equipment and a gastronomic adventurousness which was certainly not typical of any post-war generation. Perhaps cooking in Britain is heading for a renaissance.

All of a sudden, though, my house has got too big and my collection of recipes stands reproachfully on the shelf, so I have used the lull to sort out the best of my pudding recipes and put them together in the hope that they will give some ideas to other people. An interesting pudding completes a good meal. I always feel vaguely disappointed to be offered only cheese or fruit and when I go to a restaurant I make a bee line for the pudding which is new to me or which I know someone has worked to produce.

The range and versatility of British puddings are the best in the world. There are always plenty to suit both the menu and the budget. Take, for instance, the classic Queen of Puddings. Using only things which are almost always available in any kitchen – milk, bread, jam, sugar, eggs – with a little time you can concoct a delicious pudding to be eaten hot or cold and one which lends itself to an assortment of flavourings and can be dressed up or down to suit the occasion.

Many of our more elegant recipes were originally French, of course, but the French, whose gastronomy otherwise is second to none, seem to have given up on puddings. Only a few years back the French housewife would offer various fruit/batter concoctions or the odd poached pear floating palely in a cream sauce. Today they seem reduced to cheese and fruit or get seduced by the excellence of the local pâtisserie and invest all in a glossy fruit tart. We have no such temptation. If we want good puddings and tarts then we must make them and they are not difficult nowadays with all the beating, mixing, freezing and thermostatically controlled cooking equipment which so many kitchens have.

In this book you can pick and choose from the best I have found. I have used them all at one time or another on a long-suffering family. There are plenty of everyday recipes (and there is a checklist on p. 230 of 'any-time' puddings for which the ingredients are nearly always to hand) as well as more extravagant desserts for grander occasions. There are heart-warming puddings for cold winter days and light-as-air confections to whip up for summer evenings. There is also an extra index with suggestions for using up some of the things like egg whites which sometimes get left over and sit sadly in the fridge for days.

For convenience the metric conversion used is on the scale of 25 grams to 1 ounce and 6 decilitres to 1 pint. These metric measures are very slightly less than the corresponding imperial measures so your puddings will turn out marginally smaller on the metric scale.

I have dedicated *The Pudding Book* to my aunt – Lena Chronnell – as she was an important culinary influence in the impressionable years of my childhood. She and her children used to spend holidays with us in a rambling old house right on the sea shore in Anglesey. The kitchen was enormous but primitive, with a pump to raise the water – at which we all took our daily turn – and a cooker run on paraffin. She is a trained domestic scientist and, with her encouragement, I laboured in that kitchen over my first pudding. I well remember scraping away for hours at a mountain of new potatoes judged high enough to satisfy the sea-sharpened appetites of the twelve of us who were staying there. When they were eventually done she ran a prac-tised eye over them and said, 'Your potatoes have a finished air.' (So, I feel, did I, but the tribute has outlasted the fatigue.) She has a talent for vivid verbal description and all through the war she would regale us children with mouth-watering descriptions of the Florentines and Rum Babas we would make once rationing had ended. I feel much indebted to her.

To my aunt
HELENA CHRONNELL

Fruit Puddings

No apologies are made for the fact that this first chapter, despite ruthless pruning, is bursting at the seams. There is something irrefutably right about ending a meal with 'the precious fruits of the earth brought forth by the sun' and this does not mean a desiccated orange on a bare plate but, ideally, a dish to bring out the best in the fruit. No cook can resist the challenge presented by a mound of shining scarlet currants or a dewy heap of raspberries. It is difficult to imagine that anything which looks so wholesome can possibly harm our weight, our digestion or our cholesterol level.

Apple and Lemon Crisp

Child's play to start with. Nothing can go wrong. It only takes minutes to make and tastes good. Any crumbly, stale biscuits will do.

2 large cooking apples	4 oz (100 g) biscuits
sugar to taste	2 oz (50 g) margarine
1 lemon	

Peel, core and slice the apples and stew them with the grated lemon rind and a little water until soft. Stir in the juice of the lemon and sweeten to taste. Spread in a dish and leave to cool. Crush the biscuits in a polythene bag, with a rolling pin. Melt the margarine, mix into the biscuit crumbs and spread over the apples. Serve cold. *Serves 4.*

Apple and Blackberry Crumble

The basic recipe for a fruit crumble which may, of course, be made with any fruit. Crunchy and wholesome made with brown sugar and wholemeal flour.

12 oz (325 g) cooking apples	2 oz (50 g) margarine
4 oz (100 g) blackberries	2 oz (50 g) sugar
2 tablespoons golden syrup	4 oz (100 g) flour

Peel, core and slice the apples and place them with the blackberries and syrup in a buttered fireproof dish. Rub the margarine, sugar and flour together until crumbly and strew over the fruit spreading it right to the edge of the dish. Bake at Gas Mark 7 (425 °F, 220 °C) for about 30 minutes. Serve hot or cold with cream or Custard (p. 209). *Serves 4.*

Apple Betty

An old English recipe rather like an apple Queen of Puddings.

1½ lb (675 g) cooking apples	pinch of salt
4 oz (100 g) sugar	4 oz (100 g) caster sugar
1 pint (6 dl) milk	1 oz (25 g) margarine
8 oz (225 g) fresh breadcrumbs	2 eggs

Peel, core and slice the apples and stew them with the sugar and a little water until soft. Place in a buttered fireproof dish. Scald the milk and pour it, while still hot, over the breadcrumbs. Add a pinch of salt, the caster sugar and the margarine and leave the mixture for about 15 minutes to allow the crumbs to swell. Now stir in the beaten eggs (or, if you prefer a meringue topping, stir in the yolks and whisk up the whites with 2 tablespoons of caster sugar) and spread the mixture over the apples (with the meringue on top of that, if used). Bake at Gas Mark 4 (350 °F, 180 °C) for about 45 minutes. Serve hot or cold. *Serves 4 to 6.*

Apple Cake – Modern Swedish

Dry old bread crusts in the oven and roll them down to make fine breadcrumbs which will absorb the apple juices.

2 oz (50 g) fine, dry
  breadcrumbs
4 oz (100 g) brown sugar
1½ teaspoons cinnamon

8 cooking apples
2 oz (50 g) butter or margarine
½ cup cherry brandy, rum, white
  wine or orange juice

Mix the breadcrumbs, sugar and cinnamon together. Butter a fireproof dish and place a layer of sliced apples in the bottom of it. Sprinkle with the crumb mixture and some of the butter or margarine melted and continue in layers finishing with a layer of crumbs. Pour the cherry brandy or other liquid over and bake at Gas Mark 6 (400 °F, 200 °C) for about 30 minutes. Serve hot or cold with cream or Custard (p. 209). *Serves 4.*

Apple Charlotte

There are many versions of this but this particular one tastes nice and buttery.

stale bread
3 oz (75 g) butter

2 lbs (900 g) cooking apples
sugar to taste

Butter a deep fireproof dish and dust it with sugar. Cut some fingers of bread (removing the crusts). Dip them into the melted butter and arrange around the sides of the dish, overlapping them slightly. Now cut two rounds which will exactly fit the top and the bottom and dip these too in melted butter. Fit in the bottom round, fill the dish with a stiff apple purée made with very little water and sweetened to taste and place the second round on top. Bake at Gas Mark 4 (350 °F, 180 °C) for about 40 minutes. Leave for a minute or two before turning out on to a hot dish and pouring Jam (p. 211) or Custard Sauce (p. 209) around. *Serves 4 to 6.*

Apple Chausson

A very grand sort of Apple Turnover in a rich, spicy pastry. Excellent picnic fare.

6 oz (150 g) plain flour
3 oz (75 g) butter
3 oz (75 g) caster sugar
1 teaspoon cinnamon
1 egg

1 lb (450 g) apples
$\frac{1}{2}$ oz (12 g) butter
3 oz (75 g) dried fruit
rind $\frac{1}{2}$ lemon
brown or white sugar

Sieve the flour onto a board. Make a well in the centre and pour in the butter, caster sugar, cinnamon and egg. Blend these together then gradually draw in the flour from the sides using only the fingertips of one hand and working as little as possible or the mixture will become too sticky. When it just binds together form it into a ball and place in a plastic bag in the fridge for at least 30 minutes.

Peel, core and thickly slice the apples. Rub the bottom of a saucepan or a fireproof dish thickly with butter and put in the apples in layers with the dried fruit, grated lemon rind and sugar to taste. Cover closely and cook over low heat (or in a low oven) for 5 to 8 minutes until partially cooked. Turn out and cool.

Divide the pastry into two and roll each into a large round. Lay one on a baking sheet, pile on the apple mixture leaving a margin all around the edge. Brush the margin with water and lay the other round over the top sealing the edges well together. Score with a sharp knife, brush with water, sprinkle with caster sugar and bake at Gas Mark 4 (350 °F, 180 °C) for 30 to 40 minutes.
Serves 4 to 5.

Apple Custard

Simple and good. Will suit everyone from Grandpapa to the baby just embarking on solid food.

2 lbs (900 g) apples
6 oz (150 g) sugar

1 pint (6 dl) milk
3 eggs

Wash the apples, cut them up roughly and stew with 4 oz (100 g) of the sugar and 2 to 3 tablespoons water, then sieve and place in a fireproof dish. Bring the milk nearly to boiling point and put in the remainder of the sugar and the beaten egg yolks. Stir and cook gently until the mixture thickens but do not let it boil. Pour on top of the apple purée.

Now whisk the egg whites stiffly and sweeten with a little caster sugar. Pile on top of the custard, dredge with more caster sugar and bake at Gas Mark 3 (325 °F, 170 °C) for about 30 minutes. Eat hot or chilled. *Serves 4 to 6.*

Apple Dumplings

Charles Lamb said early in the last century – 'Coleridge holds that a man cannot have a pure mind who refuses apple dumplings. I am not certain but he is right'!

6 oz (150 g) short crust pastry (p. 55)
4 apples

4 cloves
4 oz (100 g) demerara sugar

Divide the pastry into four and roll each piece out large enough to enclose an apple. Peel and core the apples and place one in the centre of each round of pastry. Put a clove and a tablespoon of sugar into the centre of each apple then brush the edge of the pastry with water. Press the pastry round the sides of the apple pleating any fullness to the top. Seal the edges firmly and turn the dumplings over. Brush with lightly whisked egg white and dredge with caster sugar before baking at Gas Mark 6 (400 °F, 200 °C) for 15 minutes then at Gas Mark 3 (325 °F, 170 °C) for a further 15 minutes. Serve hot with cream or Custard (p. 209). *Serves 4.*

Apple Meringues

Lighter, more elegant than a dumpling. Sugar syrup, which crops up frequently in fruit recipes and in ices, is simply made by bringing 2 lbs (900 g) sugar and 1¼ pints (7.5 dl) water very slowly to the boil and then simmering for 4 minutes. It can be bottled and kept for use over several months.

6 apples
½ pint (3 dl) sugar syrup
2 egg whites

1 oz (25 g) caster sugar
1 oz (25 g) almonds

Peel and core the apples and poach them (whole) in the sugar syrup. Transfer them to a baking tin and coat them with the egg white stiffly whisked with the sugar. Dredge with a little more caster sugar and spike with blanched almond splinters. Brown lightly at Gas Mark 3 (325 °F, 170 °C) and pour the reduced sugar syrup around before serving hot. *Serves 6.*

Apple Pudding – Crusty

The oats and brown sugar mixed make a good crunchy contrast to the apple.

4 oz (100 g) rolled oats   1½ lbs (675 g) apples, stewed
2 oz (50 g) demerara sugar   2 oz (50 g) butter

Mix the oats and sugar together. Fill a buttered pie dish with alternate layers of stewed apple, the oat mixture and the butter, melted, finishing with a layer of oats and butter. Bake at Gas Mark 4 (350 °F, 180 °C) for about 30 minutes. *Serves 4 to 6.*

Apple Pudding – Dutch

A succulent hot pudding with a toffee-like topping for cold winter days.

6 oz (150 g) suet crust (p. 56)   brown sugar
1 lb (450 g) apples   golden syrup
1 lemon

Divide the pastry into two and roll out half of it into a round big enough to line a pie plate 10 inches (25 cm) in diameter. Peel, core and slice the apples and lay them on the pastry sprinkling with the grated lemon rind, the juice and some sugar. Roll out the rest of the pastry to form a lid. Spread about 2 tablespoons of syrup on it and sprinkle generously with brown sugar. Now bake at Gas Mark 5 (375 °F, 190 °C) for 30 to 40 minutes. *Serves 4 to 5.*

Apple Snow

This was always called 'Polanyi Pudding' when we were children as my mother was given the recipe by the late Professor Michael Polanyi. It was one of our great favourites, served in a huge, shallow, cut-glass dish on high days and holidays.

1 lb (450 g) apples   2 eggs
2 tablespoons water   1 oz (25 g) caster sugar
strip of lemon rind   vanilla essence
2 oz (50 g) sugar   4 oz (100 g) sponge cake
⅓ pint (2.5 dl) milk   almonds to decorate

Opposite Brandy Pot (*page 28*)

Wash the apples, cut up roughly and stew with the water, lemon rind and sugar until soft. Sieve. Heat the milk slightly and pour onto the beaten egg yolks. Add the sugar and vanilla essence and cook, without boiling, until the sauce begins to thicken. Arrange the sponge cake in a glass dish and pour on the custard. Whisk the egg whites stiffly and mix gradually with the apple purée, whisking thoroughly. Pile the apple snow on top of the custard and decorate with spikes of almond. Serve very cold. *Serves 6.*

Apples – Baked

There are endless variations of this. They can be filled with dried fruit, blackberries, butter and sugar, marmalade, jam, lumps of sugar soaked in rum, nuts, preserved ginger, marzipan and so on and the surrounding liquid can contain sherry, fruit juice, spices – anything you like. To prevent the apple skins bursting, cut an 'equator' around each apple with a sharp, pointed knife cutting only the skin, not the flesh. It is difficult to give a precise cooking time as apples vary but allow about 40 minutes to 1 hour.

4 large cooking apples
3 tablespoons water
1 tablespoon golden syrup

Wash the apples and core them leaving a little at the bottom to hold the filling in. Place in a buttered fireproof dish and pour the water and warmed syrup around them. Bake at Gas Mark 4 (350 °F, 180 °C) for about 40 minutes or until tender. Serve hot. *Serves 4.*

Apples – Caramelled

These need care in the cooking, but are delicious. Try serving them with pancakes or even with leftover pancakes cut in strips and crisped in butter.

1½ lbs (675 g) cooking apples
juice ½ lemon
sugar syrup (p. 17)

Peel, core and quarter the apples and lay the pieces side by side in a large pan. Sprinkle with the lemon juice and pour on enough boiling sugar syrup to just cover them. Simmer gently for 1 hour shaking the

Opposite Minty Melon (*page 41*)

pan lightly now and then to prevent the pieces from sticking to the bottom. When they are glazed to a rich brown underneath, turn them carefully with a palette knife and simmer for a further 15 minutes. Transfer them to a dish and, when quite cold, serve them on a bed of Crème de Riz (p. 133) handing whipped cream flavoured with vanilla or kirsch separately. *Serves 4 to 6.*

Apples Cooked in Butter

This demands real butter – and the flavour is sublime. Eating apples are better here as they are firmer and the flavour is important. For special occasions the apples may be flambéd in Calvados. The point of flambéing is to eliminate excess grease and impart the flavour of the liqueur. It is always easier to set alight if the liqueur is warmed a little in a separate pan before being poured around the dish, and if the dish is moved gently from side to side while being carried to the table it will keep burning.

2 lbs (900 g) eating apples
2 oz (50 g) butter

3 or 4 oz (75 to 100 g) caster sugar

Melt the butter in a heavy frying pan and lay in the apples which you have peeled, cored and sliced evenly. Sprinkle on the sugar and cook gently until the apples are golden and transparent. Best eaten hot just as they are but, for a change, try them sprinkled with a little cinnamon. *Serves 4 to 6.*

Apples – Diana's

Apples and chocolate make a delicious combination – especially ice cold.

2 lbs (900 g) cooking apples
2 tablespoons black treacle
ground cloves

2 oz (50 g) sugar
grated chocolate

Peel, core and slice the apples and cook them with the treacle, cloves and sugar until reduced to a pulp. Turn into a glass dish and, while still warm, spread with a thick layer of chocolate. Serve chilled, with a little thick cream. *Serves 4 to 6.*

Apples – Gingered

This recipe is reputed to be over a hundred years old when cooking was done on a big scale.

3 lbs (1 k 350 g) apples   ½ pint (3 dl) boiling water
2 lbs (900 g) demerara sugar   rind ½ lemon
1 oz (25 g) whole white ginger
  (bruised)

Peel, core and quarter the apples and place in layers with the sugar in a wetted earthenware jar. Leave for 2 days. Put the bruised ginger in a screw-top bottle, cover with the boiling water, screw down and leave also for 2 days. Place the apples, sugar and the strained water from the ginger in a preserving pan and cook for 1 hour until the apples are clear and the syrup rich. Add the grated lemon rind just before carefully lifting the apple slices out on to a glass dish. Serve cold. *Serves 8.*

Apples in Cider

I always think this would be a good dish with pork – but I haven't tried it yet.

2 lbs (900 g) apples
brown sugar to taste
1 pint (6 dl) cider

Peel, core and slice the apples and put them into a fireproof dish with some brown sugar and enough cider to come about halfway up them. Cover with buttered paper and bake at Gas Mark 4 (350 °F, 180 °C) for about 30 minutes. Remove the paper and leave a further 10 minutes for the top to brown. Serve hot or cold. *Serves 4 to 6.*

Apples Lexington

Whole, poached apples with a super-crisp coating.

6 cooking apples   cake crumbs
1 oz (25 g) flour   frying fat
1 oz (25 g) caster sugar   pineapple jam
1 egg

Peel and core the apples and steam them until half cooked. Leave to cool. Mix the flour and sugar together and roll each apple in the mixture. Brush with beaten egg then roll in cake crumbs and fry in hot fat until crisp and golden. Fill the centre of each with pineapple jam and pour some hot pineapple syrup around. *Serves 6.*

Apples – Scalloped

A lemony mixture with a crisp topping.

1½ lbs (675 g) apples
sugar to taste
1 lemon
2 oz (50 g) candied or glacé fruit

bread and butter
2 egg whites
2 oz (50 g) caster sugar

Peel, core and quarter the apples and place in layers in a buttered pie dish with sugar to taste, grated lemon rind, the flesh of the lemon cut into small chunks and the chopped glacé fruit. Cover with buttered paper and bake at Gas Mark 4 (350 °F, 180 °C) for about 30 minutes until the apples are soft. Now cover with thin slices of bread and butter and return to the oven to brown. Whip the egg whites stiffly, stir in the sugar and spread over the crisp, brown top. Dredge with caster sugar, leave for a few minutes then brown in a cool oven. *Serves 6.*

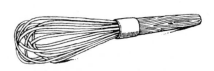

Apricots – Baked

Plums may be cooked in the same way with a little port as a welcome addition.

2 lbs (900 g) apricots
6 oz (150 g) sugar

vanilla – essence or pod
6 tablespoons water

Rinse and stone the apricots and arrange them in a baking dish. Strew with sugar (flavoured with vanilla) or add a few drops of vanilla essence, put in the water and bake, uncovered, at Gas Mark 2 (300 °F, 150 °C) for about 1 hour. Eat hot. *Serves 6.*

Avocados

It is unusual to find avocados as a sweet course. This is a Jamaican recipe well worth a try when avocados are down in price.

2 avocado pears	1 wineglass sherry
2 oz (50 g) caster sugar	grated nutmeg

Cut the avocados in half and remove the stones. Scoop out the flesh and mash it up with the sugar, sherry and freshly grated nutmeg. Pile back into the skins, chill and serve. *Serves 4.*

Banana and Rhubarb Fool

We always dubbed this 'Poor Man's Strawberries and Cream' for the taste and the texture are extraordinarily similar. You won't believe me until you try it. It is something to do with the acid element.

1 lb (450 g) rhubarb	3 bananas
3 oz (75 g) sugar	¼ pint (1.5 dl) top-of-the-milk

Peel and chop the rhubarb. Cover it in cold water in a saucepan and bring it rapidly to the boil then strain immediately. This removes some of the acid content. Now return it to the pan, add the sugar and a little water and stew until soft. Leave to cool. Peel and mash the bananas and mix with the milk or single cream. When the rhubarb has cooled stir them both together and serve chilled. *Serves 4 to 6.*

Bananas au Rhum

Bananas seem to have an affinity with rum (and with kirsch) and this is one of many recipes which combine the two. If you like coconut a sprinkling gives added interest.

4 bananas	juice of 1 lemon
3 tablespoons water	1 wineglass rum
2 oz (50 g) demerara sugar	

Peel the bananas, cut in half lengthwise and place in a fireproof dish with the water, sugar and the lemon juice. Bake at Gas Mark 4 (350 °F, 180 °C) for 10 minutes then pour the rum over them and continue cooking for another 5 minutes. *Serves 4.*

Banana Blush

Despite its rather coy name this is a luscious combination. When raspberries are not available you can make it without them and serve it as Banana Dessert.

8 oz (225 g) raspberries
6 small bananas
4 to 6 oz (100 to 150 g) caster or
  icing sugar

1 egg white
pinch of salt
$\frac{1}{3}$ pint (2.5 dl) double cream

Sieve most of the raspberries but keep back a few for decoration. Peel and mash the bananas and mix with the raspberry pureé together with 2 oz (50 g) of the sugar. Beat well and leave in a cool place for 2 to 3 hours then beat again.

Whisk the egg white with a pinch of salt until stiff and fold in 2 to 3 oz (50 to 75 g) sugar gradually. Stir lightly into the chilled fruit. Whisk the cream until thick, fold in and divide into glass dishes. *Serves 6.*

Banana Flambé

Real butter – or a mixture of butter and oil – must be used for this dish both for the flavour and to avoid burning.

$1\frac{1}{2}$ oz (37 g) butter
$1\frac{1}{2}$ oz (37 g) sugar
1 tablespoon lemon juice

6 bananas
1 small wineglass brandy

Melt the butter in a frying pan with the sugar and lemon juice and allow to cook until very slightly coloured. Add the peeled bananas, halved lengthwise, and cook for a minute or so on each side. Pour over the warmed brandy, ignite and serve immediately. *Serves 6.*

Bananes Gratinées

Even better than Bananas au Rhum as the richness of the bananas is cut by the oranges.

6 bananas
4 oranges

rum butter (p. 214)
brown sugar

Peel the bananas and cut into long, slanting slices. Grate the rind of one orange into the rum butter and mix well. Peel all the oranges and slice thinly. Arrange oranges and bananas in layers in a fireproof dish sprinkling with sugar and topping with pieces of the rum butter. Bake at Gas Mark 4 (350°F, 180°C) for 10 to 15 minutes. *Serves 6.*

Banana Pinwheels

An easy pudding which the children can make.

2 bananas	cinnamon
lemon juice	2 oz (50 g) sugar
8 large slices bread	

Peel the bananas and cut each across the middle then lengthwise so that you have four pieces from each. Sprinkle with lemon juice. Cut the crusts off the bread and butter one side of each slice generously. Sprinkle with a mixture of sugar and cinnamon. Place a banana finger on the unbuttered side of each slice, roll up and place side by side in a baking tin. Bake at Gas Mark 5 (375°F, 190°C) for about 10 minutes. *Serves 4.*

Banana Cream

If only someone would invent a banana which did not go black once it was peeled. It is true that the darkening does not impair the flavour (some people think it enriches it) but it does not look appetizing. This pudding will keep perfectly well for a couple of hours, but after that the fruit exposed on the surface may darken and the mixture separate slightly. The yogurt and egg whites give a light, almost lemony taste. Instead of the cream you can use white wine for a change.

3 bananas	1 oz (25 g) caster sugar
¼ pint (1.5 dl) yogurt (p. 142)	2 egg whites
2 tablespoons cream	

Peel and mash the bananas and mix with the yogurt, cream and sugar. Whip the egg whites until stiff and fold in. Pile into individual glasses and chill. *Serves 4 to 5.*

Bananas Baked

The simplest ways are so often the best. For baked bananas just put
one per person in its skin in the oven and bake at Gas Mark 4 (350 °F,
180 °C) for 15 to 20 minutes.

Berry Sweet (*Dodgrod med Flode*)

A simple and refreshing Scandinavian recipe rather similar to Russian
Kissels.

1 lb (450 g) redcurrants	cornflour
1 lb (450 g) raspberries	vanilla essence
1 pint (6 dl) water	flaked almonds
3 oz (75 g) caster sugar	

Lightly mash the fruit then add the water to it and bring to the boil for
a couple of minutes. Sieve, stir in the sugar and measure the juice. Mix
$1\frac{1}{2}$ oz (37 g) cornflour for each pint (6 dl) of juice with a little water.
Whisk the cornflour mixture with the juice adding a few drops of
vanilla essence. Turn into dishes, leave to set and serve very cold
sprinkled with flaked almonds and handing cream separately.
Serves 6.

Blackberry Meringue

Blackberries can get very sticky and also seem to attract flies so always
rinse them before using.

$1\frac{1}{2}$ lbs (675 g) blackberries	4 egg whites
sugar to taste	8 oz (225 g) caster sugar

Rinse the blackberries and place, with enough sugar to sweeten, in a
fireproof dish. Whisk the egg whites until stiff then whisk in the caster
sugar gradually. Cover the blackberries completely with the meringue
and bake at Gas Mark 3 (325 °F, 170 °C) for 30 to 40 minutes. Cool
then chill before serving. *Serves 6.*

Blackcurrant Oatmeal Flummery

$2\frac{1}{2}$ lbs (1 k 125 g) blackcurrants	$\frac{1}{4}$ teaspoon salt
3 pints ($1\frac{1}{2}$ l) water	4 oz (100 g) caster sugar
2 oz (50 g) fine oatmeal	rum, kirsch or brandy (optional)

Rinse the blackcurrants and strip them roughly from their stems. Stew gently with the water for 35 to 45 minutes then stir in the oatmeal. Bring to boiling point and turn into a large bowl. Cover and leave in a cool place (not the refrigerator) for 24 hours, stirring occasionally. Return to the saucepan and bring to boiling point again, stirring all the time. Strain, rubbing only lightly with a wooden spoon. Stir in salt and sugar, bring back to the boil and cook quickly for about 20 minutes until thick and reduced to about half the original volume. Skim if necessary and add more sugar if needed. May be flavoured with rum, kirsch or brandy. Divide into shallow bowls and chill. Just before serving trail a little single cream over the surface. *Serves 6.*

Blossom's Delight

Blossom's identity remains a mystery but honeyed apple pudding, caramelized and scattered with almonds, will delight many others as well.

½ pint (3 dl) water	1 lb (450 g) eating apples
1 large tablespoon honey or	1 oz (25 g) brown sugar
golden syrup	1 oz (25 g) flaked almonds

Put the water and honey or syrup together in a saucepan and cook until well reduced and syrupy. Peel, core and quarter the apples and place them in a buttered fireproof dish. Cover with the syrup and poach at Gas Mark 3 (325 °F, 170 °C) until the apples are soft but not broken. Remove and baste with the syrup. Spread the sugar and almonds on top and flash under a hot grill until the sugar caramelizes. Serve hot with cream or ice cream. *Serves 4.*

Bondepige med Slör *(Peasant Girl with Veil)*

This is a Danish pudding which has been a favourite of ours for years but, although it is economical and not difficult to make, I have not met with it anywhere else. Do try it. Granary bread is the best but wholemeal will do. On special occasions make it with real cream, otherwise top-of-the-milk is perfectly adequate.

6 oz (150 g) breadcrumbs	1½ lbs (1 k 125 g) stewed apples
2 oz (50 g) sugar	grated chocolate
½ oz (12 g) butter	double cream

Spread the nutty breadcrumbs in a baking tin and mix with the sugar and the melted butter. Leave in a very low oven until crisp and almost dry, stirring frequently. Place a layer of this in the bottom of a glass dish and cover with the well-drained, cold stewed apples. Top with the rest of the crumb mixture, sprinkle with grated chocolate and finally cover with a layer of lightly whipped cream. Serve very cold. *Serves 6.*

Brandy Pot

Over the years I have made a junk-shop collection of stone jars ranging from 6 inches to 24 inches high. They only cost me a few shillings and are ideal for the following recipe. As the summer progresses you earmark a bottle of plonky brandy from somebody's duty-free haul and gather the different fruits as they ripen.

1 bottle brandy
1 lb (450 g) sugar
mixed fruits

Tip the brandy into the jar with the sugar and add any combination (1 lb (450 g) of each, if possible) of cherries, peaches, grapes, raspberries, strawberries, blackberries, greengages, plums, etc. The jar must be well sealed and re-sealed after each addition. Leave for 3 months and spoon out as required (re-sealing after each extraction). This makes a very potent and delicious fruit salad. A little goes a long way.

The number of servings depends on how much fruit you put in.

Chartreuse de Pommes

Use a good dessert apple for this so that it will hold its shape.

1¾ lbs (775 g) Cox's orange
  pippin apples
10 oz (275 g) lump sugar
⅓ pint (2 dl) water

lemon juice
4 oz (100 g) glacé or candied
  fruit

Wash, peel, core and quarter the apples. Put the skins and cores in a saucepan with the sugar, water and a good squeeze of lemon juice. Bring to the boil and boil for 5 minutes, then strain. Now add the quartered apples to the syrup and cook gently in the covered pan for 10 to 12 minutes, stirring occasionally. Uncover and continue to cook until the syrup is almost absorbed. Cover and leave to cool then carefully add the finely chopped preserved fruits. Turn into wetted mould and leave to set. Unmould to serve and pour Jam Sauce (p. 211) over it. *Serves 6.*

Cherries au Kirsch

The affinity of cherries with kirsch is well known. Maraschino is also good. If you can persuade anyone to crack some of the cherry stones for you the kernels are delicious strewn on top.

1 lb (450 g) black cherries
sugar to taste
2 tablespoons kirsch

6 macaroons
double cream
pistachio nuts or almonds

Wash and stone the cherries and stew them gently in sugar and water so that they retain their shape. Leave to cool then add the kirsch. Place a macaroon in the bottom of each of six glasses, spoon in the cherry compôte and cover with stiffly whipped cream strewn with nuts. Serve very cold. *Serves 6.*

Black Cheese Cherries

A creamy mountain covered in glazed black cherries, the cream cheese sharpened by the addition of yogurt.

1 lb (450 g) cream cheese
2 tablespoons yogurt
1 lb (450 g) cherries – stewed or
  canned

1 oz (25 g) cornflour
2 tablespoons redcurrant jelly

Mix the sieved cream cheese and the yogurt together and shape into a mound. Strain off the cherry juice and thicken over gentle heat with the cornflour, adding the redcurrant jelly. Pour the cherries over the cheese mound and pour the cooled syrup over just before serving. *Serves 6.*

Cherry Pain Perdu

A very old French recipe.

3 slices milk loaf
1½ lbs (675 g) cherries
¼ pint (1.5 dl) water
sugar to taste

1 oz (25 g) butter
2 oz (50 g) chopped walnuts
cream

Trim the crust from the bread and cut each slice into four. Stew the stoned cherries (or stone after stewing if you find that easier) for 5 minutes, then drain. Add sugar to taste to the strained juice and boil rapidly until syrupy. Spoon enough of this liquid over the bread to soak it well. Heat the butter in a frying pan until foaming then put in the bread pieces. Dust with sugar and fry till brown on both sides. Arrange in a lightly buttered dish, cover with the cherries and any remaining cherry syrup and chill. Sprinkle with walnuts and serve with cream. *Serves 4.*

Chestnut Amber

A lot of fuss is made about peeling chestnuts but there is really no great difficulty about it and since they lie rotting on the ground so often it is worth taking the trouble. Simply score them across the rounded side with a sharp, pointed knife and then either bake them in a baking tin at Gas Mark 3 (325°F, 170°C) for 20 minutes or drop them into boiling water and boil for 8 minutes. Remove a few at a time so that the rest do not get cold and peel off both the hard outer shell and the inner brown skin with the help of your knife.

6 oz (150 g) chestnuts
1 oz (25 g) chocolate
½ pint (3 dl) milk
2 oz (50 g) butter

2 oz (50 g) flour
2 oz (50 g) cake crumbs
3 eggs
½ teaspoon vanilla essence

Peel the chestnuts and put them into a saucepan with a little water. Cook until tender then sieve. Melt the chocolate in the milk over low heat. In another pan melt the butter, stir in the flour, cook for 2 to 3 minutes then add the milk and stir until it boils. Stir in the cake crumbs and continue stirring the mixture until it leaves the sides of the pan. Cool a little then beat in the egg yolks and add the chestnut purée and vanilla essence. Whisk the egg whites stiffly, stir in gently and turn into a buttered mould. Cover with buttered paper and bake at Gas Mark 5 (375°F, 190°C) for 1 hour. Serve with Custard (p. 209). *Serves 6.*

Chestnut and Orange Compôte

All chestnut dishes are pretty rich and substantial so a little goes a long way.

1 lb (450 g) chestnuts (weighed after peeling)
6 oz (150 g) sugar

1¼ pints (7.5 dl) water
vanilla essence
3 oranges

Peel the chestnuts (p. 30). Put the sugar and water in a saucepan with a few drops of vanilla essence, dissolve over gentle heat then boil for 5 minutes. Add the chestnuts, partially cover the pan and simmer gently for about 1 hour. Cut the rind and pith from the oranges and slice them. Add the chestnuts and their syrup to the oranges when cold. Chill. *Serves 6.*

Chestnuts au Café

36 chestnuts
2 oz (50 g) sugar
2 egg yolks

¼ pint (1.5 dl) black coffee
2 tablespoons cream
1 small glass rum

Peel the chestnuts (p. 30), cover them with water in a saucepan, add 2 tablespoons of the sugar and simmer until soft. Mix the other ingredients plus the remaining sugar together in a bowl over a pan of hot water. Stir until thick then pour over the strained chestnuts and serve hot. *Serves 4.*

Gâteau de Marrons

Serve this chocolate and chestnut cake with little cups of strong black coffee (and Tia Maria?).

2½ lbs (1k 125 g) chestnuts
4 oz (100 g) chocolate
black coffee

4 oz (100 g) butter
4 oz (100 g) sugar

Peel the chestnuts (p. 30) and cook gently in water to cover until soft. Strain and sieve. Melt the chocolate in a little black coffee, stir in the butter and the sugar and then mix with the chestnut purée while both are still warm. Pour into a buttered cake tin and refrigerate for 24 hours. Turn out and serve. *Serves 6.*

Clafoutis

A famous pudding from the Limousin area of France. Use sweet black cherries.

6 oz (150 g) plain flour
3 eggs

8 oz (225 g) cherries
caster sugar

Mix together the flour and eggs with enough water to make a rather thick batter. Pour a thin layer into a buttered flan dish and let it just set on a low heat before strewing on the stoned cherries and sprinkling them with caster sugar. Pour the rest of the batter on top and bake at Gas Mark 4 (350 °F, 170 °C) for about 40 minutes. Turn out, dredge with icing sugar and eat hot or cold. *Serves 4 to 5.*

Compôte of Fruit

Compôte has come to mean almost any fruit stewed with sugar and water but this is the classic compôte with a thickened glaze. It can equally well be made with dried prunes or apricots soaked overnight.

4–6 oz (100–150 g) sugar
½ pint (3 dl) water
1–1½ lbs (450–675 g) fruit

wine, cinnamon or nutmeg
1 level teaspoon arrowroot

Dissolve the sugar in the water, bring to the boil and boil for 5 minutes. Add the prepared fruit and flavouring and cook gently until tender then lift out carefully with a spoon. Blend the arrowroot with 1 tablespoon cold water, pour into the boiling syrup, stir for 1 minute then strain over the fruit. May be eaten hot or cold. *Serves 4 to 6.*

Elderberry Purée

From the Swiss Canton of St Gallen, known there as *Toggenburger Holder-Mus*. Again – other berries can be substituted but elderberries can be found in profusion in this country in early autumn and there are few recipes available which make use of them.

1 oz (25 g) flour
1½ oz (37 g) butter
¼ pint (1.5 dl) milk

1½ lbs (675 g) elderberries
4 oz (100 g) sugar
sugar and cinnamon to top

Fry the flour gently in the butter until light golden in colour then stir in the milk. Add the rinsed elderberries and the sugar and cook over a low heat until the mixture is reduced to a thick purée. Stir constantly. Sprinkle with sugar and cinnamon and serve. *Serves 6.*

Figs in Coffee

For special occasions a tablespoon of rum makes this even better.

1 lb (450 g) dried figs	1 clove
1 pint (6 dl) sweet black coffee	brown sugar
rind ½ orange	

Soak the figs in the coffee for at least 12 hours. Cook slowly until tender, drain and arrange in a silver dish. Cook the coffee for 10 minutes longer adding the grated orange rind, the clove and a little brown sugar. When thick and syrupy pour over the figs and serve very cold with thin cream. *Serves 4 to 6.*

Fig Mould

1 lb (450 g) dried figs	1 lemon
1 pint (6 dl) water	1 oz (25 g) gelatine
4 oz (100 g) sugar	

Cut the figs into small pieces and simmer with the water, sugar and the juice and thinly pared rind of the lemon until tender. Dissolve the gelatine in 3 tablespoons water over gentle heat and stir in. Pour into a wetted mould and leave to set. Turn out and serve with cream or Custard (p. 209) or Vanilla Cream Ice (p. 174). *Serves 4 to 5.*

Fruit and Milk Pudding (*Heidelbeerbrei*)

A Swiss recipe containing bilberries. Since these are not so plentiful in this country try it with blackcurrants.

2¼ lbs (1 k) bilberries	2 oz (50 g) butter
5½ oz (135 g) sugar	½ pint (3 dl) milk
3¾ oz (100 g) bread	sugar and cinnamon for top

Wash, drain and mash the bilberries together with the sugar. Cut the bread into cubes and fry in the butter until golden. Add to the fruit with the cold milk, sprinkle with the sugar and cinnamon and serve cold. *Serves 8.*

Fruit Fools

Fruit Fools can be made of any purée of fruit stirred into sufficient real Custard (p. 209) and cream to make a smooth, creamy mixture. Serve very cold with crisp little biscuits.

Fruit – Stewed

For 1 lb (450 g) fresh fruit dissolve 4 oz (100 g) sugar in ½ pint (3 dl) water and boil for 10 minutes. Then add 1 teaspoon lemon juice and the prepared fruit, cover and cook gently until the fruit is tender.

Gooseberry Amber

Our gardens have all been prolific in gooseberries so I am always on the look-out for good gooseberry recipes.

1 lb (450 g) gooseberries	1 oz (25 g) cake crumbs
4 oz (100 g) brown sugar	1 oz (25 g) icing sugar
2 oz (25 g) butter	3 eggs

Rinse the gooseberries and cook in a covered casserole at Gas Mark 2 (300 °F, 150 °C) together with the brown sugar and butter until soft. Sieve and stir in the cake crumbs. Beat in the egg yolks, turn into a buttered pie dish and bake at Gas Mark 4 (350 °F, 180 °C) for 30 minutes. Remove, cool and chill. Beat the whites of the eggs stiffly and sift in the icing sugar. Spread over the gooseberry mixture and bake at Gas Mark 1 (275 °F, 140 °C) until the meringue is crisp and golden. Serve hot or cold. *Serves 4 to 5.*

Gooseberry Charlotte

A rather richer mixture than the one given for Apple Charlotte but the fruits are interchangeable. You can also use rhubarb, plums, blackcurrants, etc.

1 lb (450 g) gooseberries	8 oz (225 g) fresh breadcrumbs
6 oz (150 g) sugar	3 oz (75 g) suet
2 tablespoons water	1 oz (25 g) margarine

Top and tail the gooseberries and stew them with 4 oz (100 g) of the sugar and the water until tender, then strain. Mix the breadcrumbs, suet and remaining sugar together and put a third of this mixture into a buttered pie dish. Cook at Gas Mark 5 (375 °F, 190 °C) for 10 minutes then fill the dish with alternate layers of gooseberries and crumbs finishing with a layer of crumbs. Dot the top with margarine and cook at Gas Mark 4 (350 °F, 180 °C) for a further 30 minutes. Serve either hot or cold with cream or Custard (p. 209). *Serves 4.*

Gooseberry Cream

A Swedish recipe for a light, baked pudding with a delicate and unusual flavour.

1 lb (450 g) gooseberries	1 dessertspoon white wine
4 oz (100 g) sugar	2 eggs
lemon rind	1 oz (25 g) butter
¾ oz (18 g) cornflour	1 oz (25 g) breadcrumbs

Rinse the gooseberries and cook them in a little water until tender then drain and sieve. Put into a saucepan with the sugar, a little grated lemon rind and the cornflour blended with the wine. Simmer over a low heat for 3 to 4 minutes then leave to cool. Whip the eggs well and stir into the cooked purée. Add the softened butter and the breadcrumbs. Turn into a buttered dish and bake at Gas Mark 1 (275 °F, 140 °C) for about 30 minutes. Serve hot. *Serves 4 to 5.*

Gooseberry Crunch

When I consider that the French only seem to eat gooseberries with their mackerel, I thank my stars for British cooking.

4 oz (100 g) fresh breadcrumbs
2 oz (50 g) demerara sugar
2 oz (50 g) butter
1½ lbs (675 g) gooseberries

4 oz (100 g) granulated sugar
4 tablespoons water
¼ pint (1.5 dl) single cream
1 oz (25 g) chopped nuts

Mix the breadcrumbs and demerara sugar together and fry in the butter until crisp. Rinse the gooseberries and stew them with the granulated sugar and water until soft, then sieve. Place alternate layers of crumbs and gooseberries in individual glass dishes, finishing with a layer of crumbs. Chill and, before serving, top with cream and chopped nuts. *Serves 4.*

Gooseberry Kuchen

Spicy pastry spread with ground almonds mixed with egg whites, topped with gooseberries and baked makes a succulent Kuchen.

1½ lbs (675 g) gooseberries
8 oz (225 g) plain flour
3 oz (75 g) margarine
8 oz (225 g) caster sugar
cinnamon

rind ½ lemon
2 eggs (separated)
2 extra egg whites
4 oz (100 g) ground almonds

Rinse and stew the gooseberries and leave to drain. Sift the flour on to a cold surface, form into a ring and place the creamed margarine, 2 oz (50 g) of the sugar, the cinnamon, the grated lemon rind and the 2 egg yolks in the centre. Work gradually into the flour adding enough water to make a smooth dough. Line a 9 inch (23 cm) tin with greaseproof paper, roll out the pastry and line the tin with it. Whisk the 4 egg whites until stiff then fold in the ground almonds and the rest of the sugar. Spread this mixture over the pastry and top with the gooseberries. Bake at Gas Mark 8 (450 °F, 230 °C) for a further 30 minutes. Remove carefully from the tin and serve cold with whipped cream. *Serves 6.*

Gooseberry Tansy

2 lbs (900 g) gooseberries   4 oz (100 g) fresh breadcrumbs
4 oz (100 g) butter   6 oz (150 g) soft brown sugar
4 eggs   apple, redcurrant or bramble jelly

Rinse the gooseberries and cook in a covered casserole with 3 oz (75 g) of the butter at Gas Mark 2 (300 °F, 150 °C) until soft. Whip the eggs and stir in the breadcrumbs and sugar. Sieve the gooseberries into a thick pan, add the egg mixture and stir over very low heat until firm and smooth. Remove from the heat, stir in the remaining 1 oz (25 g) butter, turn into a hot dish and coat the top with the melted jelly. Delicious with fresh cream. *Serves 6.*

Caramelized Grapes

Choose big, juicy grapes. The contrasts in temperature and texture in this dish are delicious. For very special occasions try Raisins Ivrognes on p. 227.

2 lbs (900 g) white grapes   8 oz (225 g) soft brown sugar
¾ pint (4.5 dl) double cream   (pieces)

Peel and de-pip the grapes and leave in a colander for an hour or so for the excess juice to drain away. Place in a fireproof dish, cover with the stiffly whipped cream and then a generous layer of sugar. Chill overnight and just before serving place under a hot grill for the sugar to caramelize. *Serves 4 to 5.*

Kissel

You can use stewed or bottled raspberries, cherries or blackcurrants – or a mixture of all three – in this recipe. It makes a lovely thick fruit dish.

8 oz (225 g) fruit   1 glass wine
4 oz (100 g) sugar   1 oz (25 g) arrowroot
1 orange

Stew the fruit with the sugar and more water than usual so that you end up with 1¾ pints (10.5 dl) of the strained juice. Put the juice, the orange rind and the wine into a pan and bring slowly to the boil. Mix the arrowroot with the juice of the orange. Remove the orange rind from the juice and add the arrowroot to the boiling mixture, stirring vigorously. Remove from the heat and stir in the fruit. Pour into individual dishes, dust the top with sugar to prevent a skin forming and serve warm or cold but not chilled. *Serves 4.*

Kuchen

A useful German pudding which can be made with any kind of tinned or fresh fruit.

½ pint (3 dl) pancake batter (p. 147)
sugar to taste
2 tablespoons melted butter

1 lb (450 g) fruit
cinnamon
½ cup chopped walnuts

Make a batter and add a little sugar and the melted butter to it. Pour into a shallow, buttered fireproof dish and scatter the fruit over it. Sprinkle with plenty of caster sugar, some cinnamon and the walnuts and bake at Gas Mark 4 (350 °F, 180 °C) for 45 minutes. Serve with cream, custard (p. 209) or any fruit sauce. *Serves 4 to 5.*

Lemon Delight

A simple hot pudding that makes its own sauce.

2 oz (50 g) margarine
4 oz (100 g) sugar
1 oz (25 g) plain flour

juice 1 lemon
2 eggs
¼ pint (1.5 dl) milk

Cream the margarine and the sugar, stir in the flour and add the lemon juice and the egg yolks beaten with the milk. Pour into a well-buttered dish and fold in the stiffly beaten egg whites. Stand in a tin of hot water and bake at Gas Mark 5 (375 °F, 190 °C) for about 45 minutes. Serve hot. *Serves 4.*

Lemons – Filled

A really refreshing dish to serve after a substantial meal. It looks decorative served in large lemon shells cut in half lengthwise.

4 large lemons
2 tablespoons crushed pineapple
3 bananas

¼ cup rum
2 oz (50 g) sugar

Wash the lemons, cut them in half lengthwise and cut a sliver off the rounded side of each so that the shells will stand firmly. Scoop out the flesh with a grapefruit knife and remove any pips and membranes. Mix the lemon with the pineapple, chopped bananas, rum and sugar and chill. Serve piled into the shells or in small glasses. *Serves 4.*

Lemon Posset

An old English recipe. Without the wine it can be served as Lemon Whisk.

2 lemons
1 pint (6 dl) double cream
¼ pint (1.5 dl) dry white wine
sugar to taste

3 egg whites
raspberries and mint leaves or
  crystallized violets or angelica
  to decorate

Grate the lemon rind into the cream and whisk until stiff. Stir in the wine and beat again, then beat in the juice of the lemons gradually. Sweeten to taste. Whisk the egg whites stiffly and fold in. Pile into a dish and decorate. (If preparing in advance leave it in the refrigerator until required then whisk once again and decorate.) *Serves 4 to 6.*

Lemon Pudding

Another pudding to use up leftover pastry trimmings. It has a crisp meringue topping and a smooth, lemony base.

pastry trimmings
½ pint (3 dl) milk
1 oz (25 g) butter
2 oz (50 g) caster sugar

2 lemons
2 eggs
4 oz (100 g) sponge cake

Line the sides of a pie dish with the pastry. Bring the milk, butter, sugar and grated lemon rind to the boil then let it infuse, off the heat, for 15 minutes. Add the well-beaten egg yolks, the crumbled sponge cake and the juice of the lemons and pour into the pie dish. Bake at Gas Mark 4 (350 °F, 180 °C) for about 30 minutes then cover with the stiffly whisked egg whites, dredge with caster sugar and replace in the oven at Gas Mark 2 (300 °F, 150 °C) until the meringue hardens and acquires a little colour. Serve hot or cold. *Serves 6.*

Malvern Pudding

This recipe may sound a little bizarre but it is an excellent, good-natured pudding which will happily sit keeping warm while you eat the main course and can be finished off in a jiffy at the last minute.

1 lb (450 g) cooking apples
2 oz (50 g) butter
sugar to taste
½ pint (3 dl) white sauce (p. 215)

1 egg
3 oz (75 g) demerara sugar
cinnamon to taste

Peel, core and slice the apples and cook them gently with the butter and a grudging amount of sugar until soft. Spread in the bottom of a buttered fireproof dish. Make the White Sauce, thicken it with an egg at the last minute and pour over the apples. Top with a good layer of demerara sugar mixed with cinnamon and caramelize under a hot grill. *Serves 4.*

Mandarin Fruit Salad

The marmalade mixtures give a thick, rich syrup to which the ginger is a necessary contrast. Eat it very cold – *without* cream.

½ cup orange marmalade
½ cup lemon marmalade
2 tablespoons lemon juice
3 tablespoons orange juice
4 grapefruit

6 oranges
1 oz (25 g) crystallized or
  preserved ginger
4 bananas

Melt the marmalades together and stir in the juices. Cut up the grapefruit, oranges and ginger and stir into the liquid when cool. Chill and add the sliced bananas just before serving.
Serve 6.

Melon and Raspberries

A lovely combination which may be served as a summer appetizer or as a dessert. The liqueur involved can be rum, kirsch or Grand Marnier and the raspberries can either be sieved or left whole.

sugar to taste
¾ lb (325 g) raspberries

1 small glass liqueur
1 medium melon

Sprinkle the sugar over the raspberries, pour on the liqueur and leave to soak for several hours. Cut a slice from the long side of the melon (and a sliver from the opposite side so that it will stand firmly), remove the seeds and scoop out the flesh. Mix the chopped or balled flesh with the raspberries and pile back into the melon. If you want to chill it, cover it well in the refrigerator or the fragrance will permeate everything else.
Serves 4.

Minty Melon

A dish which can be used either as a starter or as a dessert.

1 medium melon
2 tablespoons lime cordial

$\frac{1}{4}$ pint (1.5 dl) sweet white wine
few sprigs chopped mint

Prepare the melon as in the preceding recipe. Mix the chopped flesh with the other ingredients, return to the shell, wrap in foil and chill.
Serves 4.

Moon Pennies

This was 'The Treat' of my childhood – partly, I suppose, because during the war fresh bananas were a rare treat. Very simple, very good.

4 bananas
1 pint (6 dl) pure orange juice or
 1 pint (6 dl) Custard (p. 209)

Slice the bananas into the sweetened orange juice (or Custard) and serve very cold. *Serves 4.*

Oranges – Baked

4 oranges
sugar to taste
juice 1 lemon

Wash the oranges, cut a slice from the top of each, stab the flesh several times with a pointed knife and pour in the lemon juice mixed with a little sugar. Replace the tops and bake in a casserole with a little water and sugar at Gas Mark 4 (350 °F, 180 °C) for about 30 minutes. Serve whipped cream separately. *Serves 4.*

Oranges – Barbecued

4 oranges
2 oz (50 g) walnuts

4 oz (100 g) raisins
2 oz (50 g) brown sugar

Slice the tops from the oranges and scoop out the flesh. Chop it into small pieces and place in a pan with any juice that has run out, the chopped walnuts, raisins and brown sugar. Cook over low heat for 5 minutes then pile back into the orange shells and serve hot. *Serves 4.*

Oranges – Caramelled

6 oranges
½ pint (3 dl) water
8 oz (225 g) sugar

Peel one of the oranges very thinly and chop the peel into fine strips. Soak in half of the water for about 1 hour then simmer for 20 minutes and leave to cool. Peel and remove the pith from the oranges then cut them into ¼ inch thick slices and arrange in a serving dish. Heat the sugar with the remaining ¼ pint of water until dissolved then boil rapidly until a rich golden brown colour. Remove from the heat and add the strained liquid from the orange strips. Stir over gentle heat for a few moments then add the orange strips and pour the mixture over the oranges. Chill for at least 8 hours and serve with crisp little biscuits. *Serves 4.*

Orange Charlotte

Good just as it is but, for variety, try it with a little thick cream stirred in and some kirsch or curaçao.

2 eggs
2 oz (100 g) caster sugar

½ orange
½ lemon

Cream the yolks of the eggs with half the sugar and the grated rind and juice of the orange and the lemon. Heat in a bowl over a pan of boiling water and when the mixture thickens remove and cool before folding in the egg whites stiffly whisked with the rest of the sugar. Pile into glasses and serve with biscuits. *Serves 4.*

Orange Fool – Boodles

4 oranges
2 lemons
1 pint (6 dl) double cream

1 oz (25 g) honey
8 oz (225 g) sponge fingers

Grate the rind of 2 oranges and 1 lemon and mix with the squeezed juice of all of them, the cream and the honey. Whip all together until frothy. Place the sponge fingers in the bottom of a glass dish, pour the fool on top and leave to stand for at least 4 hours so that the juice can penetrate the cake. *Serves 6.*

Peaches à la Cardinale

The peaches filled with raspberry purée and scattered with almonds make an eye-catching dish.

6 peaches
sugar to taste
vanilla pod

8 oz (225 g) raspberries
kirsch
1 oz (25 g) almond flakes

Halve the peaches, remove the stones and poach gently in sugared water with a vanilla pod. Let them cool in the syrup then spoon them into a glass dish and fill with the sieved raspberries sweetened and flavoured with kirsch. Sprinkle with almonds and serve.
Serves 4 to 5.

Peaches – Grilled

This dish looks better sizzling hot but tastes just as good cold.

6 peaches
1 oz (25 g) butter
2 oz (50 g) brown sugar

juice ½ lemon
grated nutmeg

Arrange the stoned peach halves cut side up in a shallow fireproof dish. Dot with butter and sprinkle with brown sugar, lemon juice and nutmeg. Bake at Gas Mark 4 (350 °F, 180 °C) for about 20 minutes. Serve hot or cold with whipped cream. *Serves 4 to 5.*

Peach Heaven

4 peaches
brandy

½ pint (3 dl) double cream
2 oz (50 g) brown sugar

Pour boiling water over the peaches, drain immediately and you will find them quite easy to peel. Peel and slice and lay them in a fireproof dish. Sprinkle well with brandy and coat with a thick layer of stiffly whipped cream. Chill for several hours so that the cream becomes fairly hard then spread brown sugar on top and caramelize under a very hot grill. Serve at once. *Serves 4.*

Peaches in White Wine

We once spent a memorable holiday in the Dordogne where the peaches were so cheap that we bought them by the crate. This was one of our favourite ways of using them.

6 peaches
sugar to taste
½ pint (3 dl) white wine

Peel the peaches (see Peach Heaven, above) and slice them into glasses. Sprinkle with sugar and top up with cold white wine. Chill only briefly or the fruit will go mushy. *Serves 4.*

Peach Melba

Real Peach Melba is a gastronomic experience which bears only the most fleeting resemblance to the ersatz effort we are usually offered.

4 peaches
sugar syrup (p. 17)
½ pint (3 dl) vanilla cream ice (p. 174)

8 oz (225 g) raspberries
¼ pint (1.5 dl) double cream

Skin the peaches (see Peach Heaven, above), halve them and poach them gently in a vanilla flavoured syrup and leave to cool. Put a good dollop of real, home-made Vanilla Ice in the bottom of each of four glass dishes, lay the cold peach halves on top, cover with the sieved raspberries and put a whirl of whisked cream on top. *Serves 4.*

Peaches with Mincemeat and Whisky

Canned peaches will do but fresh ones are better.

3 oz (75 g) sugar
½ pint (3 dl) water
3 tablespoons whisky

4 peaches
8 dessertspoons mincemeat

Make a syrup from the sugar and water (or use the drained juice of tinned peaches) and stir in 2 tablespoons of the whisky. Arrange the stoned, skinned and halved peaches flat side up in a large serving dish. Put a dessertspoon of mincemeat and a little of the remaining whisky in each. Re-heat the syrup and whisky and pour over. *Serves 4.*

Pear Delight

A soft mousse made with fresh pears spiced with ginger nuts.

4 dessert pears (well ripe)
2 egg whites
2 teaspoons caster sugar

¼ pint (1.5 dl) double cream
2 ginger nut biscuits

Peel, core and dice the pears. Whip the egg whites until stiff then whisk in the sugar. Whip the cream and fold the two together. Add the pears and pile into individual dishes sprinkling with the crumbled biscuits. *Serves 4.*

Pears – Butterscotch

A spectacular dish. Once you have mastered this try Pears in Burgundy (p. 46) which requires the same technique.

6 pears
1 oz (25 g) butter
8 oz (225 g) brown sugar

juice 2 lemons
sour cream

Choose ripe pears with a stalk and peel them. In a deep saucepan melt together the butter, brown sugar and lemon juice. Stand the pears in this sauce, cover (use foil if the lid won't fit over them) and simmer very slowly until tender (about 15 minutes). Remove the pears and boil the sauce until thick and treacly then replace the pears and, keeping the heat low, carefully baste them until they are thoroughly coated (about 5 minutes). Lift on to a serving dish, pour the sauce over and serve with sour cream. *Serves 6.*

Pears in Burgundy

The creamy pears coated with a rich red glaze look extremely glamorous.

2 lbs (900 g) pears	cinnamon
8 oz (225 g) sugar	¼ pint (1.5 dl) Burgundy
¼ pint (1.5 dl) water	whipped cream

Peel the pears but do not core them. Put them in a saucepan with the sugar, water and cinnamon and simmer, covered, for about 15 minutes. Add the Burgundy and cook, uncovered, for a further 15 minutes. Put the pears into a deep serving dish and reduce the liquid by boiling to a syrupy consistency. Spoon this over the pears and chill. Serve with whipped cream. *Serves 6 to 8.*

Pears in Cream

A good way to use some rather hard pears.

2 lbs (900 g) pears (unripe)	vanilla pod
½ oz (12 g) butter	5 tablespoons double cream
5 oz (125 g) sugar	

Peel, core and slice the pears. Pour the melted butter into a shallow fireproof dish and arrange the pears in it. Sprinkle with the sugar, add the vanilla pod and bake at Gas Mark 3 (325 °F, 170 °C) for about 25 minutes then pour in the cream and cook for a further 5 minutes. Serve hot. *Serves 6.*

Pears – with Chocolate Sauce

Poached pears served hot in a creamy sauce.

1 lb (450 g) pears	3 oz (75 g) chocolate
sugar to taste	½ oz (12 g) butter
vanilla pod	

Peel, core and quarter the pears and cook them with a very little water, some sugar and a vanilla pod until nearly done. Remove the vanilla pod. In another saucepan melt the chocolate over low heat with a tablespoon of the pear syrup, then add to the pears together with the butter and cook slowly until the pears are soft and the sauce creamy. Serve at once. *Serves 4.*

Pineapple Dumplings

A separate pudding for each person simply bursting with fruits. If you haven't any individual pudding tins you can use foil shells.

8 oz (225 g) suet crust (p. 56) sweetened
6 oz (150 g) pineapple, fresh or canned

4 tablespoons mincemeat
2 oz (50 g) candied peel
4 oz (100 g) cake crumbs
sherry

Line individual pudding tins with the rolled out pastry keeping back enough for the lids. Chop the pineapple and mix it with the mincemeat, peel, cake crumbs and a little sherry. Fill the pastry cases and cover with pastry lids sealing the edges well. Bake at Gas Mark 6 (400 °F, 200 °C) for about 30 minutes and serve with any fruit sauce. *Serves 4.*

Plum Melba

1 lb (450 g) plums
3 oz (75 g) sugar

1½ oz (37 g) semolina
vanilla essence

Stew the plums with a little sugar and very little water. Strain, stone them and place in individual dishes. Bring the juice and sugar to the boil, sprinkle in the semolina and boil, stirring, for 3 minutes. Add the vanilla essence and turn into a large bowl. When cool, beat briskly until it becomes nearly white. Pile on top of the plums and serve very cold. *Serves 4.*

Plums en Croûte

An excellent everyday sweet. It can also be made with apricots or greengages.

4 slices fresh bread (½ inch thick)
1 lb (450 g) plums

2 oz (50 g) butter
4 oz (100 g) brown sugar

Butter the bread and cover with halved raw plums, cut side up, pressing them well down into the bread. Into each plum put a little butter and sugar, place the slices of bread in a well-buttered fireproof dish, cover with buttered paper and bake at Gas Mark 4 (350 °F, 180 °C) for about 30 minutes. Serve with cream. *Serves 4.*

Pomegranate Compôte

Pomegranates are beautiful but their seeds are tiresome. Try this dish which preserves the attractive sharpness of the fruit and obliterates most of the seeds.

3 large pomegranates
rose water

6 small pomegranates
sugar to taste

Halve the large pomegranates, remove the seeds, arrange them in a shallow dish and sprinkle with rose water. Crush the smaller pomegranates over a sieve and, to the juice, add an equal quantity of water and enough sugar to make a good syrup. Thicken this over medium heat, let it cool and pour it over the pomegranates. Serve chilled. *Serves 4.*

Quince Blancmange

A Very Grand Lady who lives quite near evidently grows more quinces than she knows what to do with and every September the same piece of cardboard is tacked to her gate announcing imperiously, 'The quinces are ready.' Then we form a ragged queue with our battered baskets and pay for our share. Quinces are beautiful but, once ripe, need to be used up quickly so I was glad to come across this recipe which makes a change from the usual cheeses and marmalades.

1 lb (450 g) quinces
1 pint (6 dl) water
6 oz (150 g) sugar

$\frac{3}{4}$ oz (20 g) gelatine
$\frac{1}{4}$ pint (1.5 dl) double cream

Peel and core the quinces and simmer them in the water until soft. Strain and to the juice add the sugar and the melted gelatine and stir and boil gently. When cool stir in the cream and pour into a wetted mould to set. *Serves 4.*

Raspberry Joy

An old Gloucestershire recipe which has two great assets: the raspberries are uncooked and so retain all their flavour, and the redcurrants do not need to be painstakingly removed from their stalks. When cold the raspberries are swollen and set in a lovely jelly.

4 slices bread
1 lb (450 g) raspberries
1 lb (450 g) redcurrants

1 lb (450 g) sugar
$\frac{1}{4}$ pint (1.5 dl) water

Cover the bottom of a dish with bread cut about $\frac{1}{4}$ inch thick. On this lay the uncooked raspberries. Rinse the currants and cook rapidly in a saucepan with the sugar and water for about 20 minutes. Strain while hot over the raspberries and bread and leave to cool. *Serves 4 to 5.*

Raspberry Pudding – Russian

Raspberries are far and away my favourite summer fruit. I associate them with hot summer afternoons greedily picking under the nets of a walled nursery garden we used to visit in Anglesey. They are a pleasure to pick – very different from grubbing among muddy straw on bended knees for strawberries.

1 lb (450 g) raspberries
1 cup sour cream
2 eggs

1 oz (25 g) flour
1 oz (25 g) sugar

Heat the raspberries in a fireproof dish in a moderate oven until they are thoroughly hot and the juice is just beginning to run. Beat up the sour cream with the other ingredients and pour it over. Bake at Gas Mark 1 (275 °F, 140 °C) until the pudding is firm and pale golden – about 30 minutes. *Serves 4.*

Raspberry Shortbread

Can also be used with any other soft fruit.

1 lb (450 g) raspberries
granulated sugar to taste
2 oz (50 g) butter
6 oz (150 g) plain flour

3½ oz (90 g) brown sugar
½ teaspoon ground ginger
1 teaspoon baking powder

Spread the raspberries in a shallow fireproof dish and strew with granulated sugar. Rub the butter into the flour until crumbly and mix in the brown sugar, ginger and baking powder. Smooth this mixture lightly over the raspberries and bake at Gas Mark 4 (350 °F, 180 °C) for about 30 minutes. Serve hot or cold. *Serves 4 to 5.*

Rhubarb Strips

Rhubarb is another French blind spot. They respect it as a purgative and stick it in floral arrangements. Ah well – nobody's perfect. Rhubarb Strips make crisp, sugary rolls with a soft, tangy filling.

1 lb (450 g) rhubarb
sugar

8 oz (225 g) short crust or flaky
  pastry (p. 55)
milk

Cut the rhubarb into 4 inch (10 cm) lengths and roll them in sugar. Roll out the pastry very thinly, cut into squares 4 by 3 inches (10×8 cm) and wrap each stick of rhubarb in one, lining them up in a fireproof dish. Brush the rolls with milk, dredge generously with sugar and bake at Gas Mark 7 (425 °F, 220 °C) for about 15 minutes. Serve hot with cream or Custard (p. 209). *Serves 4 to 6.*

September Pudding

A spongy base, apple filling and crisp top make a heart-warming hot pudding.

4 oz (100 g) margarine
4 oz (100 g) plain flour
pinch of salt

2 oz (50 g) desiccated coconut
2 eggs
1 lb (450 g) stewed apples

Opposite Summer Pudding (*page 53*)

Rub the margarine into the flour and salt and stir in the coconut and the yolks of the eggs. Bake in a shallow, buttered tin at Gas Mark 4 (350 °F, 180 °C) for 15 minutes. Turn out to cool then trim it to fit into a buttered pie dish. Strain the juice from the apples and pour it over the crust. Fill the centre with the apple and cover with the stiffly whisked egg white sealing it well to the edge. Dredge with caster sugar and bake at Gas Mark 2 (300 °F, 150 °C) until the meringue is crisp – about 20 minutes. *Serves 4 to 5.*

Soup – Mixed Fruit

A Swedish dish served chilled for dessert in Sweden but sometimes to be found as an accompaniment to roast pork in America.

4 oz (100 g) dried apricots	2 oz (50 g) tapioca
4 oz (100 g) prunes	2 oz (50 g) sugar
6 cups water	2 oz (50 g) raisins
cinnamon stick	1 apple
2 slices lemon	

Soak the apricots and prunes in the water for about 30 minutes. Add the cinnamon, lemon slices, tapioca and sugar and simmer, covered, for about 30 minutes, stirring occasionally. Stir in the raisins and the apple peeled and sliced and cook for a few minutes longer. Cool and chill. *Serves 4 to 5.*

Spring Pudding

2 oz (50 g) butter	2 oz (50 g) desiccated coconut
4 oz (100 g) white breadcrumbs	6 oz (150 g) brown sugar
1 lemon	2 lbs (900 g) rhubarb
1 orange	

Melt the butter and stir in the breadcrumbs. Grate the lemon and orange rinds and squeeze out the juice. Mix both with the coconut and sugar. Put one-third of the crumbs in a buttered fireproof dish. Add half the chopped rhubarb mixed with the sugar and half the coconut, juice and rind mixture. Put the next one-third of breadcrumbs on top, then the rest of the rhubarb and sugar and the rest of the coconut mixture. Finish with the remaining breadcrumb mixture, dot with butter and bake at Gas Mark 6 (400 °F, 200 °C) for about 30 minutes. Serve with cream. *Serves 6.*

Opposite Apple and Orange Flan (*page 58*)

Strawberries

In France strawberries are never eaten with cream as they are considered too acid. Instead the whole, unhulled strawberries are plunged into cold water to cleanse them, lifted out and left to dry on a clean cloth. They are then hulled and sliced into a bowl with some fine sugar and a good dash of white wine and eaten just like that.

Strawberries – Ambrosine

Strawberries and apricots go surprisingly well together.

8 oz (225 g) apricots
juice 1 lemon
4 oz (100 g) sugar
2 egg whites

¼ pint (1.5 dl) double cream
vanilla essence
8 oz (225 g) strawberries
kirsch

Stew the apricots in water, strain and sprinkle with the lemon juice and 3 tablespoons of the sugar. Sieve and leave to get cold. Beat the egg whites with a little sugar and beat in. Spread the mousse in a shallow dish and cover with the cream whipped, sweetened and flavoured with vanilla. Soak the strawberries in a little kirsch and strew them in the dish just before serving. *Serves 4 to 5.*

Strawberries – Romanoff

Strawberries and oranges are another happy combination.

2 lbs (900 g) strawberries
4 oz (100 g) icing sugar

1 small glass curaçao
juice 2 oranges

Slice the rinsed and dried strawberries into a glass dish, dredge with icing sugar and mix in the curaçao and orange juice. Chill and serve. *Serves 6.*

Summer Pudding

One of the best puddings in the British repertoire. Although usually associated with raspberries and redcurrants it can also be made with sieved blackberries or with mulberries if you are lucky enough to have one of these lovely trees in your garden.

stale white bread	8 oz (225 g) redcurrants
2 lbs (900 g) raspberries	8 oz (225 g) sugar

Cut some slices of bread about ¼ inch thick, remove the crusts and line a soufflé dish so that there are no cracks. Put the fruit and sugar together into a saucepan and cook for about 5 minutes until the juice runs, then leave to cool. Fill up the dish reserving some of the juice. Cover with more slices of bread, then put on top a plate which will fit inside the dish and weight it. Leave overnight and then turn out onto a serving dish. Pour the reserved juice over the pudding. Serve cream separately. *Serves 8.*

Tarts & Flans

One of my sisters claims that you have to be forty to make good pastry. Experience is an advantage but there are various tips that will help you to arrive at good pastry before that!

Speed is important in the making of pastry so assemble all you need before you begin, then mix it quickly and lightly. Excessive handling leads to heavy pastry. I find that hard flour (as used for bread) is best. Everything you use (including, if possible, your fingertips) should be cool and as much air should be introduced in the mixing as possible, as cold air expands more in a hot oven and creates a lighter pastry. Use as little liquid as possible to make the pastry bind together. Excess liquid leads to hard pastry.

Pastry can be enriched by the addition of an egg or an egg yolk and may also include sugar, spices, ground almonds, oatmeal or cheese.

Many open fruit tarts demand a pastry case which has been baked 'blind' (i.e. empty). To do this successfully prick the base with a fork, line the pastry case with a piece of buttery paper (butter side down) and fill it with some dried beans, split peas, rice or lentils (kept for the purpose in an airtight jar and re-used) or stale crusts, piling them up against the sides as it is these that tend to fall in when an empty flan case is baked. Pastry needs a hot oven to start with – Gas Mark 6 (400 °F, 200 °C) for about 10 minutes. The heat may then be reduced until the pastry and its filling are cooked.

For general purposes there are four sorts of pastry that you need to know. When a recipe requires 8 oz (225 g) pastry it is the amount of flour in the pastry which is referred to.

Short Crust Pastry

This is the general, all purpose pastry. Equal quantities of margarine and lard are the usual mixture but all of either may be used. Lard alone makes a rather crumbly pastry. Use butter if the flavour of the dish is particularly delicate.

8 oz (225 g) plain flour   2 oz (50 g) lard
pinch of salt   cold water to mix
2 oz (50 g) margarine

Sift the flour and salt together and rub in the fat using the tips of the fingers until the mixture looks like fine breadcrumbs. Mix in just enough water to bind the mixture using the tip of a knife. Knead lightly until smooth on a floured board and use as required.

Flaky Pastry

8 oz (225 g) plain flour   2 oz (50 g) margarine
pinch of salt   1 teaspoon lemon juice
4 oz (100 g) lard   cold water to mix

Sieve the flour and salt into a bowl. Divide the fat into four equal portions and rub one portion into the flour using the tips of the fingers. Mix to a really slack dough with the lemon juice and water using a round-bladed knife. Turn on to a floured board and knead lightly until smooth. Roll out into a long, narrow strip keeping the ends square – roll to and fro, not from side to side. Place the second portion of the fat in small knobs on the pastry covering the bottom $\frac{2}{3}$ of the strip then fold up the bottom third on to the fat and fold down the top third so that the strip is one-third its original size. Seal the edges with a rolling pin, give the pastry a half-turn so that the fold is on your left and roll out into a strip as before. Repeat the process twice more so that all the fat is used up. Stand in a cool place for as long as possible before using.

Suet Crust

8 oz (225 g) plain flour
pinch of salt
4 oz (100 g) suet

1 teaspoon baking powder
cold water to mix

Sieve the flour and salt into a bowl, add the suet and baking powder and mix to a firm dough with the water. Turn on to a floured board and knead lightly until free from cracks.

Choux Pastry

$\frac{1}{4}$ pint (1.5 dl) water
2 oz (50 g) butter

2$\frac{1}{2}$ oz (65 g) flour
2 eggs

Bring the water and butter to the boil slowly (so that the butter has time to melt) then sift in the flour. Remove from the heat and beat vigorously. Break in the first egg and start mixing it in with a sideways cutting movement. Beat until the mixture clears and becomes smooth and thick. Mix in the second egg in the same way, then cover the mixture and leave until completely cold – without refrigerating. Then use.

Glazes

These are important for a professional finish. If you want to give your pies a gloss, brush them with a raw egg beaten with a teaspoon of salt. Any jam may be used to glaze the fruit in open flans but apricot is the most generally useful. Put 8 oz (225 g) jam into a saucepan with 2 tablespoons water and a good squeeze of lemon juice. Bring to the boil, cook until of a coating consistency and then sieve. Use hot – it sets as it cools.

Any fruit can be made into a pie – either a covered pie or an open flan – so I have not given separate instructions for, say, blackcurrant pie, plum pie, etc. Similarly any open fruit flan can be glazed and looks much more attractive for it.

It is sensible, while you are about it, to make quite a lot of pastry at the same time. Uncooked it will keep well wrapped in the refrigerator or baked flan cases will keep in an airtight tin for a week or two quite happily.

Almond Crisp Cherry Flan

Kirsch, of course, is made from cherries so it is not surprising that so many of the more interesting recipes use it. A bottle secreted in your kitchen cupboard will do wonders for your cooking.

6 oz (150 g) short crust pastry
  (p. 55)
¾ pint (4.5 dl) milk
2¼ oz (60 g) semolina
2 oz (50 g) caster sugar
1 egg

3 tablespoons kirsch
1 lb (450 g) black cherry
  preserve
2 oz (50 g) flaked almonds
icing sugar

Roll out the pastry to fit an 8 inch (20 cm) flan case and bake blind. Heat the milk, sprinkle in the semolina, bring to the boil and simmer gently for 3 minutes. Remove from the heat and stir in the sugar, beaten egg and kirsch. Leave to cool then spread in the flan case and leave until completely set. Warm the jam, spoon it over the filling and sprinkle the toasted almonds around the edge. *Serves 6.*

Angelica Tart

Some love it, some hate it – but here's a tart for the angelica addicts among you. If it seems extravagant you'd better learn how to crystallize your own.

10 oz (275 g) short crust pastry
  (p. 55)
1¼ lbs (550 g) cooking apples
12 oz (325 g) angelica

piece lemon rind
sugar syrup (p. 17)
egg white
caster sugar

Line an 8 inch (20 cm) flan dish with the pastry. Peel, core and slice the apples and cook them with the diced angelica and the lemon rind in sugar syrup until transparent. Cool, remove lemon rind and turn into the pastry case. Cover with the remaining pastry rolled out to form a lid and bake at Gas Mark 6 (400 °F, 200 °C) until a rich golden brown. *Serves 6.*

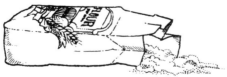

Apple and Orange Flan

Glazed orange slices overlapping around the top and orange-flavoured apple below make for a succulent tart.

3 lumps sugar
1 large orange
1½ lbs (675 g) apples
sugar to taste

6 oz (150 g) sweet short crust
  pastry (p. 55)
apricot glaze

Rub the lumps of sugar over the orange until well soaked with the zest. Peel, core and slice the apples and simmer with the lumps of sugar and a little extra sugar until well reduced. Leave to cool. Line a 8 inch (20 cm) flan case with the pastry, fill with the apple, dust with sugar and bake at Gas Mark 5 (375 °F, 190 °C) for about 30 minutes. Cut the peel and pith from the oranges, slice the flesh thinly and arrange in an overlapping circle around the edge of the flan. Make the glaze and coat the flan. Serve warm with Sabayon Sauce (p. 214). *Serves 6.*

Apple Caramel Tart

Cox's are the best apples to use here. When turned out the apple slices are varnished with the caramel and the base is a cross between vanilla flavoured sponge and rich short crust pastry.

6 oz (150 g) sugar
½ pint (3 dl) water
1½ lbs (675 g) dessert apples
butter
8 oz (225 g) plain flour
pinch of salt

2½ oz (62 g) butter or margarine
2 oz (50 g) vanilla sugar
1 egg yolk
1 tablespoon orange flower
  water

Make a caramel by dissolving the sugar in the water slowly then boiling rapidly until a rich brown colour. Pour this at once into a 9 inch (23 cm) flan tin. Peel, core and slice the apples and arrange them carefully in overlapping circles on top of the caramel. Dot with little pieces of butter and sprinkle with vanilla sugar. Make a rich pastry by sieving the flour and salt together, rubbing in the margarine or butter and mixing to a soft dough with the remaining vanilla sugar, the egg yolk and the orange flower water, adding a little cold water if necessary. Cover the apples with this crust, brush over with water, sprinkle with more sugar, make an airhole and bake at Gas Mark 6 (400 °F, 200 °C) for about 45 minutes. Invert on to a plate to serve. May be eaten hot but more delicious cold. *Serves 6.*

Apple Cheesecake

This is not a cheesecake in the contemporary use of the name but more like an appley lemon curd tart.

6 oz (150 g) short crust pastry (p. 55)
1½ lbs (675 g) apples
3 oz (75 g) sugar
1 oz (25 g) butter
1 lemon
2 eggs

Line an 8 inch (20 cm) flan tin with the pastry and bake for 10 minutes at Gas Mark 6 (400 °F, 200 °C). Wash the apples, cut up roughly and simmer with the sugar and 1 tablespoon water until tender, then sieve. Return to the pan and add the butter, the juice and grated rind of the lemon, the yolks of 2 eggs and the white of 1 and cook until the mixture thickens. Turn into the pastry case, cover with the remaining egg white stiffly whisked with a little sugar and bake at Gas Mark 4 (350 °F, 180 °C) for about 15 minutes. Serve hot. *Serves 6.*

Apple Pie

'*But I, when I undress me*
Each night upon my knees
Will ask the Lord to bless me
With apple pie and cheese.'
EUGENE FIELD (1850–95)

The classic Apple Pie is simply cooking apples, layered with sugar and either covered with or sandwiched between good short crust or flaky pastry. You will need about 1½ lbs (675 g) apples for six people. Bake at Gas Mark 6 (400 °F, 200 °C) for 15 to 20 minutes then reduce to Gas Mark 4 (350 °F, 180 °C) for a further 10 minutes or so until the apples are soft. Excellent hot or cold with cream, Custard (p. 209) or, as in the North of England, with wedges of cheese.

The variations, of course, are endless. You can add sultanas, spices, orange or lemon, blackberries or other fruit, marmalade, ginger and so on. Try it with ¼ pint (1.5 dl) soured cream poured over the apples or grated cheese mixed in with them.

Applescotch Flan

If you have a sweet tooth you will like this – and children love it.

8 oz (225 g) short crust pastry (p. 55)
4 oz (100 g) golden syrup

1 egg
1 lb (450 g) cooking apples
1 oz (25 g) butter

Line a shallow rectangular tin, 12 by 7½ inches (30 by 19 cm) with the pastry. Beat the syrup and the egg together and pour half the mixture on to the pastry. Arrange the peeled, cored and sliced apples on top and pour over the rest of the syrup mixture. Dot with butter and bake at Gas Mark 6 (400 °F, 200 °C) for about 45 minutes. *Serves 4.*

Apple Tart – German

German cookery seems to make a speciality of setting fruit and vegetables in a sort of custard. It makes a pleasant change from the more predictable British apple pie.

6 oz (150 g) short crust pastry (p. 55)
1 oz (25 g) butter
juice ½ lemon
2 oz (50 g) caster sugar

½ teaspoon mixed spice
1 egg
½ pint (3 dl) milk
1 lb (450 g) cooking apples
almonds to decorate

Line an 8 inch (20 cm) flan tin with the pastry. Mix together the melted butter, the lemon juice, the sugar, mixed spice, egg and milk and stir into this the peeled, cored and thinly sliced apples. Pour into the flan case, sprinkle with almonds and bake at Gas Mark 5 (375 °F, 190 °C) for about 30 minutes. Serve with cream, hot or cold, but better hot. *Serves 6.*

Apricot Tart (*Bourdaloue*)

'*Bourdalou*' means hat-band but I've never quite understood the culinary connection!

4 oz (100 g) short crust pastry (p. 55)
2 eggs
2 oz (50 g) sugar
orange rind
½ oz (12 g) cornflour

½ oz (12 g) flour
½ pint (3 dl) milk
1 lb (450 g) apricots
sugar syrup (p. 17)
almonds to decorate

Line a 6 inch (15 cm) flan tin with the pastry and bake it blind. Make the bourdaloue by creaming the egg yolks with 1 tablespoon of the sugar and the grated orange rind. Stir in the cornflour and the flour and pour on the milk which has been brought to the boil. Return to the pan and stir until boiling. Leave to cool then fold in the stiffly whisked egg white sweetened with the rest of the sugar. Poach the stoned apricots in the sugar syrup until soft then drain and reduce the syrup by further cooking. Pile the bourdaloue into the pastry case shaping it into a dome. Arrange the apricot halves over it and brush with the syrup to glaze them. Serve at once, scattered with almonds. *Serves 6.*

Bakewell Tart

The genuine article – and very good too.

6 oz (150 g) short crust pastry (p. 55)
raspberry jam
2 oz (50 g) butter

2 oz (50 g) caster sugar
1 egg
2 oz (50 g) ground almonds
almond essence

Line an 8 inch (20 cm) flan tin with the pastry and spread with a good layer of jam. Cream the butter and sugar together until thick and white. Stir in the egg, the almonds and a few drops of almond essence and beat well. Spread this mixture lightly on top of the jam and bake at Gas Mark 6 (400 °F, 200 °C) for about 30 minutes. Serve hot or cold. *Serves 6.*

Bakewell Tart – Mock

An everyday version of the preceding recipe. It looks similar with a filling which turns a rich brown in the baking but, lacking the ground almonds, it is sweeter.

4 oz (100 g) short crust pastry (p. 55)
jam

2 oz (50 g) butter
2 eggs
4 oz (100 g) brown sugar

Line a 7 inch (18 cm) flan tin with the pastry and spread it with a good layer of strawberry or raspberry jam. Melt the butter. Mix – but do not beat – the eggs and add, then stir in the sugar and pour on top of the jam. Bake at Gas Mark 4 (350 °F, 180 °C) for about 30 minutes. Good hot or cold. *Serves 4.*

Balmoral Tart

A useful tart which turns a few odds and ends into a really good pudding in its own right.

6 oz (150 g) short crust pastry (p. 55)
1 oz (25 g) butter
1 oz (25 g) caster sugar
1 egg

1 oz (25 g) cake crumbs
1 oz (25 g) glacé cherries
1 oz (25 g) candied peel
$\frac{3}{4}$ oz (18 g) cornflour

Line an 8 inch (20 cm) flan tin with the pastry. Cream the butter and sugar together until thick and white then stir in the egg yolk, the crumbs, the chopped cherries and peel and the cornflour. Whisk the white of the egg stiffly and stir it in lightly. Turn into the pastry case and bake at Gas Mark 4 (350 °F, 180 °C) for about 20 minutes. Eat hot or cold. *Serves 6.*

Banana Cream Flan

A dash of rum is a welcome addition to this recipe.

6 oz (150 g) short crust pastry (p. 55)
4 bananas

$\frac{1}{2}$ pint (3 dl) custard (p. 209)
$\frac{1}{4}$ pint (1.5 dg) double cream
desiccated coconut

Line an 8 inch (20 cm) flan tin with the pastry and bake it blind. Peel and slice the bananas and place them in the flan. Cover quickly – before they discolour – with the custard and, when this is cold, with whipped cream and sprinkle with coconut. *Serves 4.*

Blackberry and Cream Cheese Flan

Really a sort of cheesecake but less rich than most. The gleaming blackberries look very attractive on the creamy base.

6 oz (150 g) short crust pastry (p. 55)
6 oz (150 g) cream cheese
1 oz (25 g) icing sugar

4 tablespoons single cream
1 tablespoon lemon juice
1 lb (450 g) blackberries
glaze (p. 56)

Line an 8 inch (20 cm) flan tin with the pastry and bake it blind. Beat the cream cheese with the icing sugar until smooth and gradually stir in the cream and lemon juice. Turn into the cold flan case, spread evenly and leave in a cool place to set. When firm, arrange the rinsed blackberries on top and coat with a glaze. *Serves 6.*

Blackberry Syllabub Flan

The blackberries must be very ripe and sweet. Keep those little half-red, boot-button jobs for something else.

6 oz (150 g) short crust pastry
  (p. 55)
6 oz (150 g) blackberries
1 lemon

6 tablespoons rosé wine
2 oz (50 g) caster sugar
¼ pint (1.5 dl) double cream

Line an 8 inch (20 cm) flan tin with the pastry, bake it blind and cover, when cool, with the rinsed blackberries keeping back a few for decoration. Chill while you mix together the grated rind of the lemon and half the juice with the wine, sugar and cream. Whisk until thick and standing in peaks then pour over the blackberries and chill for a further 20 minutes. Decorate with the reserved blackberries just before serving. *Serves 6.*

Blackcurrant Meringue Pie

Many people find the taste of blackcurrants rather strong and this recipe takes the bitter edge off them.

6 oz (150 g) short crust pastry
  (p. 55)
8 oz (225 g) blackcurrants
½ pint (3 dl) blackcurrant juice
  (made up with water)

1 oz (25 g) cornflour
2 eggs
4 oz (100 g) caster sugar

Line an 8 inch (20 cm) flan tin with the pastry and bake it blind. Simmer the blackcurrants in a little water for only a few minutes then strain off the liquid and make up to ½ pint (3 dl) with water. Mix 2 tablespoons of this with the cornflour, heat the rest and, when boiling, stir in the cornflour cream and keep stirring until clear. Remove from the heat, add the blackcurrants and the egg yolks and turn into the flan case. Beat the egg whites until stiff, beat in half the sugar gradually and fold in the rest. Spread the meringue over the filled case and bake at Gas Mark 6 (400°F, 200°C) for about 10 minutes. *Serves 6.*

Butter Tart – Canadian

A clever little spicy confection.

6 oz (150 g) short crust pastry (p. 55)
1 oz (25 g) butter
3 oz (75 g) sultanas
1 oz (25 g) demerara sugar

1 teaspoon cinnamon
1 teaspoon nutmeg
1 egg
$\frac{1}{8}$ pint (0.75 dl) milk

Line a flan tin with the pastry and place the butter in small pieces in it. Sprinkle with the sultanas, sugar, cinnamon and grated nutmeg. Beat the egg into the milk and pour over. Bake at Gas Mark 4 (350°F, 180°C) for about 30 minutes. Serve hot or cold but better hot. *Serves 4.*

Cheesecake

This is the classic Curd Cheesecake – and is excellent. Cheesecakes are currently enjoying a tremendous vogue. They frequently have a crushed biscuit and butter base and are often served topped with fruit and glazed and even with additional cream. You can stir a little soured cream into the curd cheese base to give it more edge and top it with pineapple, cherries, blackcurrants, strawberries, raspberries, black-berries, plums, greengages, glaze it, strew it with chopped nuts, whirl it with cream – anything you like – it will always look decorative and always be popular. My fear is that they will get to look so elaborate and taste so bland that they will degenerate into a sort of trifle. So – beware.

8 oz (225 g) short crust pastry (p. 55)
1 lb (450 g) curd cheese
5 oz (125 g) caster sugar
2 eggs

1 tablespoon single cream
4 oz (100 g) sultanas
2 oz (50 g) plain flour
lemon rind

Line a 9 inch (23 cm) flan case with the pastry and bake it blind. Press the cheese through a sieve and mix in the sugar, egg yolks, cream, sultanas, flour and plenty of grated lemon rind. Whip the egg whites stiffly, fold gently into the cheese mixture and turn into the flan case. Brush with a little egg or milk and bake at Gas Mark ½ (250 °F, 130 °C) for about 1 hour. Serve cold. *Serves 6.*

Cherry Flan

Cherries and almonds seem to have a special affinity. In fact, wild cherry blossom smells of almonds to me.

8 oz (225 g) short crust pastry (p. 55)
1 lb (450 g) black cherries
6 oz (150 g) sugar

2 oz (50 g) ground almonds
4 oz (100 g) plain flour
pinch of salt
3 eggs

Line a 9 inch (23 cm) flan tin with the pastry and spread the stoned cherries on it. Make a batter by mixing all the other ingredients together. Spread this over the cherries, dot with a little butter and bake at Gas Mark 6 (400 °F, 200 °C) for 40 to 50 minutes. *Serves 6.*

Chester Flan

An unusual almond meringue.

6 oz (150 g) short crust pastry (p. 55)
2 oz (50 g) butter

4 oz (100 g) caster sugar
1 oz (25 g) ground almonds
3 eggs

Line a 6 inch (15 cm) flan tin with the pastry. Melt the butter and sugar in a saucepan, add the almonds then stir in the yolks of the 3 eggs and the white of 1. Stir over low heat until thickening then pour into the flan case and bake at Gas Mark 5 (375 °F, 190 °C) for 20 minutes. Whip the remaining 2 egg whites stiffly incorporating 1 tablespoon sugar, pile on top and return to the oven for a further 20 minutes. *Serves 4.*

Chestnut Flan

Worth the trouble if you are fond of chestnuts. The apricots (which could be canned) relieve the richness.

6 oz (150 g) short crust pastry (p. 55)
1 lb (450 g) chestnuts
milk
vanilla pod
2 oz (50 g) sugar

¼ pint (1.5 dl) water
1½ oz (37 g) butter
8 oz (225 g) apricots
icing sugar
rum
caster sugar

Line an 8 inch (20 cm) flan tin with the pastry and bake it blind. Peel the chestnuts (p. 30) and simmer with the vanilla pod and sufficient milk to cover until tender then strain and sieve. Boil the sugar and water to a syrup and add the chestnut purée, the butter and enough of the vanilla-flavoured milk to make a smooth cream. Halve and stone the apricots and place them, cut side up, in the flan case. Sprinkle with icing sugar and rum and cover with the chestnut cream. Sprinkle thickly with caster sugar and brown under the grill. Serve cold. *Serves 6.*

Chocolate Chiffon Pie

A good, rich chocolate filling in a nutty flan case.

4 oz (100 g) plain flour
1 oz (25 g) caster sugar
3 oz (75 g) desiccated coconut
2 oz (50 g) margarine
4 eggs
5 tablespoons cocoa

¼ teaspoon cinnamon
¼ pint (1.5 dl) milk
1 oz (25 g) butter
1 oz (25 g) gelatine
¼ pint (1.5 dl) double cream

Make a pastry by sifting the flour, stirring in the sugar and coconut, rubbing in the margarine and mixing to a smooth dough with the yolk of 1 of the eggs and a little water. Roll out and line an 8 inch (20 cm) flan case and bake it blind. Now mix the cocoa and cinnamon to a smooth paste with a little of the milk. Add the rest of the milk, the 3 remaining eggs and the butter and cook very gently until the mixture lightly coats the back of the spoon. Dissolve the gelatine in a little hot water, mix in and chill, stirring occasionally, until the mixture is partly set, then beat and fold in the whipped cream and the stiffly whisked egg whites. Pour into the baked flan case and chill until set. *Serves 6.*

Coffee Meringue Tart

There seems no reason why Lemon Meringue Pie should get all the attention – this is just as good.

6 oz (150 g) short crust pastry (p. 55)
1 oz (25 g) cornflour
½ pint (3 dl) milk
5 oz (125 g) caster sugar

1 teaspoon vanilla essence
2 eggs
1 teaspoon instant coffee powder

Line a 7 inch (18 cm) flan tin and bake it blind. Blend the cornflour with 3 tablespoons of the milk. Bring the rest of the milk to the boil and stir into the cornflour cream. Return to the saucepan and stir over gentle heat until thick and smooth. Mix in 1 oz (25 g) sugar, the vanilla essence and the egg yolks, stir into the milk and turn the whole into the flan case. Now whisk the egg whites very stiffly incorporating half the remaining sugar. Dissolve the coffee in ½ teaspoon boiling water and fold into the meringue with the rest of the sugar. Pile on to the pastry filling and bake at Gas Mark ½ (250 °F, 130 °C) for 45 minutes. Serve cold. *Serves 4.*

Cottage Cheese and Honey Pie

This is a Greek recipe – *Mizithropita me meli* – which can be eaten warm or cold.

6 oz (150 g) short crust pastry (p. 55)
1 lb (450 g) cottage cheese
6 oz (150 g) honey

4 oz (100 g) sugar
4 eggs
1½ tablespoons cinnamon
icing sugar

Line an 8 inch (20 cm) flan tin with the pastry. Sieve the cottage cheese and mix with the honey, sugar, eggs and half the cinnamon. Blend thoroughly and spread in the pastry case. Bake at Gas Mark 4 (350 °F, 180 °C) for about 40 minutes and dredge with icing sugar and the rest of the cinnamon before serving. *Serves 6.*

Currant Almond Flan

Cut slices look very appetizing with the almond layer sandwiched between redcurrant jam and fresh redcurrants.

6 oz (150 g) short crust pastry (p. 55)
2 tablespoons redcurrant jelly
1 egg white

4 oz (100 g) caster sugar
3 oz (75 g) ground almonds
½ teaspoon almond essence
4 oz (100 g) redcurrants

Line an 8 inch (20 cm) flan tin with the pastry and spread the redcurrant jelly on it. Whisk the egg white stiffly, lightly fold in the sugar, ground almonds and almond essence. Turn into the flan case and bake at Gas Mark 4 (350 °F, 180 °C) for about 20 minutes then spread the redcurrants on top and return to the oven for a further 10 minutes. Serve hot or cold. *Serves 4.*

Date and Almond Flan

A richly dark topping chewy with almonds covering a creamy layer.

6 oz (150 g) short crust pastry (p. 55)
1 egg yolk
1 oz (25 g) caster sugar
½ oz (12 g) plain flour
about ⅓ pint (2 dl) milk

almond essence
1 oz (25 g) butter
3 teaspoons brown sugar
2 oz (50 g) dates
2 oz (50 g) chopped almonds

Roll out the pastry to fit an 8 inch (20 cm) flan case, bake blind and place on a serving dish. Whisk the egg yolk and sugar together until thick then beat in the flour, 1 tablespoon of the milk and the almond essence. Heat the remaining milk and, when nearly boiling, whisk gradually into the egg mixture. Return to the pan and heat gently, stirring, until boiling. Remove, beat in ½ oz (12 g) of the butter and leave to cool, stirring occasionally, then pour into the pastry case. Melt the remaining butter and mix in the brown sugar, chopped dates and toasted almonds and spread over the flan. Serve chilled. *Serves 4 to 5.*

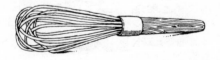

Date Tart

Dates, being dried and fleshy, soak up a pleasing amount of the liquor in this recipe.

6 oz (150 g) short crust pastry (p. 55)
4 oz (100 g) dates
rum or brandy

3 egg whites
2 oz (50 g) ground almonds
4 oz (100 g) caster sugar
extra sugar

Line a 7 inch (18 cm) flan tin with the pastry. Stone the dates, cut into four and soak in rum or brandy for 30 minutes. Beat the egg whites to a froth, add the ground almonds, sugar and drained dates and fill the flan case with the mixture. Sprinkle with caster sugar and bake at Gas Mark 4 (350 °F, 180 °C) for about 30 minutes. *Serves 4.*

Duke of Cambridge Flan

Crystallized fruit may be used instead of candied peel and both are improved by soaking in kirsch.

6 oz (150 g) short crust pastry (p. 55)
2 oz (50 g) candied peel

3 oz (75 g) caster sugar
3 oz (75 g) butter
2 egg yolks

Line a 7 inch (18 cm) flan tin with the pastry and scatter the candied peel over the bottom of it. Now put into a small saucepan the sugar, butter and egg yolks and when it boils pour immediately over the peel. Bake at Gas Mark 5 (375 °F, 190 °C) for about 20 minutes and serve hot. *Serves 4.*

Elizabethan Flan

Here glazed orange slices are arranged over a cream and brandy filling. It looks spectacular and tastes delicious.

2 large thin-skinned oranges
2 tablespoons honey
¼ pint (1.5 dl) water
6 oz (150 g) short crust pastry (p. 55)

¼ pint (1.5 dl) double cream
1 tablespoon brandy
2 oz (50 g) sugar

Wash the oranges, slice thinly and soak overnight in the honey and water. Next day simmer the mixture for about 20 minutes, drain and leave to cool. Line an 8 inch (20 cm) flan tin with the pastry and bake it blind. Whip the cream until just stiff, stir in the brandy and spread over the bottom of the cooled flan case. Arrange the orange slices in overlapping circles on top. Add the sugar to ¼ pint (1.5 dl) of the honey liquid and heat gently until the sugar has dissolved then boil rapidly until syrupy. Pour carefully over the flan. *Serves 5.*

Gainsborough Tart

Also known as Lincoln Tart. Rather like a coconut version of Bakewell Tart.

6 oz (150 g) short crust pastry (p. 55)	1 egg
jam	2 oz (50 g) caster sugar
1 oz (25 g) butter	4 oz (100 g) desiccated coconut
	¼ teaspoon baking powder

Line an 8 inch (20 cm) flan tin with the pastry and spread with jam. Melt the butter and stir in the beaten egg, sugar, coconut and baking powder and pour into the flan case. Bake at Gas Mark 5 (375 °F, 190 °C) for 30 minutes. *Serves 4.*

Gooseberry Cream Flan

A Gooseberry Fool set in a pastry case.

6 oz (150 g) short crust pastry (p. 55)	½ pint (3 dl) Custard (p. 209)
12 oz (325 g) gooseberries	¼ oz (6 g) gelatine
4 oz (100 g) sugar	¼ pint (1.5 dl) double cream

Line an 8 inch (20 cm) flan case with the pastry and bake it blind. Simmer the gooseberries with the sugar and a very little water until soft then drain briskly, sieve and mix with the custard. Dissolve the gelatine in a little hot water and stir in. Finally fold in the whipped cream, turn into the flan case and leave to set. *Serves 6.*

Grape Flan

The pale green grapes arranged on an almond base and set in a glaze look enchanting.

8 oz (225 g) short crust pastry
 (p. 55)
2 egg whites
6 oz (150 g) ground almonds
4 oz (100 g) caster sugar

3 oz (75 g) soft breadcrumbs
almond essence
12 oz (325 g) white grapes
apricot glaze

Roll out the pastry thinly and line a 10 inch (25 cm) flan tin with it. Prick the base and bake blind. Whip the egg whites stiffly and stir in the ground almonds, sugar, breadcrumbs and enough almond essence to give a good flavour. Spread evenly in the cold flan case. Peel, halve and de-pip the grapes and arrange them carefully in circles, cut side down, on top. Glaze and serve cold. *Serves 6.*

Hampshire Flan

A fluffier and more refined version of Mock Bakewell Tart.

6 oz (150 g) short crust pastry
 (p. 55)
jam
3 oz (75 g) caster sugar

3 oz (75 g) butter
3 egg yolks
2 egg whites

Line a 7 inch (18 cm) flan tin with the pastry and spread generously with jam. Whisk together the sugar, melted butter and eggs, spread on top and bake at Gas Mark 4 (350 °F, 180 °C) for about 30 minutes. *Serves 4.*

Hazelnut Pie

A Hungarian recipe. Mix your usual short crust pastry (p. 55) with sour cream instead of water and add an egg yolk and a little sugar.

8 oz (225 g) Hungarian short
 crust pastry.
4½ oz (112 g) roasted and ground
 hazelnuts

3½ oz (95 g) caster sugar
½ oz (12 g) cocoa
4 egg whites

Divide the pastry into two and line an 8 inch (20 cm) tin with half of it. Mix the nuts, sugar and cocoa together, fold in the stiffly beaten egg

whites and spread on to the pastry. Roll out the rest of the pastry, cut it
into long strips and make a criss-cross pattern on top of the filling.
Bake at Gas Mark 4 (350 °F, 180 °C) for 20 to 25 minutes. *Serves 5.*

Lemon Butter Pie

Marshmallows are a strange form of life but if you like their particular
texture you will like this American pie.

6 oz (150 g) short crust pastry (p. 55)	2 oz (50 g) butter
2 lemons	1 oz (25 g) cornflour
3 oz (75 g) caster sugar	3 eggs
	4 oz (100 g) marshmallows

Line an 8 inch (20 cm) flan tin with the pastry and bake blind. Put the
juice and grated rind of the lemons, the sugar, butter, cornflour, 2
whole eggs and 1 egg yolk into a saucepan and cook over very gentle
heat – stirring all the time – until the mixture just comes up to the boil.
Remove and cool slightly before folding in the remaining egg white,
stiffly whisked, and the marshmallows. Pour into the flan case and
brown lightly under grill for 3 to 4 minutes. Serve chilled.
Serves 6.

Lemon Chiffon Pie

You can substitute an orange for the lemon and make this into Orange
Chiffon Pie.

6 oz (150 g) short crust pastry (p. 55)	1 lemon
2 eggs	pinch of salt
3 oz (75 g) caster sugar	1 teaspoon gelatine
	2 tablespoons double cream

Line an 8 inch (20 cm) flan tin with the pastry and bake blind. Beat the
yolks of the eggs with 2 oz (50 g) of the sugar and add the juice of the
lemon and the salt. Whisk over gentle heat until thick then remove
and add the grated rind of half the lemon and the gelatine dissolved in
a little water. Continue whisking until light and fluffy and on the point
of setting. Whisk the whites with the rest of the sugar and fold into the
mixture together with the whipped cream. Whisk until it will hold its
shape then pile into the pastry case and chill. *Serves 6.*

Lemon Meringue Pie

Originally American but has become an international star.

6 oz (150 g) short crust pastry
  (p. 55)
1 oz (25 g) cornflour
½ pint (3 dl) milk

1 oz (25 g) sugar
2 eggs
1 lemon
4 oz (100 g) caster sugar

Line an 8 inch (20 cm) flan tin with the pastry and bake it blind. Mix the cornflour with a little of the milk, heat the remainder and pour on. Return to the saucepan and boil, while stirring, for 3 to 4 minutes. Add the sugar, cool a little, then beat in the egg yolks and the grated rind and juice of the lemon. Turn into the flan case and set for a few minutes in a low oven. Whip the egg whites until stiff and dry, whisk in 1 tablespoon of the caster sugar then fold in the remainder lightly and pile on top of the pie. Dust with a little more caster sugar and finish off at Gas Mark 1 (275 °F, 140 °C) for 10 to 15 minutes. *Serves 6.*

Lemon Tart

This makes a very runny mixture but it sets in the cooking to a golden, lemon-curdy consistency.

6 oz (150 g) short crust pastry
  (p. 55)
6 oz (150 g) caster sugar

3 eggs
2 lemons
4 oz (100 g) butter

Line a 7 inch (18 cm) flan tin with the pastry. Cream the sugar and eggs together and stir in the juice and grated rind of the lemons. Add the melted butter and pour the mixture into the flan case. Lay a few very thin slices of lemon on top and bake at Gas Mark 6 (400 °F, 200 °C) for about 30 minutes. Serve hot or cold. *Serves 4.*

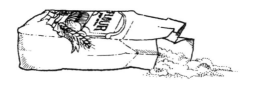

Lent Pie

Almost a custard pie but the ground rice gives it a rather different texture.

6 oz (150 g) short crust pastry (p. 55)
½ oz (12 g) ground rice
1 pint (6 dl) milk

2 oz (50 g) sugar
1 egg
nutmeg

Line a 7 inch (18 cm) flan case with the pastry. Mix the ground rice with a little milk and then put ½ pint of it on to heat and, when almost boiling, stir in the ground rice mixture. Boil for 1 to 2 minutes then stir in 1 dessertspoon of the sugar and pour into the pastry case. Now heat the remaining milk with the egg and the rest of the sugar up to blood heat then strain into the pastry case on top of the ground rice. Sprinkle well with grated nutmeg and bake at Gas Mark 4 (350 °F, 190 °C) for 40–60 minutes. *Serves 4.*

Marmalade Pie

5 oz (125 g) short crust pastry (p. 55)
8 oz (225 g) fresh white breadcrumbs

3 tablespoons marmalade
3 tablespoons undiluted lemon squash
caster sugar

Line a 7 inch (18 cm) pie plate with the pastry. Mix together the breadcrumbs, marmalade and lemon squash and spread on the pastry. Decorate with scraps of pastry cut into leaves, sprinkle with sugar and bake at Gas Mark 6 (400 °F, 200 °C) for 20 to 30 minutes. *Serves 4.*

Mint Pasty

Like a large Eccles Cake but the mint makes it different.

8 oz (225 g) flaky pastry (p. 55)
8 oz (225 g) currants
2 oz (50 g) sugar

2 cups hot water
3 oz (75 g) chopped mint
beaten egg

Roll out the pastry thinly and use half of it to line an 8 inch (20 cm) tin. Mix the currants with the sugar, pour the hot water over and leave to swell for a few minutes then spread over the pastry, sprinkle with the mint and cover with a lid made from the remaining pastry. Brush with beaten egg and bake at Gas Mark 7 (425 °F, 220 °C) for about 20 minutes. *Serves 4.*

Neapolitan Pie

The Italians are clever at making delicious dishes out of nothing very much. It is surprising how good this pie is.

8 oz (225 g) short crust pastry
 (p. 55)
2 egg yolks
2 oz (50 g) sugar

2 oz (50 g) flour
½ pint (3 dl) milk
almond essence
roast almonds

Divide the pastry into two and line a 7 inch (18 cm) tin with half of it. Beat the egg yolks with the sugar until creamy then add the flour and carry on beating. Stir into the boiled milk and heat gently until thick – do not boil. Stir in a few drops of almond essence. Now put the mixture into the refrigerator until very cold. If it is not very cold at the time of cooking it will curdle. Turn the filling into the pastry case and cover with the remaining pastry, sealing well so that no air can get in. Bake at Gas Mark 7 (425 °F, 220 °C) for 20 minutes and serve sprinkled with roast almonds, either hot or cold. *Serves 4.*

Orange Cream Tart

A very sharp pointed knife is needed to cut this elegantly.

4 oz (100 g) short crust pastry
 (p. 55)
2 oz (50 g) butter
4 oz (100 g) icing sugar
2 egg yolks

4 tablespoons cream
4 oranges
kirsch (optional)
glacé cherries

Roll out the pastry thinly, line an 8 inch (20 cm) fireproof plate with it and bake blind. Cream the butter and sugar until light and fluffy and gradually beat in the egg yolks and cream. Peel the oranges removing all the pith, and slice thinly. Spread half the cream over the pastry, cover with half the sliced orange, sprinkle with kirsch and cover with the remaining cream and orange slices. Sprinkle with more kirsch and decorate with cherries. *Serves 4.*

Orange Tart

The chopped peel gives this a very strong orange flavour.

6 oz (150 g) short crust pastry (p. 55)	3 oz (75 g) caster sugar
2 oranges	2 eggs
3 oz (75 g) butter	½ teaspoon vanilla essence

Roll out the pastry and line an 8 inch flan tin. Peel the oranges thinly and chop the rind finely. Cream the butter and sugar together, beat in each yolk separately, add 2 tablespoons orange juice, the orange rind and vanilla essence. Whisk the egg whites stiffly and fold in lightly. Turn into the flan case and bake at Gas Mark 4 (350 °F, 180 °C) for about 20 minutes. When nearly done dredge with caster sugar. Serve hot or cold. *Serves 4*.

Parisian Tart

A smooth filling tasting lemony and faintly spiced.

6 oz (150 g) short crust pastry (p. 55)	2 tablespoons milk
3 oz (75 g) butter	1 oz (25 g) cornflour
3 oz (75 g) caster sugar	1 oz (25 g) ground almonds
2 eggs	2 oz (50 g) cake crumbs
	½ teaspoon cinnamon

Roll out the pastry and line an 8 inch (20 cm) flan case. Cream the butter and sugar together until thick, add the eggs separately and beat well. Mix the milk and cornflour smoothly together and add. Now stir in the ground almonds, crumbs, cinnamon and lemon juice. Turn into the pastry case and bake at Gas Mark 4 (350 °F, 180 °C) for 20 minutes. Dredge with sugar before serving. *Serves 6*.

Pecan Pie

Since pecan nuts are Mississippi hickories we don't get hold of them every day of the week but when you do have some try this sweet pie.

8 oz (225 g) short crust pastry (p. 55)	4 oz (100 g) honey
2 oz (50 g) butter	3 eggs
4 oz (100 g) brown sugar pieces	4 oz (100 g) shelled pecan nuts

Line a pie plate with the pastry and decorate the edges. Cream the butter and sugar and add the honey, beaten eggs and chopped nuts. Spread over the pastry and bake at Gas Mark 6 (400 °F, 200 °C) for 10 minutes then reduce to Gas Mark 2 (300 °F, 150 °C) for a further 30 minutes. *Serves 6.*

Pinch Pie

A good way of using up leftover egg whites. It makes a crisp and glamorous shell for some special fruit. An electric mixer is a help in the making.

1 teaspoon water	4½ oz (112 g) icing sugar
1 teaspoon white vinegar	½ teaspoon baking powder
1 teaspoon vanilla essence	pinch of salt
3 egg whites	

Mix the water, vinegar and vanilla essence together in a small cup. Whisk the egg whites stiffly and add, very slowly, the icing sugar sifted with the baking powder and salt. As you beat in this mixture add alternately with it a few drops of the mixture in the cup and when all has been mixed together go on beating for several minutes. Heap this meringue into a buttered and floured flan tin and, with a spatula, shape it into the form of a tart. Bake at Gas Mark ½ (250 °F, 130 °C) until crisp (an hour or more) and fill with any well-drained fresh, stewed or canned fruit when cold. *Serves 6.*

Pineapple Flan

The pineapple is set in the custard and topped with meringue.

6 oz (150 g) short crust pastry (p. 55)	1 oz (25 g) caster sugar
8 oz (225 g) can crushed pineapple	2 eggs

Line an 8 inch (20 cm) flan tin with the pastry and bake blind. Strain the syrup from the pineapple and place ¼ pint of it (1.5 dl) in a saucepan with the sugar. Bring to the boil and simmer for 5 minutes. Let it cool slightly then add the egg yolks and stir over a very low heat until thickening. Arrange the pineapple in the flan case, cover with the custard and spread the stiffly whisked whites on top. Bake at Gas Mark 3 (325 °F, 170 °C) for about 30 minutes. Serve hot or cold. *Serves 5.*

Praline Flan

Try and get big fat raisins (not sultanas) for this flan.

8 oz (225 g) short crust pastry
  (p. 55)
1 pint (6 dl) Custard (p. 209)
2 oz (50 g) ground almonds

1 egg
2 oz (50 g) raisins
1 oz (25 g) caster sugar

Roll out the pastry to fill a 7 inch (18 cm) flan case and bake it blind.
Add the almonds and yolk of the egg to the custard and beat well.
Arrange the raisins in the flan case and pour the custard over. Beat the
white stiffly with the caster sugar and spread on top. Bake at Gas Mark
2 (300 °F, 150 °C) until the meringue is crisp and golden – about 30
minutes. Serve hot or cold. *Serves 4.*

Pumpkin Pie

Pumpkin is pretty bland and there is an awful lot of it. This recipe
makes a nice spicy pie. The peeled pumpkin should first be simmered
until soft.

4 oz (100 g) flaky pastry (p. 55)
¼ pint (1.5 dl) sweet milk
2 cups well drained cooked
  pumpkin
2 eggs
2 oz (50 g) flour

2 oz (50 g) brown sugar
1 teaspoon salt
1½ teaspoons cinnamon
½ teaspoon ginger
egg white

Line an 8 inch (20 cm) tin with the pastry. Stir the milk into the
pumpkin, add the beaten eggs, flour, sugar, salt and spices and beat
well for 5 minutes. Brush the inside of the pastry with white of egg,
turn in the filling and bake at Gas Mark 7 (425 °F, 180 °C) for 20 to 30
minutes more. The filling should be set and browned. *Serves 6.*

Raspberry and Redcurrant Tart

One of the very best of the summer tarts. Use a rich short crust pastry (p. 55), sweetened and mixed with an egg.

6 oz (150 g) rich short crust
  pastry
1½ lbs (675 g) raspberries

8 oz (225 g) redcurrants
6 oz (150 g) sugar
1 tablespoon redcurrant jelly

Roll out the pastry thinly, line a 10 inch (25 cm) flan tin with it and bake blind. Cook the fruit with the sugar for a few minutes until the juice runs then strain and spread in the flan case. Add the redcurrant jelly to the juice and cook, while stirring, until thick. Pour over the fruit when it has cooled and leave the glaze to set. *Serves 6.*

Raspberry Pie – Dutch

The raspberries are set in a rich cream.

2 lbs (900 g) raspberries
4 oz (100 g) sugar
½ oz (12 g) butter
1 oz (25 g) flour
pinch of salt

¼ teaspoon cinnamon
13½ oz (440 g) tin evaporated
  milk
4 oz (100 g) flaky pastry (p. 55)

Place the raspberries in a pie dish then mix the other ingredients together and pour over. Cover with the pastry, make 2 or 3 cuts in the top and bake at Gas Mark 7 (425 °F, 220 °C) until the crust is golden brown. Serve warm, sprinkled with sugar. *Serves 6.*

Rhubarb and Date Pie

The acidity of the rhubarb is counterbalanced by the sweetness of the dates.

10 oz (275 g) short crust pastry
  (p. 55)
1½ lbs (675 g) rhubarb

8 oz (225 g) dates
orange rind
4 oz (100 g) caster sugar

Line an 8 inch (20 cm) flan tin with half the pastry and fill it with the chopped rhubarb and dates, grated orange rind and sugar in layers. Cover with the rest of the pastry and bake at Gas Mark 4 (350 °F, 180 °C) for about 30 minutes. *Serves 6.*

Rhubarb Butterscotch Pie

Equally good with washed, topped and tailed gooseberries. The fruit sets in a toffee-like mixture.

6 oz (150 g) short crust pastry (p. 55)
1 lb (450 g) rhubarb
4 oz (100 g) brown sugar
1 oz (25 g) flour
1 tablespoon water
pinch of salt
2 eggs

Line an 8 inch (20 cm) flan tin with the pastry and fill it with the chopped rhubarb. Mix the other ingredients together and pour over. Bake at Gas Mark 7 (425 °F, 220 °C) for 10 minutes then at Gas Mark 3 (325 °F, 170 °C) for 30 minutes more. Serve hot or cold. *Serves 4.*

Rum Pie

The first time I made this the top sank into the bottom without a trace, so let the bottom set *firm* before continuing.

6 oz (150 g) short crust pastry (p. 55)
2 eggs
2 oz (50 g) sugar
pinch of salt
1 teaspoon cornflour
½ pint (3 dl) milk
¼ oz (6 g) gelatine
2 tablespoons rum
4 oz (100 g) chocolate
⅛ pint (0.75 dl) double cream
sugar to taste
few drops of rum

Line an 8 inch (20 cm) flan tin with the pastry and bake blind. Beat the yolks of the eggs with the sugar and salt, stir in the cornflour and gradually add the hot milk. Cook until thick then add the gelatine dissolved in a little hot water. Cool and then fold in the stiffly beaten egg whites and stir in the rum. Leave to set firm. Make the topping by melting the chocolate in a little water over gentle heat. Mix the whipped cream with a little sugar and rum and add the cooled chocolate. Cover the pie with this and chill. *Serves 6.*

Strawberry Cream Tart

Glazed strawberries set upon a sort of crème patissière.

6 oz (150 g) short crust pastry   ½ pint (3 dl) milk
   (p. 55)   vanilla essence
3 egg yolks   ¼ pint (1.5 dl) double cream
3 oz (75 g) caster sugar   8 oz (225 g) strawberries
1½ oz (37 g) flour   redcurrant jelly

Line an 8 inch (20 cm) flan tin with the pastry and bake blind. Blend the egg yolks and sugar together until creamy then work in gradually the sieved flour and the milk. Place in a saucepan and bring slowly to the boil stirring all the time. Boil for a few minutes to cook the flour then add the vanilla essence and leave to cool. Fold in the lightly whipped cream and turn into the flan case. Arrange the strawberries on top and glaze with the warmed redcurrant jelly. *Serves 4.*

Strawberry Surprise Flan

A thick layer of firm mousse lightly flavoured with orange sandwiched between two layers of strawberries.

6 oz (150 g) short crust pastry   1 orange
   (p. 55)   ½ oz (12 g) gelatine
8 oz (225 g) strawberries   juice 1 lemon
2 eggs   ¼ pint (1.5 dl) evaporated milk
2 oz (50 g) caster sugar

Line an 8 inch (20 cm) flan case with the pastry and bake blind. When cool cover the base with sliced strawberries reserving a few for decoration. Put the egg yolks, sugar and grated orange rind into a bowl over a pan of hot water and whisk until thick. Dissolve the gelatine in the juice of the orange and the lemon and stir in. Whip the evaporated milk until frothy and thickening and fold in, then the stiffly whisked egg whites. Turn the mixture into the flan case and leave to set. Decorate with the reserved strawberries cut in half before serving. *Serves 4.*

Strawberry Yogurt Flan

In this unusual recipe the yogurt is set with strawberry jelly, spread with strawberries and glazed with the rest of the jelly.

6 oz (150 g) short crust pastry (p. 55)
½ pint (3 dl) strawberry jelly
1 oz (25 g) caster sugar

¼ pint (1.5 dl) plain yogurt (p. 142)
8 oz (225 g) strawberries

Line an 8 inch (20 cm) flan tin with the pastry and bake blind. Pour half the liquid jelly on to the sugar and stir until dissolved then stir in the yogurt. Cool then pour into the flan case and leave to set. Halve or slice the strawberries and arrange them on top of the yogurt jelly and pour the rest of the strawberry jelly over. Leave to set thoroughly. *Serves 6.*

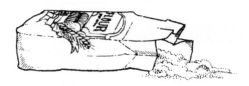

Treacle Flan

A change from the usual Treacle Flan which is simply syrup, bread-crumbs and a little lemon.

6 oz (150 g) short crust pastry (p. 55)
4 oz (100 g) breadcrumbs
4 oz (100 g) mixed dried fruit
1 dessert apple
1 lemon

mixed spice
ground ginger
1 oz (25 g) sugar
2 tablespoons milk
2 tablespoons golden syrup

Line an 8 inch (20 cm) flan tin with the pastry and fill with all the other ingredients well mixed together. Criss-cross with thin pastry strips and bake at Gas Mark 7 (425 °F, 220 °C) for 10 minutes then at Gas Mark 4 (350 °F, 180 °C) for a further 15 minutes. *Serves 6.*

Opposite Grape Flan (*page 71*)

Treacle Tart – Norfolk

Treacle has become a misnomer these days for although we still refer to Treacle Pudding and Treacle Tart most of us now prefer the less strong flavour of golden syrup. All these things are immensely popular with children.

4 oz (100 g) short crusty pastry
  (p. 55)
4 tablespoons golden syrup
½ oz (12 g) butter

2 tablespoons cream
rind ½ lemon
1 egg

Roll out the pastry and line a 7 inch (18 cm) flan tin. Warm the syrup, remove from the heat and stir in the other ingredients. Mix thoroughly and pour into the flan case. Bake at Gas Mark 4 (350 °F, 180 °C) for about 30 minutes. *Serves 4.*

Opposite Cœur à la Crème (*page 90*)

Creams &
Mousses

Some of these are frankly extravagant as they rely heavily upon cream or eggs to set them. Many of them contain gelatine. Nowadays powdered gelatine is easy to obtain and easy to use. It must, however, be dissolved slowly and completely or you will detect the taste of it.

Creams and mousses always look attractive and are always popular. Presentation is important. Collect some pretty glass serving dishes and also some individual ones. Beware of pouring hot mixtures straight into glass dishes. A cold metal spoon placed in the dish before you pour will help to cool the mixture quickly and prevent cracking.

These puddings do not need a refrigerator to set them but some are improved, to my mind, by being served chilled. Petits fours or plain, sweet biscuits are often served with them.

Almond Cream

Nibs of browned almonds among the cream make this particularly toothsome. Add a dash of almond essence if you like.

2 oz (50 g) almonds
½ oz (12 g) gelatine

1 oz (25 g) sugar
½ pint (3 dl) double cream

Blanch the almonds by covering them with cold water in a small saucepan, bringing them to the boil for a few seconds, allowing them to stand in the hot water for a further few seconds then straining them and sliding off the skins. Chop the almonds then grill or bake them in the oven until golden brown. Dissolve the gelatine and sugar in 3 tablespoons hot water. Whip the cream stiffly and stir in the other ingredients. Turn into a glass dish and chill until set. *Serves 4.*

Almond Sweetmeat

A bit heavy on the eggs perhaps but the sight of this caramel-glazed ring mould and its nutty-creamy texture will quell your feelings of extravagance.

caramel

4 oz (100 g) sugar
¼ pint (1.5 dl) water

8 oz (225 g) caster sugar
7 tablespoons water
3 eggs
4 egg yolks
6 oz (150 g) chopped almonds

Make a caramel (p. 58) and pour it into a wetted ring mould. Dissolve the caster sugar in the water over gentle heat to make a syrup. Beat the egg and the yolks together, pour in the syrup when it has cooled slightly (or the yolks will curdle) and stir in the almonds. Pour into the mould, stand the mould in a tin of hot water and bake at Gas Mark 4 (350 °F, 180 °C) for about 20 minutes. Allow to cool before serving. *Serves 4.*

Apple Mousse

There are several ways of preventing cut apple from going brown – it can be sprinkled with lemon juice or immersed in sugar syrup or in plain water, water and lemon juice or water and salt. Do not let it stand in any of these last three for a long time or flavour will be lost.

4 large apples
1 lemon
½ oz (12 g) gelatine

3 eggs
2–3 oz (50–75 g) sugar
½ pint (3 dl) double cream

Wash the apples, cut them up roughly (no need to peel and core) and cook them with the rind of the lemon and a little water until soft. Sieve. Melt the gelatine with the juice of the lemon and a little hot water and add it to the apple purée. Whisk the eggs in a bowl over a pan of hot water until thick. Cool, stirring occasionally, then add to the apple mixture, sweeten to taste and fold in the cream. Turn into an 8 inch (20 cm) cake tin, leave to set then turn out and decorate with very thin slices of a red-skinned eating apple. *Serves 4 to 5.*

Apricot Cream

In my opinion the only thing to do with really ripe, fresh apricots is – eat them. For this, therefore, I suggest you use any that are past their prime or use canned or stewed, dried apricots.

½ pint (3 dl) apricot purée
½ pint (3 dl) double cream
¾ oz (20 g) gelatine
¼ pint (1.5 dl) apricot syrup

1½ oz (37 g) caster sugar
1 teaspoon lemon juice
cochineal

Whip the cream stiffly and stir into the purée. Dissolve the gelatine in a little hot water and stir into the apricot syrup. Add the sugar and lemon juice and leave to cool then stir into the apricot cream and add a few drops of cochineal to give a rosy colour. Turn into a wetted mould and leave to set. *Serves 4 to 5.*

Apricot Mousse

Less extravagant than the Cream and makes a light and delectable sweet course. Useful for using up the whites of eggs which many of the recipes in this chapter leave behind.

8 oz (225 g) dried apricots
½ lemon
2 cooking apples
sugar to taste

3 egg whites
grated chocolate or flaked
  almonds

Soak the apricots overnight then stew them with the pared rind and the juice of the lemon and the apple roughly cut up. Drain and sieve the purée, sweetening to taste. Whip the whites stiffly and whisk gradually into the purée. Pile into serving dishes and decorate. *Serves 4 to 5.*

Bavaroise

Escoffier and Larousse define 'Bavaroise' as a frothy confection based on tea, coffee or chocolate, sugar syrup and cream. It is nowadays used much more loosely to describe various sorts of cold creams.

$\frac{3}{4}$ pint (4.5 dl) milk
flavouring (chocolate, orange or
  vanilla pod)
3 egg yolks
1$\frac{1}{2}$ oz (37 g) caster sugar

$\frac{1}{2}$ oz (12 g) gelatine
3 tablespoons water or fruit
  juice
2 tablespoons double cream

Bring the milk to the boil with whatever flavouring is to be used. Cream the egg yolks and sugar well together and pour on the milk. Return to the pan and thicken without boiling. Strain and allow to cool. Dissolve the gelatine in the fruit juice or water over gentle heat and stir into the custard. Continue stirring the mixture until beginning to thicken then fold in the whipped cream, turn into lightly oiled mould and chill. Turn out when required and serve with any fruit or Chocolate (p. 207) sauce. *Serves 4 to 5.*

Blanc-Manger à la Princesse

To make almond milk blanch 4$\frac{1}{2}$ oz (112 g) almonds (p. 85) and pound to a smooth paste mixing in gradually nearly $\frac{1}{2}$ pint (3 dl) cold water. Place in a cloth and wring out the moisture into a small pan. Add 3$\frac{1}{2}$ oz (90 g) sugar and stir over gentle heat until dissolved.

3 tablespoons almond milk
piece orange rind
1 oz (25 g) gelatine

4 tablespoons water
$\frac{1}{2}$ pint (3 dl) double cream

Dissolve the gelatine in the water over low heat. When clear and syrupy add it to the almond milk and stir over ice until the mixture begins to thicken. Whip the cream and whip it gradually into the mixture until smooth. Turn into a wetted mould and chill. Unmould when set. *Serves 4.*

Brown Bread Cream

Try the contrast between the nutty crispness of the baked crumbs and the smoothness of the cream.

3 oz (75 g) brown breadcrumbs
3 egg yolks
1½ oz (37 g) sugar
¾ pint (4.5 dl) milk
vanilla or grated lemon to
  flavour

1 oz (25 g) gelatine
juice 1 lemon
2 tablespoons double cream

Bake the crumbs in the oven until crisp. Cream the egg yolks and sugar together and pour on the hot, flavoured milk to form a custard. Dissolve the gelatine in the lemon juice over gentle heat adding a little water if necessary. Add to the custard. Stir over ice until beginning to thicken then fold in the crumbs and the whipped cream. Turn into a mould to set. Unmould and serve as it is or with a fruit sauce. *Serves 4 to 5.*

Butterscotch Mould

You start off as though making toffee but stop when the mixture is *golden* – or you will have toffee.

1 oz (25 g) butter
2 oz (50 g) sugar
½ pint (3 dl) milk

1 oz (25 g) cornflour
grated chocolate to decorate

Melt the butter, stir in the sugar and cook until golden. Add the milk and bring to the boil. Blend the cornflour with 1 tablespoon water, add and cook for 2 minutes stirring continuously. Pour into dishes, leave to cool and decorate just before serving. *Serves 4.*

Chestnut Cream

1 lb (450 g) chestnuts
1½ pints (9 dl) milk
rind 1 lemon
vanilla pod
4 oz (100 g) caster sugar

¾ oz (20 g) gelatine
3 egg yolks
1 tablespoon Maraschino
½ pint (3 dl) double cream
cochineal

Peel the chestnuts (p. 30) and put them into a saucepan with 1 pint of the milk (6 dl), the lemon rind and vanilla pod. Simmer until tender then sieve. Dissolve the sugar and gelatine in the rest of the milk over gentle heat, cool slightly and add the egg yolks. Stir over very low heat until thickening then leave to cool and mix with the purée, the Maraschino, the whipped cream and enough cochineal to make a rosy mixture. Pour into a wetted mould and leave until set. Turn out and serve. *Serves 6.*

Chocolate Chinchilla

A super-light mousse.

6 egg whites	1 dessertspoon finely ground
4 oz (100 g) chocolate	coffee

Beat the egg whites stiffly and grate the chocolate into them. Fold in lightly together with the coffee. Turn into a buttered soufflé dish and steam – uncovered – for about 1 hour. Leave to cool then turn out and serve with cream. *Serves 4.*

Chocolate Cream

When turned out this looks good masked in single cream and decorated with Fanny Cradock's Chocolate Leaves. For these all you do is gather some small, well-shaped leaves (rose leaves are particularly good), tow them face down over a saucer of melted chocolate so that the upper surface is coated, lay them face up on a plate to dry and then peel off the leaf. The veins of the leaf will be perfectly imprinted on your chocolate replica. They keep well in an airtight tin and are useful for decorating both puddings and cakes.

$\frac{1}{4}$ pint (1.5 dl) milk	$\frac{3}{4}$ oz (20 g) gelatine
4 oz (100 g) chocolate	vanilla essence
2 egg yolks	$\frac{1}{4}$ pint (1.5 dl) double cream

Simmer the milk and chocolate together until smoothly mixed. Let it cool slightly then add the egg yolks and stir over gentle heat until thickening. Dissolve the gelatine in 1 tablespoon hot water, strain into the custard and add the vanilla essence. Whip the cream stiffly and stir it in lightly. Turn into a wetted mould and leave to set. *Serves 4.*

Chocolate Mousse

This is the basic, infallible and excellent Chocolate Mousse. It can be varied by adding a little strong black coffee, or rum, liqueur, the grated rind or juice of a Seville orange or chopped nuts.

4 eggs
4 oz (100 g) bitter chocolate

Melt the chocolate with very gentle heat then beat in the egg yolks. Whisk the whites stiffly and fold them in lightly. Spoon into individual glasses and serve – or chill if preferred. *Serves 4 to 5.*

Cœur à la Crème

Traditionally in Belgium this is made in special, perforated, heart-shaped moulds but you can compromise by using a sieve or colander lined with muslin. It is rich and delicious.

8 oz (225 g) cottage cheese
½ pint (3 dl) double cream
2 oz (50 g) icing sugar

2 egg whites
strawberries

Sieve the cottage cheese and stir into it the cream and icing sugar. Beat well then fold in the beaten egg whites. Press into moulds, sieve or colander and leave to drain over suitable receptacle in the refrigerator overnight. Unmould and serve with strawberries dredged with caster sugar. *Serves 6.*

Coffee and Rum Flip

The best way to flavour most coffee dishes is to make a coffee syrup by collecting leftover coffee and, when you have a bottleful, boil it down until thickish. Re-bottled and tightly corked it will keep for months and makes a strong and genuine coffee flavouring.

¼ pint (1.5 dl) double cream
1 dessertspoon rum
sugar to taste

1 teaspoon gelatine
2 tablespoons coffee syrup
3 egg whites

caramel
3 oz (75 g) sugar
¼ pint (1.5 dl) water

Whip the cream with the rum and sugar and turn into a glass bowl. Dissolve the gelatine in the coffee syrup over gentle heat. Keep warm while you make the caramel (p. 58) then mix the two together. Whip up the egg whites and whisk the hot mixture into them. When thick and setting slightly pile into the dish on top of the cream and leave to set. *Serves 4 to 5.*

Coffee Cream

2 egg yolks
½ pint (3 dl) milk
2½ oz (65 g) caster sugar

¾ oz (20 g) gelatine
½ pint (3 dl) double cream
teaspoon coffee syrup or essence

Beat the egg yolks and stir them into the milk when it is nearly boiling. Stir until thickening then add the sugar and cool slightly. Dissolve the gelatine in 1 tablespoon water over gentle heat and add. Whip the cream stiffly, stir it into the custard when nearly cold, add the coffee to taste and turn into a wetted mould. Turn out when set. *Serves 4 to 6.*

Coffee Cream – Roman

Since proper Italian Ricotta cheese is difficult to get you can make your own cream cheese for this. The ultra-hygienic milk we are supplied with today does not sour in the way it used to, so the best method is to put about 4 pints of milk (to make 1½ lbs cheese) into a large bowl in a warm place for 30 minutes. Then stir in 2 teaspoons rennet and after 3 or 4 hours in the warm the curd will have separated from the whey. Tie it up in a cloth and hang it to drain for 24 hours, stirring once or twice to redistribute the cream. It is then ready for use but, if required, will keep for 2 or 3 days in a cold place.

1½ lbs (675 g) Ricotta, cream or
  cottage cheese
4 oz (100 g) caster sugar

4 tablespoons double cream
2 oz (50 g) finely ground coffee
1 tablespoon cognac

Beat all the ingredients together, pile into individual glasses and chill for at least 1 hour. *Serves 6 to 7.*

Coffee Walnut Mousse

Instead of the coffee you can use ¼ pint (1.5 dl) coffee syrup (p. 90) and ¾ pint (4.5 dl) milk if you like.

½ pint (3 dl) strong black coffee
½ pint (3 dl) milk
2 oz (50 g) semolina
½ oz (12 g) gelatine
3 oz (75 g) caster sugar

2 eggs
vanilla essence
2 oz (50 g) chopped walnuts
¼ pint (1.5 dl) double cream

Heat the coffee and milk together. Stir in the semolina, bring to the boil and cook gently for 5 minutes. Dissolve the gelatine in a little water over low heat and add. Stir well, remove from the heat and beat in the sugar and egg yolks. Cool, then add vanilla, walnuts and cream. Whisk the egg whites until stiff and fold in gently. Turn into a dish and chill. *Serves 4 to 6.*

Convent Cream

This is an old family recipe, jealously guarded, which I publish with reluctance so that it may not be lost. It is really too good for us to keep to ourselves. Heaven alone knows how it got its name.

13½ oz (440 g) tin condensed
   milk
2 oz (50 g) sugar
1 oz (25 g) cornflour

2 eggs
almond essence
4 oz (100 g) ratafias

Mix the condensed milk with enough water to make it up to 1½ pints (9 dl). Heat well but do not let it boil. Mix the sugar and cornflour together and whisk up with the eggs until light. Add the hot milk and stir over gentle heat until thick. Flavour with almond essence. Put most of the ratafias into a dish reserving a few for decoration. Pour in the cream while still hot and leave to cool. Decorate and serve. *Serves 6.*

Cream Cheese Dessert

Lovely with strawberries, raspberries or a few white grapes.

1 lb (450 g) cream cheese
4 oz (100 g) caster sugar

1 large glass white wine
juice 1 lemon

Sieve the cream cheese and blend in the other ingredients. Pile into glass dishes and serve with little biscuits. *Serves 6.*

Crème Bacchique

Like a baked and chilled Zabaglione.

6 egg yolks
3 oz (75 g) caster sugar
1 pint (6 dl) sweet white wine

Cream the egg yolks and sugar together until thick. Bring the wine to simmering point and stir it gradually into the mixture. Pour into little fireproof pots, cover with foil, stand them in a baking tin filled with hot water and bake at Gas Mark 3 (325 °F, 170 °C) for about 40 minutes. Serve cold. *Serves 6.*

Crème Beau Rivage

To 'set the custard on ice' stand the custard in a pudding basin inside a larger bowl containing ice cubes, crushed ice or a mixture of ice and iced water.

3 egg yolks
1½ oz (37 g) caster sugar
1 level teaspoon arrowroot
4 lumps sugar
1 orange

¾ pint (4.5 dl) milk
1 oz (25 g) gelatine
1 egg white
3 tablespoons double cream
4 tablespoons redcurrant jelly

Cream the yolks with the sugar and arrowroot. Rub the lumps of sugar over the rind of the orange, add to the milk and bring to boiling point. Pour on to the yolks, return to the pan and thicken over gentle heat. Strain and leave to cool. Dissolve the gelatine in 2 to 3 tablespoons water and add it to the custard. Set the custard on ice and stir until thickening then fold in the whipped cream and the stiffly whisked egg white. Turn into a bowl and leave to set. Melt the redcurrant jelly in a saucepan with 2 to 3 tablespoons water. Bring to the boil and leave to cool. Peel the orange, slice thinly and arrange on top of the cream when it has set. Spoon the jelly sauce on top.
Serves 6 to 8.

Flamri de Semoule

'Flummery' is an expressive but mysterious word.

½ pint (3 dl) water
¼ pint (1.5 dl) white wine or
  lemon juice and water mixed
little lemon juice

3 oz (75 g) semolina
1½ oz (37 g) caster sugar
2 egg whites

Mix the liquids and bring to the boil. Sprinkle in the semolina and simmer for about 5 minutes stirring frequently. Remove from the heat and add the sugar. The mixture should be of a soft, dropping consistency. If too thick, add a little more water. Cool slightly then fold in the stiffly whisked egg whites and turn into an oiled mould. Leave to set. When required, turn out. Serve with Melba Sauce (p. 212) or a purée of strawberries. *Serves 6.*

Floating Islands

These are really in a category of their own. I believe they are originally Hungarian although I have been offered them in France. There is also a French version which involves a sponge cake soaked in liqueur, masked in Crème Chantilly, sprinkled with nuts and launched upon a similar sauce. The method sounds most unorthodox but they are, in fact, quite easy to make. The sauce may be flavoured with chocolate or coffee.

2 eggs
2½ oz (65 g) caster sugar
1 pint (6 dl) milk

vanilla pod
2 egg yolks
1 teaspoon flour

Beat the egg whites with 1 oz (25 g) of the sugar until really stiff. Have ready a large saucepan containing boiling water. Drop spoonsful of the mixture on to the surface (a few at a time – they must have room to expand) and simmer gently until well risen then flip over with a spoon and cook the other side for about 30 seconds. Lift out on to a large sieve or cake rack to drain – they are now of a spongy, marshmallow texture and quite easy to handle. Bring the milk to the boil with the vanilla pod and 1 oz (25 g) of the remaining sugar. Cream the rest of the sugar with the 4 egg yolks and the flour and slowly pour on the hot milk, stirring constantly. Return to gentle heat and stir until thickening. Remove and keep stirring until nearly cold. Extract the vanilla pod and pour the cream into a large serving dish floating the islands on top. Serve cold. *Serves 4 to 5.*

Fudge Cream

1 oz (25 g) gelatine
2 oz (50 g) bitter chocolate
4 oz (100 g) sugar

2 oz (50 g) butter
3 eggs
¼ pint (1.5 dl) double cream

Dissolve the gelatine in a little water over low heat. Melt the chocolate, sugar and water together and stir in the gelatine. Add the butter, stir until smooth and remove from the heat. Beat in the egg yolks one at a time. Whisk the egg whites until they form soft peaks. Fold in carefully. Turn into an oiled mould and leave to set. Unmould and decorate with the whipped cream. *Serves 6.*

Genoese Cream

Enough to make one wish oneself born in Genoa and weaned on such delicacies.

2 oz (50 g) macaroons
1 tablespoon brandy
½ pint (3 dl) milk
2 oz (50 g) caster sugar
rind ½ orange

½ oz (12 g) gelatine
2 egg yolks
1 oz (25 g) mixed glacé fruit
¼ pint (1.5 dl) double cream

Crush the macaroons and sprinkle with the brandy. Put the milk, sugar and thinly pared orange rind into a saucepan, bring to the boil and simmer for 10 minutes then add the gelatine and the beaten egg yolks and stir on very low heat until they thicken. Strain over the macaroons and brandy, add the prepared fruit and, when cool, stir in the chopped glacé fruits. Stir until on the point of setting then turn into a wetted mould. Leave to set in a cool place and unmould when required. *Serves 4 to 6.*

Geranium Cream

So many people grow sweet-scented geraniums in their homes that this subtle sweet presents no problem. It is delicious either on its own or with fresh fruit such as blackberries, raspberries or sliced greengages.

½ pint (3 dl) single cream
4 oz (100 g) caster sugar

2 sweet-scented geranium leaves
8 oz (225 g) cream cheese

Put the cream into a bowl over a saucepan of hot water together with the sugar and the geranium leaves. Steam gently and let the mixture get thoroughly hot then leave to cool with the geranium leaves still infusing in it. Sieve the cream cheese and mix in gradually. Cover and leave in the refrigerator for 12 hours. Remove the geranium leaves just before serving. *Serves 4 to 5.*

Ginger Cream

The combination of the hot ginger and the cool, smooth cream is irresistible.

2 egg yolks
$\frac{1}{4}$ pint (1.5 dl) milk
1 oz (25 g) caster sugar
$\frac{3}{4}$ oz (20 g) gelatine

2 tablespoons ginger syrup
2 oz (50 g) preserved ginger
$\frac{1}{2}$ pint (3 dl) double cream

Beat the egg yolks and add to the milk when nearly boiling. Stir until thickening then add the sugar and leave to cool. Dissolve the gelatine in 1 tablespoon water and mix in the ginger syrup and the chopped ginger and pour into the custard. Whip the cream stiffly and stir into the cooled custard. Turn into a wetted mould and leave to set. *Serves 4 to 6.*

Halva

The famous Greek sweetmeat. Pine kernels may be omitted if unobtainable. Serve cut into small squares with strong coffee.

12 oz (325 g) sugar
1 pint (6 dl) water
4 oz (100 g) honey
cinnamon stick
3 cloves
$\frac{1}{4}$ pint (1.5 dl) olive oil

8 oz (225 g) flour
2 oz (50 g) chopped walnuts
2 oz (50 g) pine kernels
2 oz (50 g) sultanas
1 teaspoon cinnamon
2 teaspoons sugar

Boil the sugar, water, honey, cinnamon and cloves to a thin syrup. Heat the oil until bubbling and stir in the flour gradually. Keep stirring with a wooden spoon until the flour starts to colour then add the nuts, pine kernels and sultanas. Continue cooking gently until the flour turns light brown. Remove from the heat and add the hot, strained syrup. Cover the saucepan and place on very low heat until all the syrup has been absorbed. Stir well and pack into a mould. When required, turn out and sprinkle with cinnamon and sugar. *Serves 4 to 6.*

Lemon Cream

Simple and excellent. A glass of sherry added will not come amiss.

1 pint (6 dl) double cream
2 tablespoons lemon juice
1 oz (25 g) ground almonds

1 oz (25 g) caster sugar
1 teaspoon grated lemon rind

Whip the cream stiffly, fold in the other ingredients and pile into individual glasses. *Serves 8.*

Norwegian Cream

To make caraque chocolate grate some good quality chocolate and place on a plate over a pan of hot water. Work it with a palette knife as it melts then spread thinly on a cold surface (marble is ideal) and leave until practically set. With a long, sharp knife shave it off slantwise so that the chocolate forms long scrolls and flakes.

2 tablespoons apricot jam
3 eggs
1½ oz (37 g) sugar
½ teaspoon vanilla essence

¾ pint (4.5 dl) milk
3 tablespoons double cream
caraque chocolate

Spread the bottom of a soufflé dish with the jam. Cream 2 whole eggs and 1 egg yolk with the sugar and vanilla essence then pour on the hot milk. Mix well together and strain into the dish and stand in a baking tin of hot water. Cover and bake at Gas Mark 3 (325 °F, 170 °C) for about 20 minutes until set. Leave to cool. Whip the remaining egg white stiffly and fold into the whipped cream. Cover the dish with the caraque chocolate and decorate with the cream. *Serves 4 to 5.*

Orange and Sherry Cream

1 oz (25 g) gelatine
1 pint (6 dl) milk
4 egg yolks
grated rind ½ orange
5 oz (125 g) sugar

4 oz (100 g) macaroons
½ wineglass sherry
¼ pint (1.5 dl) cream
glacé cherries

Soak the gelatine in a little warm water. Bring the milk to the boil and add to it the egg yolks, the orange rind, the sugar and the macaroons. Stir until the mixture thickens then add the gelatine and the sherry.

Leave to cool then stir in the cream and a few chopped glacé cherries. Pour into a mould to set and serve cold. *Serves 4 to 5.*

Orange Cream – Brazilian

A lovely dish for a hot summer evening.

caramel
4 oz (100 g) sugar
4 tablespoons water

½ pint (3 dl) orange juice
grated rind 1 orange
3 eggs
3 egg yolks
3 oz (75 g) caster sugar

Make the caramel (p. 58) and coat four small moulds with it. Heat the orange juice and rind together slowly. Whisk the eggs, yolks and sugar until light and creamy and strain into the hot orange juice. Stir well, pour into the moulds, cover and stand in a baking tin of hot water. Bake at Gas Mark 4 (350 °F, 180 °C) for about 25 minutes. Chill and turn out into individual dishes when required. *Serves 4.*

Orange Fluff

4 eggs
4 oz (100 g) sugar
2 oranges

2 lemons
cochineal
½ oz (12 g) gelatine

Beat the yolks of the eggs with half the sugar until fluffy. Add the grated rind of the oranges, the juice of the oranges and the lemons and a few drops of cochineal and stir until well blended. Dissolve the gelatine in a little hot water and add. Chill for about 30 minutes until the mixture is beginning to set, stirring occasionally. Beat the whites of the eggs until foamy, gradually add remaining sugar and continue beating until stiff then fold lightly into the orange mixture. Chill until set. *Serves 6.*

Orange Mousse

Another good home for superfluous egg whites. It can also be made with any other fruit juice or chocolate or coffee. Serve within about an hour of making or it will separate.

4 egg whites
4 oz (100 g) caster sugar
¼ pint (1.5 dl) orange juice

Simply whip up the egg whites stiffly then beat in the sugar and orange juice, pile into glasses and chill. *Serves 4.*

Passion Fruit Cream

I have a Passion Fruit that rambles all over the back of the house spangled with elaborate flowers from June to November. The first year it bore fruit I guarded them fiercely. They hung on the vine like luminous, smooth apricots for weeks and when I finally picked one and cut it open it was to find no flesh to speak of, just a strange, desiccated heart full of seeds and flax. Regretfully I decided that the passion fruit which we grow here are virtually inedible so for this recipe you will have to use imported ones – fresh or tinned.

6 oz (150 g) passion fruit purée   ½ pint (3 dl) double cream
1 oz (25 g) caster sugar   2 oz (50 g) gelatine
1 teaspoon lemon juice

Sieve the passion fruit to make the purée and to eliminate the seeds. Stir in the sugar and lemon juice and leave in a covered bowl for about 1 hour. Whip the cream stiffly and fold in. Dissolve the gelatine in a little hot water and add. Pour into a mould and serve iced. *Serves 4 to 5.*

Peach Cream

May be made with very ripe fresh peaches or apricots, or canned ones.

½ pint (3 dl) peach purée   1 oz (25 g) caster sugar
½ oz (12 g) gelatine   ½ pint (3 dl) double cream
¼ pint (1.5 dl) sugar syrup (p.
  17)

Sieve enough peaches to make the purée. Dissolve the gelatine in the warmed syrup and stir in the sugar, purée and stiffly whipped cream. Turn into a mould and leave to set. *Serves 4 to 5.*

Pineapple Mousse

3 eggs
3 oz (75 g) caster sugar
1 tin pineapple

1½ oz (37 g) gelatine
juice 1 lemon
½ pint (3 dl) double cream

Put the yolks of the eggs, the sugar and ¼ pint (1.5 dl) of the pineapple juice into a bowl over hot water and whisk until thick and creamy. Remove and continue whisking for 5 minutes. Dissolve the gelatine in the juice of the lemon and stir in. When the mixture is on the point of setting stir in the lightly whipped cream and the stiffly whisked egg whites. Turn into a dish and decorate with the pieces of pineapple. *Serves 6.*

Prune Mousse

One of the very few mousses which does not demand several eggs.

8 oz (225 g) prunes
tea to cover
sugar to taste
½ lemon

½ oz (12 g) gelatine
2–3 tablespoons double cream
1 egg white

Soak the prunes overnight in the tea then simmer until tender with enough sugar to taste and the grated rind of the lemon. Drain (reserving the liquor), sieve and stir in the juice of the lemon. Now dissolve the gelatine in the strained liquid and stir into the purée testing again for sweetness. Whip the cream and stir in when the purée has cooled adding the stiffly whisked egg white at the very end. Turn into a wetted mould and leave to set. *Serves 4 to 5.*

Raspberry and Redcurrant Mousse

The combination of these two fruits is the very quintessence of summer. This mousse may be eaten hot or cold.

8 oz (225 g) raspberries
8 oz (225 g) redcurrants

6 oz (150 g) sugar
2 egg whites

Pass the fruit through a sieve and add the sugar and stiffly whisked egg whites. Whisk over gentle heat for about 3 minutes when the mixture will start to thicken. Whip again before serving if using cold. *Serves 4 to 6.*

Raspberry Cream

2 tablespoons raspberry jam
cochineal
$\frac{1}{2}$ oz (12 g) gelatine
$1\frac{1}{2}$ oz (37 g) caster sugar

$\frac{1}{4}$ pint (1.5 dl) milk
1 lemon
1 pint (6 dl) double cream

Sieve the jam and dilute with water to make it up to $\frac{1}{4}$ pint. Add cochineal to give a good, strong colour. Dissolve the gelatine and sugar in the warmed milk, stir in the juice of the lemon and the raspberry syrup and finally fold in the stiffly whipped cream. Turn into a mould and leave to set. *Serves 4 to 6.*

Rum Cream

$\frac{1}{2}$ pint (3 dl) milk
1 bay leaf
2 oz (50 g) sugar

2 egg yolks
$\frac{1}{4}$ oz (6 g) gelatine
1 wineglass rum

Bring the milk to the boil and infuse the bay leaf in it for about 20 minutes. Add the sugar and egg yolks and stir over gentle heat until thickening then put in the gelatine previously dissolved in a little hot water. Remove the bay leaf and add the rum. Leave to cool, stirring occasionally, then pour into a wetted mould and allow to set. *Serves 4.*

Russian Rum Pudding

2 eggs
vanilla essence
3 tablespoons rum
3 oz (75 g) caster sugar

1 teaspoon gelatine
$\frac{1}{2}$ pint (3 dl) double cream
grated chocolate

Beat the yolks of the eggs, vanilla essence, rum and sugar together until light and foamy. Dissolve the gelatine in a little hot water then beat in. Whisk the egg whites until stiff and whip the cream. Fold the cream into the egg mixture then gently stir in the whites. Turn into a serving dish and decorate with chocolate. *Serves 4 to 5.*

St Valentine's Cream

Not expensive to make and very good to eat. It can be flavoured with grated orange rind or chocolate or coffee essence. Do not use cottage cheese as the texture is too grainy.

4 oz (100 g) cream cheese
2 eggs
2 oz (50 g) sugar

2 dessertspoons single cream
flavouring

Sieve the cream cheese and beat into it the yolks of the eggs, the sugar and cream. Flavour, and fold in the stiffly beaten egg whites. Pile into individual glasses and chill. *Serves 4.*

Strawberry Bavaroise

The most delicious possible filling for a Charlotte Russe.

1 lb (450 g) strawberries
1 lemon
4 oz (100 g) icing sugar

1 oz (25 g) gelatine
½ pint (3 dl) double cream

Sieve the strawberries and add to them the juice of the lemon and the icing sugar. Melt the gelatine in a little hot water and stir in then add the stiffly whipped cream. Mix well and turn into a wetted mould to set. *Serves 4 to 6.*

Strawberry Cream

The up-stage version of what we, as children, called Eton Mess. Ours was simply strawberries mashed up with sugar and top-of-the-milk. It has the twin advantages of making the strawberries stretch farther and bringing out the flavour. The following, however, was dreamed up in the French kitchen of the Second Empire. Raspberries or wild strawberries can also be used.

12 oz (325 g) strawberries
½ pint (3 dl) double cream

1 egg white
2–3 oz (100–125 g) caster sugar

Rinse and sieve the strawberries. Whip the cream and fold into it the stiffly whisked egg white and then the strawberry purée. Sweeten and turn into a bowl. *Serves 4.*

Tea Cream

Try Earl Grey or China tea to give a delicate flavour.

½ pint (3 dl) milk
1 oz (25 g) tea
½ pint (3 dl) double cream

¾ oz (20 g) gelatine
sugar to taste

Bring the milk to the boil, pour it over the tea and let it infuse for about 20 minutes. Strain and add half the cream. Dissolve the gelatine in a little hot water, stir into the cream and sweeten to taste. Whip the rest of the cream stiffly and stir in when the mixture has cooled. Turn into a wetted mould and leave to set. *Serves 4 to 5.*

Vanilla Cream

A basic recipe which happily accepts any flavour you like to add.

¼ pint (1.5 dl) cream
¾ pint (4.5 dl) milk
1 oz (25 g) caster sugar

1 teaspoon vanilla essence
½ oz (12 g) gelatine

Whip the cream and mix it gradually with the milk. Add the sugar and vanilla essence. Dissolve the gelatine in a little hot water and, when cool, strain into the cream, mix well and turn into a wetted mould to set. *Serves 4 to 5.*

Wine Mould

½ pint (3 dl) water
⅛ pint (0.75 dl) white wine
3 oz (75 g) semolina

1½ oz (37 g) caster sugar
2 egg whites
⅓ (pint 2 dl) double cream

Bring the water and wine to the boil, add the semolina and simmer for 10 minutes. Leave to cool then beat in the sugar, stiffly beaten egg whites and cream. Turn into wetted mould, leave to set and serve with fresh raspberries, loganberries or blackberries. *Serves 4.*

Yogurt Cœur à la Crème

A more everyday version of the Belgian Cœur à la Crème.

12 oz (325 g) cottage cheese   2 oz (50 g) caster sugar
5 oz (125 g) plain yogurt   1 oz (25 g) gelatine

Pass the cottage cheese through a sieve and blend it with the yogurt, sugar and gelatine dissolved in 2 tablespoons hot water. Press into moulds or yogurt cartons perforated with a skewer and leave to drain overnight. Delicious with fresh peaches or raspberries.
Serves 4 to 6.

Yogurt Pudding

A Dutch idea. Very refreshing.

8 oz (450 g) raspberries   1 pint (6 dl) plain yogurt
sugar to taste   juice 1 lemon
½ oz (12 g) gelatine   ¼ pint (1.5 dl) double cream
2 oz (50 g) caster sugar   cochineal

Cook the raspberries gently with a little sugar for a few minutes only then strain – reserving the juice. Dissolve the gelatine in the hot raspberry juice. Add the sugar and blend into the yogurt with the lemon juice. Stir in a few drops of cochineal and leave to set. Turn out and decorate with whipped cream. *Serves 4.*

Soufflés & Sweet Omelettes

Soufflés have acquired the reputation of being tricky and temperamental. They are not really either and have the considerable advantages that they are quickly made, economical, light and nutritious and use ingredients that are generally available in the kitchen. It is the egg whites which enable the soufflé to rise (and the base which bears the flavour) and soufflés usually require more egg whites than yolks. For a hot soufflé some sort of deep fireproof dish is needed. Modern ones are made of fine fireproof china which allows quick penetration of the heat. We always used to be told to fix a paper collar around the outside of the dish to hold the rising mixture up. It is a bothersome business and quite unnecessary. If the dish is filled to the brim and scraped off level with a metal spatula the mixture is locked to the rim of the dish and cannot do anything but rise. The dish, however, must be generously buttered. It is important that the oven is pre-heated to the required temperature and that the soufflé is not overcooked or it will shrink and be dry. A few of the lighter mixtures are steamed and not baked.

Omelettes are a boon to the busy cook as they are so quick to make. Do keep a pan specially for omelettes. It should be fairly small and thick. You will also need a good rotary whisk.

Almond Soufflé

| 4 eggs | 4 oz (100 g) ground almonds |
| 5 oz (125 g) caster sugar | juice 1 lemon |

Beat the yolks of the eggs and the sugar together in a basin over a pan of boiling water until creamy. Remove from the heat and stir in the ground almonds and lemon juice then fold in the stiffly beaten egg whites. Pour into a prepared soufflé dish and cook at Gas Mark 3 (325 °F, 170 °C) for 30 minutes. Serve at once. *Serves 4.*

Apple Soufflé

An unusual recipe from Hungary.

1 lb (450 g) apples	4 eggs
2 oz (50 g) butter	breadcrumbs
3½ oz (90 g) flour	apricot jam
1 pint (6 dl) milk	sultanas
7 oz (175 g) sugar	cinnamon and sugar
grated rind 1 lemon	

Peel, core and quarter the apples and cook for a few minutes in a very little water with a touch of sugar and lemon juice. Melt the butter, add the flour and cook for a few moments before stirring in the milk. Bring to the boil, stirring, and cook for 3 minutes. Mix in the sugar, grated lemon rind, the yolks of the eggs and then the stiffly beaten whites. Butter a soufflé dish, line it with breadcrumbs and put 1 inch (2½ cm) layer of this mixture in the bottom. Put in the apples spreading them with a little apricot jam and sprinkling them with sultanas then pour on the rest of the sauce and bake at Gas Mark 4 (350 °F, 180 °C) for 40 minutes. 10 minutes before the end of cooking sprinkle the surface with a little sugar mixed with cinnamon. May be eaten hot or cold. *Serves 6.*

Apricot Soufflé

Keep some dried apricots in store and when you have extra egg whites to use up try this.

8 oz (225 g) dried apricots	2 tablespoons double cream
2 oz (50 g) caster sugar	5 egg whites
2 egg yolks	

Cover the apricots with cold water and leave them to soak overnight then cook uncovered at Gas Mark 2 (300 °F, 150 °C) for about 1 hour. Strain, sieve and stir in the sugar, egg yolks and cream. Beat the egg whites stiffly and fold into the mixture when it is cold. Turn into a prepared soufflé dish and bake at Gas Mark 4 (350 °F, 180 °C) for 25 minutes. Serve hot. *Serves 4.*

Banana Soufflé

The richness of bananas is well counterbalanced in this hot soufflé.

6 bananas
1 orange
lemon juice
4 oz (100 g) caster sugar

1½ oz (37 g) nuts
4 egg whites
pinch of salt

Peel the bananas, mash them well and mix in the grated rind of the orange, its juice and a little lemon juice, the sugar and the chopped nuts. Whip the whites stiffly with the salt, fold in and turn into a prepared soufflé dish. Bake at Gas Mark 4 (350 °F, 180 °C) for 25 minutes. Serve at once. *Serves 6.*

Chestnut Soufflé

A tin of chestnut purée may be used and the milk omitted.

8 oz (225 g) chestnuts
¼ pint (1.5 dl) milk
vanilla pod
3 oz (75 g) caster sugar

1 small glass Maraschino
2 oz (50 g) butter
5 eggs

Peel the chestnuts (p. 30) and cook them in the milk with the vanilla pod, sugar, Maraschino and butter until soft, then sieve. Beat the yolks of the eggs and stir them into the cooled mixture then whip the whites stiffly and fold them in lightly. Pour into a prepared soufflé dish and bake at Gas Mark 5 (375 °F, 190 °C) for 25 minutes. Sprinkle with icing sugar and serve at once. *Serves 6.*

Chocolate Soufflé – Cold

Toasted almonds make all the difference to this chocolate soufflé.

3 eggs
2 oz (50 g) caster sugar
2 oz (50 g) chocolate
½ oz (12 g) gelatine

1 oz (25 g) almonds
vanilla essence
½ pint (3 dl) double cream

Whisk the yolks of the eggs and the sugar together in a bowl over a pan of hot water until thick and creamy, then remove. Melt the chocolate in a little water over gentle heat, add the gelatine and heat until dissolved then stir in the whisked mixture together with the toasted, shredded almonds and the vanilla essence. Fold in the whipped cream lightly and then the stiffly whisked egg whites. Turn into a prepared soufflé dish and leave to set. *Serves 4.*

Chocolate Soufflé – Hot

This recipe and the one before are pleasing as they utilize both the yolks and the whites of the eggs.

4 oz (100 g) cooking chocolate
2 tablespoons water
2 oz (50 g) butter

4 eggs
4 oz (100 g) icing sugar

Melt the chocolate in the water over very gentle heat then beat in the softened butter. Whisk together the yolks of the eggs and the sifted icing sugar until white and foamy and pour on to the chocolate. Beat together over low heat then mix in the stiffly beaten egg whites. Turn into a prepared soufflé dish and cook at Gas Mark 7 (425 °F, 220 °C) for 20 minutes. *Serves 4 to 5.*

Coffee Soufflé

A cold soufflé which is similar to but lighter than the Coffee Cream in the preceding chapter. Rather less Coffee Syrup (p. 90) may be substituted.

3 eggs
3 oz (75 g) caster sugar
¼ pint (1.5 dl) strong black coffee

½ oz (12 g) gelatine
½ pint (3 dl) double cream

Put the yolks of the eggs in a large bowl together with the sugar and coffee and whisk over hot water until thick and frothy. Dissolve the gelatine in a little hot water and add to the mixture when cold. Stir in the stiffly whisked cream and the whipped egg whites, turn into a serving dish and leave to set. *Serves 4.*

Custard Soufflé

A hot, light pudding that can be made any day of the week as it requires no special ingredients.

2 oz (50 g) butter
2 oz (50 g) flour
½ pint (3 dl) milk

2 oz (50 g) caster sugar
3 eggs

Melt the butter, stir in the flour, add the milk and cook for about 5 minutes stirring all the time. Add the sugar and beat in the yolks of the eggs. Whisk the egg whites stiffly, stir them in lightly and pour into a buttered dish. Bake at Gas Mark 6 (400°F, 200°C) for 20 minutes. Serve hot with Wine (p. 215) or any fruit sauce. *Serves 4.*

Fruit Soufflé

Very good made with blackcurrant or gooseberry purée.

4 eggs
2 oz (50 g) sugar
½ pint (3 dl) fruit purée

¼ pint (1.5 dl) double cream
1 teaspoon lemon juice
½ oz (12 g) gelatine

Put the yolks of the eggs, sugar and fruit purée in a bowl and whisk over hot water until thick and creamy. Remove from the heat. Whisk the cream slightly and stir in with the lemon juice. Dissolve the gelatine in a little hot water and add. Stir until the mixture begins to thicken then fold in the stiffly beaten egg whites as lightly as possible. Turn into a prepared dish and leave to set. Decorate with cream and chopped nuts. *Serves 4 to 5.*

Honey Chinchilla

4 oz (100 g) clear honey
6 egg whites
1 oz (25 g) walnuts

Put the honey to warm over gentle heat. Beat the egg whites stiffly and mix in the honey and chopped walnuts. Turn into a buttered soufflé dish and steam for 1 hour. Cool and turn out.
Serves 4.

Jam Soufflé

Use a well-flavoured jam. Pineapple, for instance, is too bland.

8 oz (225 g) jam
8 egg whites

1 teaspoon lemon juice
1 tablespoon liqueur (optional)

Sieve the jam, whip the egg whites very stiffly and whip in the jam. Add the lemon juice and the liqueur, if used, turn into a prepared soufflé dish and bake at Gas Mark 7½ (435 °F, 230 °C) for 15 minutes. Serve at once.
Serves 6.

Lemon Soufflé – Cold

Otherwise known as Milanaise Soufflé.

6 oz (150 g) caster sugar
3 eggs
2 lemons

½ oz (12 g) gelatine
⅓ pint (2 dl) double cream

Cream the sugar gradually into the yolks of the eggs and add the grated rind and the juice of the lemons. Whisk over low heat until thick then remove and continue to whisk for a few minutes more. Dissolve the gelatine in a little hot water and stir in. Whisk the egg whites stiffly and fold in together with the lightly whipped cream. Turn into a soufflé dish and leave to set. *Serves 4 to 5.*

Lemon Soufflé – Hot

Good with lemon-flavoured shortbread.

4 eggs
3 oz (75 g) caster sugar
1 lemon

Beat the yolks of the eggs with the sugar and the grated rind and juice of the lemon then whip the whites stiffly and fold them in lightly. Turn into a prepared soufflé dish and bake at Gas Mark 5 (375 °F, 190 °C) for about 10 minutes.
Serves 4.

Liqueur Soufflé

A sort of rich, hot trifle soufflé.

8 oz (225 g) sponge cake
5 tablespoons kirsch
2½ oz (70 g) mixed glacé fruits
2 oz (50 g) butter

1 oz (25 g) flour
¼ pint (1.5 dl) milk
2 oz (50 g) sugar
3 eggs

Break up the sponge cake and leave to soak in 1 tablespoon kirsch. Chop the glacé fruits finely and put to soak in another tablespoon kirsch. Melt the butter, add the flour and beat well. Gradually add the milk and cook, stirring well, for 5 minutes. Cool slightly then beat in the sugar, the yolks of the eggs and the rest of the kirsch. Fold in the stiffly beaten egg whites and pour half the mixture into a prepared soufflé dish. Now add the sponge cake and glacé fruit and finish with the rest of the soufflé mixture. Cook at Gas Mark 8 (450 °F, 230 °C) for 15 minutes then at Gas Mark 5 (375 °F, 190 °C) for a further 30 minutes. Serve at once. *Serves 5.*

Martini Soufflé

2 oz (50 g) caster sugar
2 oz (50 g) flour
rind 1 lemon
pinch of salt
¼ pint (1.5 dl) milk

2 egg yolks
1 oz (25 g) butter
6 tablespoons dry martini
3 egg whites

Put the sugar, flour, grated lemon rind and salt together in a saucepan over gentle heat and gradually stir in the milk. Bring to the boil stirring continuously and beat for 1 minute over low heat. Now add the egg yolks, butter and martini. Stir and remove from the heat. Beat the egg whites stiffly, fold in lightly and turn the mixture into a prepared soufflé dish. Cook at Gas Mark 5 (375 °F, 190 °C) for 40 minutes sprinkling with a little caster sugar after 20 minutes. Serve at once. *Serves 4.*

Noodle Pudding Soufflé

A richer mixture than most soufflés.

4 eggs
½ pint (3 dl) sour cream
4 oz (100 g) cottage cheese
⅓ pint (2 dl) milk
2½ oz (67 g) sugar
vanilla essence

4 oz (100 g) egg noodles
rind 1 lemon
2 oz (50 g) butter
handful of cherries
cinnamon

Mix the yolks of the eggs, the sour cream, cheese, milk, sugar and a little vanilla essence smoothly together. Boil the noodles until tender, drain and add the mixture together with the grated lemon rind. Beat the egg whites until stiff and fold in lightly. Melt the butter in a casserole, turn the mixture in and cook at Gas Mark 4 (350 °F, 170 °C) for 1 hour then scatter with the pitted cherries and cinnamon, and serve. *Serves 4 to 5.*

Omelette Soufflé

Quick and easy and can be enhanced by adding mashed bananas, stewed fruit, jam, chocolate, liqueurs, rum, even ice cream – if you're quick.

3 eggs
1 oz (25 g) caster sugar
1 tablespoon water

1 teaspoon flour
vanilla essence
½ oz (12 g) butter)

Cream the yolks of the eggs with the sugar until thick then add the water, flour and a few drops of vanilla essence. Fold in the stiffly whisked egg whites as lightly as possible. Heat the butter in an omelette pan and pour in the mixture. Cook over fairly moderate heat for about 10 minutes then place desired filling in the centre, fold over and serve, or simply fold over, sprinkle well with caster sugar and serve at once. *Serves 4.*

Orange Soufflé – Hot

Looks attractive baked in large orange or grapefruit shells.

2 oranges	1½ oz (37 g) butter
½ pint (3 dl) milk	2 oz (50 g) flour
1 oz (25 g) caster sugar	3 eggs

Grate the rind of the oranges into the milk and bring to the boil with the sugar. Melt the butter in a fairly large saucepan, stir in the flour and add the hot milk. Whisk until smooth then beat in the yolks of the eggs and leave to cool. Whisk up the whites of the eggs stiffly, fold them into the mixture and turn into a prepared soufflé dish. Bake at Gas Mark 6 (400 °F, 200 °C) for 35 to 40 minutes. Dredge with icing sugar and serve. *Serves 6.*

Pineapple Soufflé – Hot

½ pint (3 dl) milk	3 eggs
vanilla pod	4 oz (100 g) caster sugar
4 oz (100 g) butter	4 oz (100 g) fresh, canned or
4 oz (100 g) flour	crystallized pineapple

Bring the milk and vanilla pod to the boil, remove from the heat and leave to infuse for about 30 minutes. Melt the butter in a saucepan, stir in the flour and cook for 5 minutes then add the strained milk, stir and boil well. Let it cool slightly before beating in the yolks of the eggs, the sugar, the chopped pineapple and, finally, the stiffly whisked egg whites. Turn into a prepared soufflé dish and steam very gently for 45–60 minutes. Serve at once. *Serves 6.*

Prune Soufflé

8 oz (225 g) prunes	4 oz (100 g) caster sugar
1 lemon	1 oz (25 g) flour
3 eggs	½ oz (12 g) almonds

Cover the prunes in cold water and leave to soak for 3 to 4 hours then cook with the thinly pared lemon rind until tender. When cold, remove the stones and chop the prunes finely. Cream the yolks of the eggs with the sugar, stir in the flour, add half the shredded almonds, 1 teaspoon lemon juice and the prunes. Whisk the egg whites to a stiff froth and fold half of them into the mixture. Turn into a prepared soufflé dish and bake at Gas Mark 4 (350°F, 180°C) for about 15 minutes then pile the rest of the egg whites on top, dredge with caster sugar, scatter with the rest of the almonds and return to the oven for a further 15 minutes. Serve at once. *Serves 6.*

Raspberry Soufflé

---

8 oz (225 g) raspberries
⅛ pint (0.75 dl) double cream
2 oz (50 g) ground rice

2 oz (50 g) caster sugar
3 eggs
2 oz (50 g) cake or bread crumbs

Put the raspberries, cream, ground rice and sugar into a bowl and mash them to a pulp with a wooden spoon. Beat in the yolks of the eggs and the cake crumbs and fold in the stiffly whisked egg whites. Turn into a prepared soufflé dish and cook at Gas Mark 6 (400°F, 200°C) for about 30 minutes. Serve at once. *Serves 4 to 6.*

Rice and Apple Soufflé

---

1 lb (450 g) cooking apples
4 oz (100 g) caster sugar
1 oz (25 g) butter
rind ½ lemon
1 clove

cinnamon stick
2 oz (50 g) ground rice
¾ pint (4.5 dl) milk
2 eggs

Cook the apples with half the sugar, the butter, the thinly pared lemon rind, the clove and cinnamon stick until soft, then sieve. Mix the ground rice smoothly with a little of the milk, boil the remainder, add the ground rice cream and simmer gently for 15 minutes. Stir in the sugar, let the mixture cool a little then beat in the egg yolks and lightly stir in the stiffly whisked egg whites. Fill a prepared soufflé dish with alternate layers of rice and apple purée finishing with a layer of rice. Dredge well with caster sugar and bake at Gas Mark 4 (350°F, 180°C). *Serves 4 to 6.*

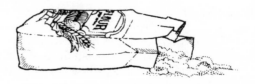

Opposite Coffee Cream – Roman (*page 91*)

Rice Soufflé

A useful soufflé but a bland one so serve with a Chocolate (p. 207), Wine (p. 215) or other well-flavoured sauce.

6 tablespoons water
1 pint (6 dl) milk
3½ oz (95 g) sugar
lemon rind
½ oz (12 g) butter

4 oz (100 g) rice
2 eggs
½ teaspoon flour
1½ oz (37 g) raisins

Bring the water and milk to the boil with half the sugar, a piece of lemon rind and the butter. Rinse the rice, add, return to the boil and leave on very low heat for about 25 minutes until the rice has absorbed the liquid. Remove the lemon rind. Cream the yolks of the eggs with the rest of the sugar and mix into the cooled rice then add the flour, the raisins and the stiffly beaten egg whites. Turn into a prepared soufflé dish and bake at Gas Mark 4 (350 °F, 170 °C) for about 30 minutes. Turn out and serve. *Serves 6.*

Rum Omelette

3 eggs
1 tablespoon double cream
1 teaspoon caster sugar
pinch of salt

½ oz (12 g) butter
1 small glass rum

Beat the eggs well with the cream, sugar and salt. Heat the butter in an omelette pan and pour the mixture in. Stir until beginning to set then fold over and cook a little longer. Slide on to a hot dish, pour the rum around, light it and serve. *Serves 4.*

Semolina Soufflé

rind ½ lemon
½ pint (3 dl) milk
1 oz (25 g) caster sugar

1½ oz (37 g) semolina
2 eggs

Simmer the lemon rind in the milk for a few minutes then add the sugar and semolina and cook until thick. Remove the rind and let the mixture cool a little before beating in the yolks of the eggs and then folding in the stiffly whisked whites. Pour into a buttered mould and steam gently for 1 hour. *Serves 4.*

Opposite Chocolate Soufflé – Cold (*page 108*)

Soufflé de Normandie

Although this is also an apple soufflé it is an altogether lighter confection than the earlier one.

1 lb (450 g) apples	cinnamon
4 oz (100 g) sugar	4 eggs
2 oz (50 g) butter	2 oz (50 g) almonds

Peel, core and slice the apples and cook them with the sugar and a little water until tender. Mix in the butter, cinnamon, the beaten egg yolks and, finally, the stiffly whisked egg whites. Turn into a prepared soufflé dish, sprinkle with the chopped almonds and cook at Gas Mark 6 (400 °F, 200 °C) for about 30 minutes. Serve at once. *Serves 4.*

Soufflé Rothschild

A very superior soufflé worth treating yourself to in high summer when peaches and strawberries are not exorbitant.

3 peaches	sugar to taste
8 oz (225 g) strawberries	3 eggs
2 slices pineapple	1 oz (25 g) sugar
2 small glasses Cointreau	2 tablespoons double cream

Slice the fruit, pour the Cointreau over, dust with sugar and leave for 1 hour. Cream the yolks of the eggs with the tablespoon of sugar, add 2 tablespoons of the liquid from the fruit and the whipped cream. Whip the egg whites firmly and fold in lightly. Put the soufflé mixture and the fruit (lightly drained) in layers in a prepared soufflé dish finishing with a layer of soufflé. Cook at Gas Mark 5 (375 °F, 190 °C) for 15 minutes and after 10 minutes dredge with icing sugar and continue cooking. Serve at once. *Serves 6.*

Strawberry Soufflé – Cold

May also be made with raspberries or loganberries.

6 oz (150 g) caster sugar	$\frac{1}{4}$ pint (1.5 dl) strawberry purée
2 lemons	$\frac{1}{2}$ pint (3 dl) double cream
2 eggs	4 oz (100 g) redcurrant jelly
$\frac{1}{2}$ oz (12 g) gelatine	

Whisk the sugar, juice and grated rind of the lemons and the egg yolks in a bowl over hot water until thick. Dissolve the gelatine in a little hot water and add, then stir in the fruit purée. Cool then fold in the stiffly whisked cream and the egg whites. Pour into a prepared soufflé dish and chill for 2 hours. Melt the redcurrant jelly over gentle heat, cool and when the surface of the soufflé is firm, pour it over. *Serves 6.*

Strawberry Soufflé – Hot

A hot strawberry dish is unusual. You might try this in winter with canned, bottled or frozen strawberries.

1 lb (450 g) strawberries	¼ pint (1.5 dl) milk
sugar to taste	2 oz (50 g) caster sugar
1½ oz (37 g) butter	3 eggs
2 oz (50 g) flour	cochineal (optional)

Take about three-quarters of the strawberries and sieve them, sweetening to taste. Melt the butter, stir in the flour, add the milk and boil well, stirring, before adding the sugar and strawberry purée. Remove from the heat and beat in the egg yolks, add a few drops of cochineal to brighten the colour and stir in the remaining strawberries, cut up small. Fold in the stiffly whisked egg whites. Turn into a prepared soufflé dish and cook at Gas Mark 6 (400 °F, 200 °C) for 30 to 40 minutes. *Serves 6.*

Tangerine Soufflé

This means real tangerines which have far more flavour than the currently popular clementines. The preponderance of pips does not matter in this recipe.

3 eggs	3 tangerines
2 egg yolks	½ oz (12 g) gelatine
1½ oz (37 g) caster sugar	juice 1 lemon
½ oz (12 g) lump sugar	3 tablespoons double cream

Mix the eggs and the 2 yolks with the caster sugar. Rub the lumps of sugar over the rind of the tangerines until they have absorbed the oil then crush and add to the eggs. Whisk in a bowl over hot water until thick and then remove and whisk for a further 5 minutes. Dissolve the gelatine in the juice of the lemon and add together with the squeezed juice of the tangerines and 2 tablespoons water. Stir over ice until almost setting then fold in the lightly whipped cream, turn into a prepared soufflé dish and leave to set. *Serves 6.*

Tansy

An English recipe dated 1856.

6 egg yolks	½ pint (3 dl) madeira
1 pint (6 dl) double cream	nutmeg
2 egg whites	icing sugar

Mix the egg yolks into the cream and beat in the egg whites. Add the madeira by slow degrees then flavour with grated nutmeg and icing sugar. Turn into a prepared soufflé dish, stand in a baking tin of hot water and cook at Gas Mark 4 (350°F, 180°C) for 30 to 40 minutes. Serve cold dredged with icing sugar. *Serves 6.*

Walnut Soufflé

2 eggs	¼ oz (7 g) gelatine
2 oz (50 g) caster sugar	¼ pint (1.5 dl) double cream
2 tablespoons coffee syrup	1 oz (25 g) walnuts

Whisk the yolks of the eggs and the sugar together over a pan of hot water until thick. Remove and whisk until cool. Heat the coffee and dissolve the gelatine in it. Stir into the egg mixture and then fold in the whipped cream and stiffly whisked egg whites. Turn into a prepared soufflé dish and leave to set. Decorate with the chopped walnuts. *Serves 4.*

Jellies

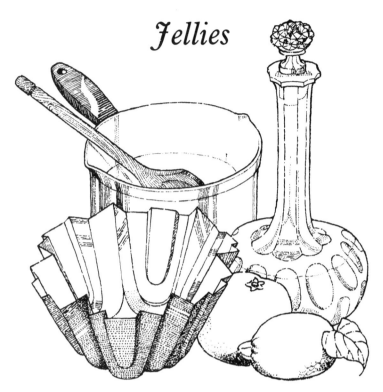

We have all come to associate jelly with a rectangular box, rubbery cubes and children's parties. The modern child seems to spurn jelly so perhaps it is *our* turn and time we realized that it doesn't have to come in a cardboard box and that it can taste of any of the twenty-five-odd flavours which follow. Try Maraschino, Crab Apple or Gooseberry Jelly, serve it in wineglasses or any pretty individual dishes with little biscuits to round off a substantial meal and discover what we have all been missing. Jellies are economical, glamorous, light (they can be made with artificial sweeteners) and tasty. They are quick and easy to make and only need time to set. Almost any of these can be turned into milk jelly by substituting evaporated or top-of-the-milk for some of the liquid.

    Home-made jelly used to be made to set with isinglass (got from some fresh-water fish) or agar-agar (a product of seaweed). The powdered gelatine available in any supermarket today is much easier to use and if you always have some in your store cupboard you always have a pudding course available. It should be sprinkled on to hot liquid or water (whatever is used in the recipe) and stirred until dissolved. If it fails to dissolve completely stand the cup in a saucepan of hot water over gentle heat and stir until clear. Jellies set faster in a refrigerator or cool larder.

Some of these recipes require a cloth for straining the jelly. Double muslin baby nappies are ideal or, failing that, a piece of clean cotton.

Unmoulding is sometimes a bit tricky and if the jelly does not unmould easily immerse it in hot water, remove immediately, tipping any water off the surface, invert and jerk it sharply on to the serving dish. It sometimes helps to ease the top surface away from the sides with the tips of the fingers. Moulds need careful maintenance as they will not part gracefully with their contents unless scrupulously clean and smooth. Porcelain ones seem to attract dust into their grooves. They should be brushed with liquid paraffin and stored upside down. Metal ones may rust, so they must be thoroughly dried and then also wiped with liquid paraffin.

Egg shells are sometimes included to help clear the mixture (as in consommé) and are then, of course, strained out.

Amber Jelly

Simply could not be easier to make.

$\frac{3}{4}$ pint (4.5 dl) water
1 glass sherry
$\frac{1}{4}$ pint (1.5 dl) lemon juice
6 oz (150 g) sugar

1 oz (25 g) gelatine
3 egg yolks
rind 1 lemon

Put all the ingredients into a saucepan and whisk over gentle heat until nearly boiling. Strain into a mould and leave to set. *Serves 4 to 5.*

Apple Jelly

Particularly good made with crab apples which impart a lovely colour and flavour.

1 lb (450 g) cooking apples
3 oz (75 g) sugar
$\frac{1}{2}$ pint (3 dl) water

1 lemon
$\frac{1}{2}$ oz (12 g) gelatine

Wash the apples, cut up roughly and stew with the sugar, water and the juice and thinly pared rind of the lemon. When soft, sieve. Melt the gelatine in 2 tablespoons hot water, stir into the apples and turn into a wetted mould to set. *Serves 4 to 5.*

Apricot Jelly

May also be made with nectarines if you can ever get your hands on those lovely fruit.

18 ripe apricots
1 pint (6 dl) water
1 lb (450 g) sugar

3 tablespoons lemon juice
1½ oz (37 g)) gelatine

Remove the stones from the apricots and slice them thinly. Make a sugar syrup (p. 17), add the lemon juice, pour over the apricots and leave to cool. Dissolve the gelatine in a little hot water. Strain the apricots through a fine cloth, stir in the gelatine, pour into a wetted mould and leave to set. *Serves 4.*

Banana Jelly

A cream jelly with pistachio nuts. If these are unobtainable chopped walnuts, hazelnuts or flaked almonds will serve.

1 pint (6 dl) Lemon Jelly
 (p. 124)
6 bananas

¼ pint (1.5 dl) double cream
nuts

Peel and mash the bananas and stir them into the cooling jelly. Add the lightly whipped cream and mix well together. Strew the nuts in the bottom of the mould, pour on the mixture and leave to set. *Serves 4 to 5.*

Blueberry Dessert

As far as I can gather blueberries, bilberries and whortleberries are all one and the same thing or if not, strictly speaking, botanically identical, any of them could certainly be used for this jelly.

8 oz (225 g) fresh blueberries
5 oz (125 g) sugar
1 tablespoon lemon juice

½ oz (12 g) gelatine
1 cup water

Rinse the blueberries and place in a large bowl with the sugar and lemon juice and beat well. Dissolve the gelatine in the water over gentle heat and add. Chill and serve. *Serves 4.*

Brandy Jelly

The eggshells help to give a clear and sparkling jelly.

4 oz (100 g) sugar
1 oz (25 g) gelatine
1 lemon
2 egg whites and shells
1 bay-leaf

2 cloves
1 blade of mace
1 pint (6 dl) water
1 wineglass brandy

Put all the ingredients except the brandy into a saucepan, whisk until nearly boiling then allow to simmer gently for 5 minutes. Strain through a fine cloth, add the brandy and pour into a wetted mould. *Serves 4 to 5.*

Claret Jelly

Lovely with fresh fruit (grapes, sliced pears, raspberries) set in it.

$\frac{1}{4}$ pint (1.5 dl) claret
$1\frac{1}{4}$ pints (7.5 dl) water
$\frac{1}{4}$ pint (1.5 dl) lemon juice
rind 2 lemons

6 oz (150 g) sugar
$1\frac{1}{2}$ oz (37 g) gelatine
2 egg whites and shells
cochineal

Put all the ingredients except the cochineal into a saucepan and bring to the boil while stirring. Simmer for about 10 minutes then strain through a cloth. Add a few drops of cochineal to improve the colour, pour into a wetted mould and leave to set. *Serves 4 to 6.*

Coffee Jelly

If using coffee syrup (p. 90) use rather less and a little extra water.

$\frac{1}{2}$ pint (3 dl) water
$\frac{1}{2}$ oz (12 g) gelatine

$\frac{1}{2}$ pint (3 dl) strong black coffee
sugar to taste

Heat the water in a small saucepan and when it is hot but not boiling sprinkle in the gelatine and stir over gentle heat until completely dissolved. Remove from the heat, add the coffee, sweeten to taste and pour into small glasses to set. *Serves 4.*

Cranberry Jelly

Now that cranberries are often available in better greengrocers and supermarkets you can try this one.

8 oz (225 g) cranberries
1½ pints (9 dl) water

1½ oz (37 g) gelatine
sugar to taste

Simmer the cranberries in 1¼ pints (7.5 dl) of the water until soft. Dissolve the gelatine in the rest of the water, warmed, and add, with the sugar, to the cranberries. Strain through muslin and, when nearly cold, pour into a wetted mould. *Serves 4.*

Dutch Flummery

1 oz (25 g) gelatine
1 lemon
1 pint (6 dl) water

2 eggs
1 glass sherry
sugar to taste

Soak the gelatine and the rind of the lemon in the water for 20 minutes then simmer gently until the gelatine has dissolved. Beat the eggs and add the sherry, the juice of the lemon, the water and gelatine and sweeten to taste. Stir over low heat until thickening then turn into a wetted mould and leave to set. *Serves 4 to 6.*

Fruit Squash Jelly

A useful one for the children.

½ oz (12 g) gelatine
⅛ pint hot water
¼ pint (1.5 dl) undiluted fruit
  squash

1 tablespoon lemon juice
cold water

Dissolve the gelatine in the hot water and stir into the fruit squash and lemon juice. Make up to 1 pint with cold water. Turn into a mould and leave to set. *Serves 4.*

Gooseberry Jelly

Other fruit purées may be used instead of gooseberry.

1 lb (450 g) gooseberries
3 oz (75 g) caster sugar
½ pint (3 dl) water

rind 1 lemon
¾ oz (18 g) gelatine

Rinse the gooseberries and stew them with the sugar, water and thinly pared lemon rind until tender then rub them through a sieve. Dissolve the gelatine in 2 tablespoons of hot water and stir it in. Pour into small dishes to set. *Serves 4 to 6.*

Jelly Flip

Similar to the first pudding I ever made in the deprived days of the Second World War, but the gelatine here (which I think we could not get then) makes setting easier.

½ pint (3 dl) water, fruit juice or
   black coffee
2 oz (50 g) sugar

½ oz (12 g) gelatine
4 oz (100 g) dried milk
1 oz (25 g) cocoa

Heat half the liquid and dissolve the sugar and gelatine in it then add the remainder. Cool slightly then whip on to the other ingredients and continue whipping until spongy. Pile in individual glasses and when cold and firm sprinkle with grated chocolate. *Serves 4.*

Lemon Jelly

Sparkling and tangy.

1½ pints (9 dl) water
3 lemons
1½ oz (37 g) gelatine

6 oz (150 g) sugar
2 egg whites and shells

Put the water, the grated lemon rind and the juice of the lemons, the gelatine, sugar and the egg whites slightly beaten and their shells into a saucepan. Bring to the boil while whisking and simmer for 10 minutes then strain through a cloth and leave to set. *Serves 6.*

Maraschino Jelly

1½ pints (9 dl) water
4 oz (100 g) sugar
1¼ oz (30 g) gelatine

juice 2 lemons
2 egg whites and shells
4 tablespoons maraschino

Put all the ingredients except the maraschino into a saucepan and whisk until boiling. Simmer gently for a few minutes then strain, add the maraschino and pour into a wetted mould. Leave to set, turn out and decorate with maraschino cherries, if available. *Serves 6.*

Milk Jelly

A very old recipe which produces a creamy and delectable sweet.

1 pint (6 dl) milk
vanilla pod
grated nutmeg

1 egg
sugar to taste
1 oz (25 g) gelatine

Bring the milk slowly to the boil with the vanilla pod and leave to infuse – off the heat – for 15 minutes. Dust the surface well with nutmeg. Beat up the egg, pour on the milk (extracting the vanilla pod), whip, sweeten to taste, slowly mix in the gelatine dissolved in a little hot water and strain into a wetted mould to set. *Serves 4.*

Orange Jelly

½ pint (3 dl) water
3 oz (75 g) sugar
¾ oz (20 g) gelatine

4 oranges
juice 1 lemon

Put the water, sugar, gelatine and the pared rind of the oranges into a saucepan and heat gently. Cover and leave to infuse over low heat for about 10 minutes. Squeeze the juice from the oranges and the lemon and make up to ½ pint (3 dl) with more water. Add and then strain the whole into a wetted mould and leave to set. Turn out and decorate, if desired, with whipped cream and pistachio nuts. *Serves 4.*

Pineapple Snow

Tins of crushed pineapple – which come cheaper than cubes or rings – are ideal for this.

1 oz (25 g) gelatine
8 oz (225 g) tin pineapple
3 oz (75 g) lump sugar

1 wineglass sherry
3 egg whites

Dissolve the gelatine in the syrup from the pineapple and a little water over low heat. Add the pineapple (chopped if necessary) and sugar and simmer for 10 minutes. Stir in the sherry and allow to cool. Whisk the egg whites to a stiff froth, add to the mixture and whisk until nearly set. Pile roughly in a glass dish and serve chilled. *Serves 4.*

Port Wine Jelly

Should be a delectable ruby red colour.

½ pint (3 dl) water
1 oz (25 g) sugar
1 tablespoon redcurrant jelly

½ oz (12 g) gelatine
¼ pint (1.5 dl) port wine
cochineal

Put the water, sugar, redcurrant jelly and gelatine into a saucepan and stir over low heat until dissolved. Add half the port, a few drops of cochineal and strain through a cloth. Stir in the rest of the port at the end and leave to set. *Serves 4.*

Punch Jelly

Strictly for the grown-ups!

1 pint (6 dl) water
8 oz (225 g) sugar
2 lemons
1½ oz (37 g) gelatine
1 wineglass rum

1 wineglass sherry
1 wineglass kirsch
½ cinnamon stick
20 coriander seeds
1 egg white and shell

Boil the water and sugar to a syrup and add the finely pared rind of the lemons and the gelatine and stir until the gelatine has dissolved completely. Now add the juice of the lemons, the rum, sherry, kirsch, cinnamon stick and coriander seeds, bring to the boil and leave to cool. Beat up the white and shell of the egg and add to the mixture. Whisk over low heat until boiling and simmer very gently for 10 minutes. Strain through a cloth into a wetted mould and leave to set. *Serves 6.*

Raspberry Jelly

12 oz (325 g) raspberries
½ pint (3 dl) water
sugar to taste

2 oz (50 g) cornflour or
  arrowroot
juice 1 lemon

Simmer the raspberries in the water until tender then sweeten to taste and strain, reserving the juice. Mix the cornflour or arrowroot with a little cold water, stir into the raspberry juice, add the juice of the lemon and bring all to the boil, stirring. Boil gently for about 2 minutes then turn into a wetted mould and leave to set. *Serves 4.*

Rhubarb Jelly

Add a dash of cochineal to give this a rosy glow.

1 lb (450 g) rhubarb
½ pint (3 dl) water
4 oz (100 g) caster sugar

rind 1 lemon
¾ oz (20 g) gelatine

Wash and chop the rhubarb and simmer in the water with the sugar and lemon rind until soft. Rub through a sieve. Dissolve the gelatine in 2 tablespoons hot water and add. Turn into a wetted mould and leave to set. *Serves 4.*

Strawberry Jelly

Makes a pound of strawberries go a long way.

1 lb (450 g) strawberries
8 oz (225 g) sugar
2 pints (1.1 l) water
¼ pint (1.5 dl) lemon jelly

2 oz (50 g) gelatine
juice 1 lemon
2 egg whites and shells

Rinse the strawberries and crush ¾ lb (325 g) of them to a pulp. Boil the sugar and 1 pint (6 dl) of the water together until syrupy and pour over the strawberries. Leave for 30 minutes. Coat a jelly mould thinly with lemon jelly and decorate with the remaining strawberries cut in halves. Dissolve the gelatine in the other pint of water and add the strawberry mixture and the juice of the lemon. Cool then stir in the whites of the eggs and the shells. Re-heat, whisk until boiling then strain through a cloth, turn into a wetted mould and leave to set. *Serves 6.*

Tea Jelly

The best tea to use is Lapsang Souchong with its special smoky flavour.

1 pint (6 dl) water
1 oz (25 g) China tea
juice 1 lemon
juice 1 orange

1 oz (25 g) gelatine
2 egg whites
sugar to taste

Boil the water and pour it on to the tea. Infuse, strain and add the fruit juices, gelatine and egg whites. Place over low heat and whisk until boiling. Strain through muslin, sweeten to taste and pour into a wetted mould to set. *Serves 4 to 5.*

Wine Jelly

So called because the egg shells lend it the brilliance of a sparkling white wine, but it may safely be set before a teetotal great-aunt.

2 pints (1.1 l) water
4 oz (100 g) sugar
2½ oz (65 g) gelatine
1 orange

1 lemon
½ oz (12 g) coriander seeds
2 egg whites and shells

Put the water, sugar, gelatine, juice and rind of the orange and the lemon and the coriander seeds into a saucepan and heat gently until the sugar and gelatine have dissolved. Whisk the whites and the shells of the eggs together lightly, add them to the rest of the ingredients and whisk over the heat until boiling. Simmer gently for 10 minutes then strain through a cloth into a wetted mould and leave to set. *Serves 6.*

Milk Puddings

These are an invaluable standby in any household. The ingredients are practically always available, they are easy to make, economical and good, wholesome fare. Some – the rice ones in particular – take a longish time to cook so keep them in mind when you already have the oven on for something else – or use a pressure cooker in which they take a fraction of the time.

Included in this chapter are several cold moulds (e.g. Chocolate Farina, Cornflour Blancmange, Jamaican Cream) which are perhaps not what most people visualize when they think of Milk Puddings but they are included here because they contain a large proportion of milk and rarely cream, so do not qualify for inclusion in the chapter on Creams and Mousses.

Sago, semolina and tapioca are used in several of them as well as macaroni and even spaghetti. These are all inexpensive and good ingredients for adding bulk to the pudding. Italian recipes in particular often make use of semolina which, in these roughage-conscious days, may be due for a comeback: semolina is made from the hard wheat grains left over when flour is sifted. Sago comes from the pitch of certain Eastern palms and tapioca from a West Indian root called cassava. They have both been used in British cooking since the days of the Empire.

Milk puddings tend to be fairly bland which is why – apart from their nutritional and digestible qualities – they often appeal as invalid fare. Good flavourings are grated nutmeg, cinnamon, grated lemon, vanilla essence, powdered cloves and vanilla pod – which you infuse in the milk to flavour it and then remove, rinse, dry and store in a screw top jar to use again.

Almond Fruit Cream

A Cassata for cold days. I always like these lightly flavoured puddings with a variety of fruit and nuts mixed in. They both look and taste interesting.

1 pint (6 dl) milk	2 oz (50 g) ground almonds
rind 1 orange	1 oz (25 g) chopped candied peel
1 oz (25 g) caster sugar	2 oz (50 g) dates
2 oz (50 g) semolina	1 egg

Put the milk, grated orange rind and sugar together in a saucepan and heat until almost boiling. Sprinkle in the semolina and stir until boiling. Continue to cook until thick then remove from the heat and stir in the almonds, peel, chopped dates and lightly whisked egg. Turn into a buttered pie dish and bake at Gas Mark 4 (350 °F, 170 °C) for about 30 minutes until set and lightly browned. *Serves 6.*

Almond Pudding

Similar to Bread Pudding but milkier and with the welcome addition of almonds.

6 thin slices bread	cinnamon
1 oz (25 g) butter	1 pint (6 dl) milk
2 oz (50 g) ground almonds	1 oz (25 g) sugar
rind 1 lemon	2 eggs

Butter the bread sparingly and fit two slices into the bottom of a buttered pie dish. Mix together the almonds, grated lemon rind and cinnamon and sprinkle half of this on top of the bread. Fit in another layer of bread and repeat the process. Bring the milk to the boil and stir the sugar into it. Beat the eggs and pour on the hot milk, stirring

Opposite Wine Jelly (*page 128*), Banana Jelly (*page 121*), Lemon Jelly (*page 124*)

well, then pour the mixture into the dish. Let it stand for 30 minutes then bake at Gas Mark 2 (300 °F, 150 °C) for about 1 hour.
Serves 4 to 5.

Arrowroot Pudding

1 oz (25 g) arrowroot	rind ½ lemon
1 pint (6 dl) milk	2 eggs
1 oz (25 g) moist sugar	

Mix the arrowroot smoothly with a little of the milk then boil the rest and pour it on stirring all the time. Stir and cook gently until thick then cool slightly before adding the sugar, grated lemon rind and well-beaten eggs. Pour into a buttered basin, cover and steam gently for 1½ hours. Serve with Lemon (p. 212) or Melba (p. 212) Sauce.
Serves 4 to 5.

Chocolate Farina

Excellent eaten very cold with a swirl of cream. 2 oz (50 g) gelatine may be used in place of the cornflour to give a rather lighter texture.

4 oz (100 g) cornflour	8 oz (225 g) block chocolate
2 pints (1.1 l) milk	vanilla essence
2 oz (50 g) sugar	

Mix the cornflour smoothly with a little of the milk. Heat the remainder, add the sugar and the chocolate broken into small pieces and stir until dissolved. Pour this mixture on to the cornflour and simmer very gently for about 10 minutes stirring continuously. Add vanilla essence to taste and pour into a rinsed mould. Leave to set and turn out when required. Decorate with chopped nuts or grated chocolate.
Serves 6.

Chocolate Pudding – Baked

This was a regular wash-day pudding when we were children as it is so quick and easy. My mother never knew the luxury of a washing machine and did the washing for seven of us with a boiler and a thing called a 'dolly-legs' – a kind of hand-operated spaddle. The washing, consequently, took most of Monday to do and most of Tuesday to iron – but was always whiter than mine has ever been!

Opposite Rice Pudding (*page 139*),
Petits Pots de Crème (*page 138*)

1¼ oz (30 g) cornflour   1 oz (25 g) sugar
1 oz (25 g) cocoa   1 pint (6 dl) milk

Mix the dry ingredients with a little of the milk. Bring the rest of the milk to the boil and pour on. Return to the pan and cook for 2 minutes stirring all the time. Pour into a buttered pie dish and set at Gas Mark 2 (300 °F, 150 °C) for 15 minutes. Eat hot thickly strewn with sugar. *Serves 4.*

Coffee Delight

This can be served as it is or can be poured into a pie dish and topped with a crumbly mixture made from equal quantities of oats, bread-crumbs, brown sugar rubbed together with half the amount of margarine and baked for 10 minutes in a hot oven. This makes a good contrast in texture to the main part of the pudding.

1½ pints (9 dl) milk   2 oz (50 g) sugar
1 oz (25 g) instant coffee powder   3 oz (75 g) semolina

Bring the milk to the boil and blend the instant coffee with a little of it. Add to the rest of the milk. Stir in the sugar and semolina. Cook for 10 minutes, stirring occasionally, and serve very hot. *Serves 4 to 5.*

Cornflour Blancmange

Instead of being moulded and allowed to set this pudding can also be baked in a low oven for about 30 minutes and eaten hot.

2½ oz (65 g) cornflour   1 oz (25 g) sugar
2 pints (1.1 l) milk   cinnamon stick or vanilla pod

Mix the cornflour smoothly with a little of the milk. Boil the remainder of the milk with the sugar and the cinnamon stick or vanilla pod. When it reaches boiling point remove the flavouring and stir in the cornflour. Cook gently for 10 minutes stirring continuously to avoid lumps forming then pour into a wetted mould and leave to set. Turn out and serve cold with jam or stewed or tinned fruit. *Serves 5 to 6.*

Crème Caramel

One of the few puddings still served in France. It is much better than any packaged equivalent and is an economical and excellent pudding.

caramel
3 oz (75 g) granulated sugar
about ¼ pint (1.5 dl) water

3 eggs
1 oz (25 g) caster sugar
½ pint (3 dl) milk
vanilla essence

Crème Caramel

Make the caramel (p. 58) and pour at once into a warmed pudding basin. Beat the eggs well with the sugar and pour on the warmed milk mixed with a little vanilla essence. Strain into the pudding basin, cover and steam gently for 1 hour. Can be eaten hot or leave it to cool in the basin then chill, turn out and serve with cream. *Serves 4.*

Crème de Riz

A cold rice cream – very good with jam and cream or cold stewed fruit.

2½ oz (72 g) short grain rice
1¼ pints (7.5 dl) milk
vanilla pod

sugar to taste
1 egg white
top-of-the-milk

Rinse the rice in cold water to remove surface starch and add it to the milk with the vanilla pod. Simmer very gently until the rice is soft and creamy, stirring occasionally (this may take up to 1 hour). Turn into a bowl to cool, sweeten to taste and remove vanilla pod. Cover the top surface with a piece of wet greaseproof paper to prevent a skin forming, and chill. Just before serving whip the egg white, stir it into the top-of-the-milk and stir into the rice cream. *Serves 4 to 5.*

Crème Frite

A most unusual and intriguing pudding. The crisp outer coating makes a delectable contrast to the soft, creamy interior.

1 pint (6 dl) milk
vanilla pod
3 egg yolks
3½ oz (80 g) caster sugar

1¼ oz (30 g) plain flour
beaten egg for coating
fine breadcrumbs
butter for frying

Make a crème pâtissière by bringing the milk to the boil with the vanilla pod in it, removing it from the heat and keeping it warm while you cream the egg yolks and sugar together until white and add the sieved flour. Stir in the milk a little at a time and cook, whipping well, until the mixture boils. Cook the cream rather longer than usual so that it is really thick then pour on to a buttered tin so that it is lying about ½ inch (1 cm) thick and leave to cool. Cut into small squares, dip them in beaten egg and then in the breadcrumbs and fry quickly in butter. Serve hot with Chocolate Sauce (p. 207). *Serves 4 to 5.*

Custard – Baked

May be flavoured with coffee, chocolate, nutmeg, orange or almond or vanilla essence. It can also be used as a filling for a baked pastry flan.

1 pint (6 dl) milk	1 oz (25 g) sugar
2 eggs	flavouring
pinch of salt	

Pour the hot milk on to the beaten eggs and salt, beating as you do so. Strain into a buttered pie dish. Add the sugar and flavouring. Bake at Gas Mark 1 (275 °F, 140 °C) for about 50 minutes. Serve hot or cold. *Serves 4.*

Empress Pudding

Another one to use up leftover pastry trimmings.

pastry trimmings	1 oz (25 g) sugar
4 oz (100 g) short-grain rice	pinch of salt
2 pints (1.1 l) milk	jam or stewed fruit
2 oz (50 g) butter	

Line the sides of a good-sized fireproof dish with the pastry trimmings. Rinse the rice and simmer it in the milk until tender and fairly dry. Stir in the butter, sugar and salt. Spread a thin layer on to the pastry base, cover thickly with jam or stewed fruit and repeat until all is used up letting the top layer be of rice. Bake at Gas Mark 4 (350 °F, 180 °C) for about 30 minutes and serve with Custard (p. 209). *Serves 6.*

Ground Rice Blancmange

A useful accompaniment to fruit or specially good jam. For a change the fruit or jam may be stirred into the mixture to set.

1½ oz (37 g) ground rice
1 pint (6 dl) milk
1½ oz (37 g) caster sugar

vanilla pod, lemon rind or other flavouring

Mix the ground rice smoothly with a little of the milk and bring the rest to the boil with the flavouring. Strain on to the rice mixture stirring thoroughly. Return to the pan and simmer gently for 10 minutes. Add the sugar and strain into a wetted mould. Leave to set. *Serves 4 to 5.*

Ground Rice Pudding

1½ oz (37 g) ground rice
1 pint (6 dl) milk
flavouring
1½ oz (37 g) sugar
1 egg

Mix the ground rice to a paste with a little of the milk and boil up the rest with a suitable flavouring. Remove flavouring if necessary and pour the milk slowly on to the rice mixture stirring all the time to avoid lumps. Return to the saucepan and cook gently until thick, stirring continuously. Pour into a pie dish and add the sugar and, when the mixture has cooled a little, the beaten egg. Bake at Gas Mark 1 (275 °F, 140 °C) for 40 minutes. *Serves 4 to 5.*

'Ice Cream' Pudding

Like a rich, baked custard. The butter rises to the surface and forms a golden glaze. Very good 'straight' or you can serve it with jam or stewed fruit and single cream.

2 oz (50 g) butter
3 oz (75 g) sugar
1 egg

1 oz (25 g) flour
1 pint (6 dl) milk
1 teaspoon vanilla essence

Cream the butter (margarine will not do here as it does not mix properly) and the sugar and beat in the egg and the flour. Bring the milk to the boil and add it gradually to the mixture together with a few drops of vanilla essence. Pour into a pie dish and bake at Gas Mark 4 (350°F, 180°C) for about 30 minutes. Serve hot or cold. *Serves 4 to 5.*

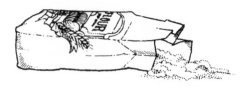

Jamaican Cream

An unusual mould. Can be served with grated chocolate or sliced bananas.

1 pint (6 dl) milk
1 tablespoon black treacle
½ oz (12 g) gelatine

Simply heat the ingredients up together in a saucepan. When well mixed and thoroughly hot (do not let it boil) pour it into a bowl and leave to set. *Serves 4.*

Noodle Pudding

10 oz (300 g) medium egg
  noodles
½ teaspoon cinnamon
pinch of salt
3 oz (75 g) sultanas

3 oz (75 g) sugar
1 teaspoon almond essence
3 eggs
¾ pint (4.5 dl) milk
4 oz (100 g) butter

Boil the noodles until just tender then strain and rinse with cold water. Mix with the cinnamon, salt, sultanas, sugar and almond essence. Beat the eggs, add the milk and strain on to the noodle mixture. Melt the butter and pour half of it into the bottom of a pie dish and stir the rest into the mixture. Turn the pudding into the dish and bake at Gas Mark 3 (325°F, 170°C) for about 45 minutes. *Serves 4.*

Oatmeal Pudding

Since this contains no sweetener serve it with syrup, cream and sugar or stewed fruit.

1 oz (25 g) fine oatmeal
½ oz (12 g) flour
1¼ pints (7.5 dl) milk

salt to taste
1 egg

Mix the oatmeal and flour smoothly with a little of the milk. Bring the rest of the milk to the boil and add. Return to the heat and cook gently for 5 minutes stirring all the time and adding salt to taste. Let it cool a little then stir in the egg. Turn into a buttered pie dish and bake at Gas Mark 2 (300°F, 150°C) for about 20 minutes. *Serves 4.*

Pasta Dolce

The nuts may be replaced by jam, honey, syrup, sliced bananas – whatever you like.

8 oz (225 g) macaroni
1¼ pints (7.5 dl) milk
1½ oz (37 g) white sugar
1½ oz (37 g) brown sugar

¼ teaspoon nutmeg
½ teaspoon cinnamon
chopped nuts to garnish

Boil the macaroni gently in the milk for 8 minutes. Add both the white sugar and the brown sugar and cook for a further 10 minutes, stirring all the time. Mix in the spices and serve hot garnished with the nuts. *Serves 4 to 5.*

Petits Pots de Crème

Small individual fireproof pots are needed for this. It can be flavoured with melted chocolate, coffee or vanilla.

1 pint (6 dl) milk
1 oz (25 g) sugar
4 egg yolks

1 whole egg
flavouring

Scald the milk with the sugar and pour on to the yolks and the egg beaten together. Add flavouring and strain into the pots. Cover each one carefully with foil and stand the pots in a baking tin of boiling water. Set at Gas Mark 4 (350 °F, 180 °C) for about 20 minutes. Remove, chill and eat from the pots with single cream, grated chocolate – or just as they are. *Serves 6.*

Rice Caramel

The rich caramel topping makes this look enticing, and it can be even more festive with raspberries strewn around the base or sliced bananas lined up around the outside.

caramel
4 oz (100 g) granulated sugar
¼ pint (1.5 dl) water

3 oz (75 g) short-grain rice
1 pint (6 dl) milk
2 eggs
1 oz (25 g) caster sugar
vanilla essence

Make the caramel (p. 58) and pour at once into a warmed pudding basin. Simmer the rice gently in the milk until tender, cool slightly then stir in the beaten eggs, caster sugar and vanilla essence. Turn into the basin, cover and steam for 1 hour. Turn out and serve either hot or cold. *Serves 4 to 5.*

Rice Meringue Pudding

1 pint (6 dl) milk
2 oz (50 g) short-grain rice
bay leaf

1 oz (25 g) caster sugar
1 oz (25 g) butter
2 eggs

Put the milk, rice and bay leaf into a saucepan and cook gently until the rice is tender. Let it cool slightly before adding the sugar, butter and beaten egg yolks. Remove the bay leaf and turn the mixture into a buttered pie dish. Whisk the egg whites stiffly and pile them on top well dredged with caster sugar. Bake at Gas Mark 4 (350 °F, 180 °C) for about 20 minutes and serve hot. *Serves 4 to 5.*

Rice Pudding

A well-made rice pudding which is creamy and not stodgy is always popular. It is pretty good just eaten straight or with jam and/or single cream but the sugar may be replaced by 3 oz (75 g) honey or the pudding may be flavoured with melted chocolate or coffee or even mixed with raisins.

3 oz (75 g) short-grain rice   pinch of salt
1½ oz (37 g) sugar   grated nutmeg
1 pint (6 dl) milk

Rinse the rice and place it in a generously buttered pie dish with the sugar, milk and salt. Sprinkle the surface with nutmeg and bake at Gas Mark 1 (275 °F, 140 °C) for about 2 hours. *Serves 4.*

Rice Tyrolhof

2½ oz (63 g) short-grain rice   1 eating apple
1 pint (6 dl) milk   3 oz (75 g) grapes
1½ oz (37 g) sugar   1 dessertspoon rum (optional)
1 rounded teaspoon gelatine   1 egg white
juice 1 orange

Simmer the rice in the milk until tender adding more milk if it becomes too dry. Stir in the sugar. Dissolve the gelatine in the orange juice and add together with the chopped apple and the peeled and pipped grapes. Add the rum – if used. Whisk the egg white stiffly and fold in then pour into a lightly oiled mould and leave to set. Turn out and pour Melba Sauce (p. 212) around. *Serves 4 to 5.*

Sago Pudding

Good with hot fruit which you have cooked with butter and brown sugar in a casserole in the oven alongside it.

¼ oz (6 g) butter   1 oz (25 g) sugar
1½ oz (37 g) sago   ¾ pint (4.5 dl) milk

Grease a pie dish with the butter and place the sugar and sago in it. Pour on the milk and let it stand for 1 hour then bake at Gas Mark 2 (300 °F, 150 °C) for 1 hour. Serve hot. *Serves 4.*

Semolina Crispie

An interesting-looking dish far removed from most people's idea of semolina.

1 pint (6 dl) milk	2 oz (50 g) sugar
3½ oz (80 g) semolina	rind ½ lemon
3 eggs	1½ oz (35 g) butter

Pour the milk over the semolina and let it stand for 1 hour. Cream together the egg yolks, sugar and grated lemon rind and mix in then beat the egg whites stiffly and fold them in too. Heat the butter in a frying pan, pour the mixture in and allow it to brown on the bottom without stirring then break it up with a fork and move it around until it has browned a little all over. Pile on to a dish to serve and scatter with chopped nuts, handing some sort of jam separately.
Serves 4 to 5.

Semolina Pudding

¾ pint (4.5 dl) milk	1 oz (25 g) sugar
rind ½ lemon	1 egg
¾ oz (18 g) semolina	

Infuse the lemon rind in the milk over gentle heat for about 5 minutes then bring to the boil and sprinkle in the semolina. Cook slowly until it thickens – about 15 minutes. Remove the lemon rind and add the sugar. Cool slightly and stir in the yolk of the egg then the stiffly beaten white. Turn into a buttered pie dish and bake at Gas Mark 2 (300 °F, 150 °C) for about 30 minutes. *Serves 4.*

Semolina Whip

May be flavoured with 2 tablespoons honey or jam or 3 oz (75 g) melted chocolate if desired.

1 pint (6 dl) milk	1 oz (25 g) sugar
1½ oz (37 g) semolina	vanilla essence

Bring the milk to the boil, sprinkle in the semolina and cook for 10 minutes, stirring, until thick. Remove from the heat and add the vanilla essence and other flavouring as desired. Turn into a basin and whip until cold. Pile in individual glasses and decorate. *Serves 4.*

Spaghetti Pudding

The same recipe may be used with macaroni or vermicelli.

1 oz (25 g) spaghetti
pinch of salt
1 pint (6 dl) milk
1 oz (25 g) sugar

1 oz (25 g) butter
rind ½ lemon
2 eggs

Break the spaghetti into ½ inch lengths and put them and the salt into the milk when it is boiling. Simmer until tender. Add the sugar, butter, grated lemon rind and the well-beaten yolks of the eggs and stir on very low heat for a few minutes without letting it boil. Stir in the stiffly whisked egg whites and turn into a buttered pie dish. Bake at Gas Mark 2 (300 °F, 150 °C) for about 30 minutes. *Serves 4.*

Tapioca Cream

School tapioca was never like this – this is almost a party pudding.

2 oz (50 g) tapioca
1 pint (6 dl) milk
vanilla pod
1½ oz (37 g) caster sugar

½ pint (3 dl) double cream
12 ratafias
2 tablespoons sherry
chopped nuts

Gently cook the tapioca in the milk with the vanilla pod and sugar until quite soft. Remove the pod, pour into a basin and allow to cool. Whisk the cream lightly and fold in. Put half the ratafias in the bottom of a glass dish and pour the sherry over them. Turn the tapioca cream on to them and decorate with the remaining ratafias and the chopped nuts. *Serves 4 to 5.*

Tapioca Pudding

You can vary the basic recipe by coating a basin with caramel (as for Rice Caramel p. 138), pouring in the tapioca mixture and steaming in a buttered basin for 1 hour then turning into a hot dish.

1½ oz (37 g) tapioca
¾ pint (4.5 dl) milk
rind ½ lemon

1 oz (25 g) sugar
1 egg

Soak the tapioca in the milk with the lemon rind for about 30 minutes then cook over gentle heat for a further 30 minutes, stirring occasionally. Add the sugar and cool slightly. Remove the lemon rind and stir in the beaten egg. Turn into a buttered pie dish and bake at Gas Mark 3 (325 °F, 170 °C) for 30 minutes. *Serves 4.*

Tenby Cream

A light and delicate cream which, in fact, contains no cream.

4 oz (100 g) sugar
½ oz (13 g) gelatine
1 tablespoon water

2 lemons
1 pint (6 dl) milk
2 eggs

Mix together over very gentle heat the sugar, gelatine, hot water and the grated rind of the lemons. When dissolved add the milk and the beaten egg yolks, stir well and continue to cook gently until the mixture begins to thicken slightly. Add the juice of the lemons and fold in the stiffly beaten egg whites then turn into a bowl and chill. *Serves 4 to 5.*

Yogurt

There is no need to invest in expensive yogurt-making kits. Invest in one pot of plain yogurt and from it you can make about 6 pints. After that the culture grows too weak and you have to buy another pot but this is infinitely cheaper. You can flavour it with a vast variety of juice left over from stewed or canned fruit, jam, fresh fruit, nuts, chocolate, coffee – anything (even – and especially – that strawberry jam that did not set!).

1 pint (6 dl) milk
1 tablespoon plain yogurt

Bring the milk to the boil, pour it into a bowl and let it cool to blood heat (i.e. when you dip your little finger into it you do not notice any difference in the temperature). Mix a spoonful of the milk with the yogurt and stir the resulting cream into the boiled milk. The problem now is to keep the mixture warm for 24 hours. Try covering the bowl, wrapping around with a towel and putting it in the airing cupboard. Once this is done you can chill it before serving. *Serves 4.*

Fritters &
Pancakes

Batter is a mixture of flour, egg, and milk or milk and water. Sometimes fat may be included, sometimes sugar and the consistency will vary according to what it is being used for.

Pancakes store perfectly well wrapped in foil in the refrigerator if you sandwich them between layers of greaseproof paper. Fritters should be drained on kitchen paper then placed on a warm dish and served piping hot.

Strong heat is needed for the cooking of batters or the result will be soggy. A special heavy pan should be kept for pancakes and, between use, should not be washed but cleaned with an oiled cloth.

Almond Fritters

2 eggs	vanilla essence
1 oz (25 g) caster sugar	$\frac{1}{2}$ oz (12 g) cornflour
2 oz (50 g) ground almonds	frying fat

Stir the yolks of the eggs and the sugar together until creamy then add the almonds, a few drops of vanilla essence, the cornflour and the stiffly whisked whites of the eggs. Drop teaspoonsful of the mixture into hot fat and fry until crisp and golden. Drain and serve as hot as possible. *Serves 5.*

Apple Fritters

1 lb (450 g) apples
sugar
2 tablespoons flour
pinch of salt

1 dessertspoon oil
2 tablespoons water
1 egg white
frying fat

Peel and core the apples and slice them into even rings. Sprinkle well with sugar and let them stand for 30 minutes. Sift the flour and salt into a bowl, add the oil and the warm water gradually, stir until well mixed then beat. Let the mixture stand for at least 1 hour before folding in the stiffly whisked egg white. Now dip each apple ring into the batter, pick it out on the point of a skewer and drop into hot fat. Fry rather slowly until the outside is crisp and brown and the apple is tender. Drain, dredge with caster sugar and serve very hot.
Serves 5.

Apple Pancakes

Other fruit may also be used – plums, apricots, etc.

1 lb (450 g) apples
2 oz (50 g) sultanas
¾ teaspoon cinnamon

basic pancake mixture (p. 147)
icing sugar

Stew the apples with a little sugar and water then sieve and mix in the sultanas and cinnamon. Turn each pancake as it is cooked on to a sugared paper, place a spoonful of the apple mixture in the middle, roll up and transfer to a hot dish. Dredge with icing sugar before serving. *Serves 4.*

Apricot Fritters

This yeast batter may be a little more trouble to prepare but it is particularly light and crisp.

¼ oz (6 g) yeast
milk
8 oz (225 g) flour
pinch of salt
½ teaspoon caster sugar

1½ oz (37 g) butter
12 apricots
caster sugar
cinnamon
frying fat

Cream the yeast with a little of the milk, warmed. Add 2 oz (50 g) of the flour, mix into a light dough and leave to rise in a warm place. When it has nearly doubled in bulk add the salt, sugar, melted butter, flour and as much warm milk as is needed to form a light dough. Leave to rise another 30 minutes. Halve the apricots and remove the stones. Cover each completely with a thin coating of dough, leave in a warm place for 30 minutes then fry in hot fat until golden brown. Drain, sprinkle with caster sugar and cinnamon and serve. *Serves 4.*

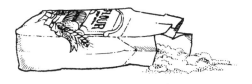

Apricot Pancakes

basic pancake mixture (p. 147)
1 lb (450 g) apricots – or large
  tin

1 oz (25 g) almonds
sugar to taste
cream

Make the pancakes and keep hot. Halve the fresh apricots and remove the stones then cook with sugar and a little water until soft. Remove the fruit and reduce the syrup. (If using tinned apricots heat them in their syrup, remove and reduce the syrup in the same way.) Toast the shredded almonds. Arrange the pancakes in a pile in a shallow fireproof dish sandwiched together with the apricot compôte and with the syrup poured over. Cut into the required number of segments with a sharp knife then sprinkle with the almonds and spoon a little cream on top. Serve very hot. *Serves 4.*

Banana Fritters

6 bananas   frying fat
coating batter (p. 146)   caster sugar

Cut each banana across, then lengthwise. Coat completely in the
batter and fry in hot fat until crisp and brown. Dredge well with caster
sugar and serve. *Serves 6.*

Banana Pastries

A Spanish recipe. Traditionally the pastry contains a teaspoon of anise
liqueur (or a pinch of ground aniseed). It is very flaky pastry and the
banana melts in the cooking into a creamy filling.

8 oz (225 g) flour   5 bananas
1 teaspoon salt   frying fat
½ cup olive oil   caster sugar
½ cup water

Sieve the flour and the salt, make a well, pour in the liquid and mix
well together. Roll into a ball and chill before using. Roll the pastry
out very thinly. Cut the bananas across the middle and then
lengthwise and wrap each one in a piece of pastry. Seal the edges very
well and fry in deep, hot fat until browned all over. Dredge with caster
sugar and serve hot. *Serves 5 to 6.*

Batter for Coating

A lighter batter than the one used for pancakes but made in the same
way. There are many variations but here are two. The second makes a
crisper coating.

1   ½ oz (12 g) butter
4 oz (100 g) plain flour   1 tablespoon milk
pinch of salt   ⅛ pint (0.75 dl) warm water
1 egg yolk   2 egg whites

Sift the flour and salt into a bowl, add the egg yolk, melted butter and
milk stirring until smooth then add the water gradually. Beat well,
leave for 30 minutes then add the stiffly whisked egg whites and use as
required.

2

4 oz (100 g) plain flour
3 tablespoons olive oil
pinch of salt

¼ pint (1.5 dl) warm water
1 egg white

Sieve the flour and stir in the olive oil and salt. Gradually add the water, stirring thoroughly. Leave for 2 hours and stir in the stiffly whisked egg white just before using.

Batter for Pancakes – Basic

4 oz (100 g) plain flour
pinch of salt
2 eggs

½ pint (3 dl) milk
frying fat

Sieve the flour and salt into a bowl. Make a well in the centre and put in the eggs and a little of the milk. Stir, drawing in the flour gradually and when all is mixed in beat well. Add the rest of the milk gradually, stirring and beating well. When the fat in the pancake pan is really hot pour off any surplus and reserve for the next pancake then pour in just enough batter to cover the bottom of the pan thinly. Let it cook for a few moments and when it moves when you shake the pan flip it over (if you can toss it it is too thick – you should be able to 'read your lover's letters through them'!) and cook the other side for a few moments. This quantity makes 8 pancakes in a 7 inch (18 cm) pan. At their simplest, of course, they are just served with sugar and quarters of lemon.

Beetroot Fritters

We are not in the habit of associating beetroot with a pudding course but they are rich in sugar and this old recipe for fritters is worth a try. You can make them with thick slices of cooked beetroot coated in batter and fried – or by the following method.

1 large cooked beetroot
1 oz (25 g) flour
3 egg yolks
grated lemon rind

nutmeg
sugar to taste
coating batter (p. 146)
frying fat

Sieve the beetroot and mix with the flour, the egg yolks, a little grated lemon rind and nutmeg and sweeten to taste. Stir over low heat for 10 minutes and then leave to cool. Drop the mixture in dessertspoonsful into the batter and fry in hot fat until crisp and lightly browned. Drain and dredge with caster sugar. *Serves 4 to 5.*

Beignets de Nancy

12 macaroons
apricot jam
kirsch

coating batter (p. 146)
frying fat

Sandwich the macaroons together in pairs with the apricot jam flavoured with kirsch. Dip in the batter and fry in deep fat. Drain well and serve with cream or Sabayon Sauce (p. 214). *Serves 3.*

Beignets de Pruneaux

Everyone will gobble up prunes cooked this way. Vanilla sugar is caster sugar in which you have stored a vanilla pod for flavour.

1 lb (450 g) prunes
weak tea
rum
almonds

coating batter (p. 146)
frying fat
grated chocolate
vanilla sugar

Soak the prunes in the tea for 2 hours, drain and stone then sprinkle well with rum and leave for a further hour. Strain again and add the liquor to the coating batter. Place an almond in the centre of each prune then dip in the batter and fry until golden. Roll in a mixture of grated chocolate and vanilla sugar. Serve at once. *Serves 4 to 6.*

Beignets Soufflés

Also called Pets de Nonnes, these are made with choux paste which is fried. They can be filled (after frying) with crème pâtissière, whipped cream, chocolate cream, coffee cream or jam.

$\frac{1}{3}$ pint (2 dl) water
3 oz (75 g) butter or margarine
4 oz (100 g) flour

3 eggs
$\frac{1}{2}$ oz (12 g) sugar
vanilla essence

Boil the water and butter together, tip in the flour and beat until smooth. Cool, then beat in the eggs one at a time and the sugar and vanilla essence. Drop in spoonsful into hot, deep fat and fry gently for about 7 minutes. Drain, roll in caster sugar and serve hot with Jam (p. 211) or any fruit sauce. *Serves 4 to 5.*

Bread and Butter Fritters

An excellent way of using up leftover bread and butter.

8 thin slices bread and butter   coating batter (p. 146)
jam   frying fat

Make the bread and butter into sandwiches with the jam and cut each into four. Dip into the batter, drop into hot fat and fry until crisp and lightly browned. Drain, dredge with caster sugar and serve hot. *Serves 4.*

Chestnut Balls

A Greek recipe – *Kastana Krokettes*. The mixture is coated in fine dried breadcrumbs instead of batter.

2 lbs (900 g) chestnuts   2 egg yolks
½ pint (3 dl) milk   2 oz (50 g) breadcrumbs
cinnamon stick   frying fat
6 oz (150 g) sugar   icing sugar
2 oz (50 g) candied peel   cinnamon
2 oz (50 g) glacé cherries

Peel the chestnuts (p. 30) and place in a saucepan with the milk, cinnamon stick and 3 tablespoons of the sugar. Simmer until all the milk is absorbed then remove the cinnamon stick and sieve the mixture. Mix in the rest of the sugar and the chopped peel and cherries and form into nut-sized balls. Dip in the beaten egg yolks and cover thickly in crumbs. Fry in deep, hot fat until golden then drain and dredge with icing sugar and cinnamon. *Serves 5.*

Chufletes

Delectable Spanish fritters.

1 lb (450 g) soft breadcrumbs   2 eggs
1 oz (25 g) caster sugar   frying oil
¼ pint (1.5 dl) white wine

Mix the breadcrumbs, sugar, wine and egg yolks together and leave to stand for 30 minutes then fold in the stiffly beaten egg whites. Drop spoonsful into slightly smoking oil and fry until golden. Drain and serve dusted with vanilla-flavoured caster sugar. *Serves 6.*

Cottage Cheese Crêpes

This batter is actually made with cottage cheese. It forms a light, spongy mixture with a particularly subtle taste.

3 eggs   1 oz (25 g) plain flour
8 oz (225 g) cottage cheese   pinch of salt
2 oz (50 g) butter   redcurrant jelly

Beat the eggs well and stir in the sieved cottage cheese then add the butter, melted. Sift in the flour and salt, stir well and drop in table-spoons on to a hot griddle or frying pan greased with a little oil (butter tends to burn). The pancakes will be softer than the usual sort and therefore difficult to flip over unless you keep them small – about 4 inches across. When one side is cooked spread a little redcurrant jelly on it while the other side is cooking then fold over, line up on a hot oval dish and sprinkle with caster sugar before serving. *Serves 4.*

Cowslip Pancakes

A traditional Wiltshire recipe – Paigle Fry. The cowslip flowers give a wonderful, delicate flavour. It is quite simple – to every cupful of batter you stir in ¼ cupful of cowslip flower heads. Serve sprinkled with caster sugar.

Crêpes Suzette

Justly famous and well worth making at home when you have some curaçao and rum available. The pancake batter should be enriched with a little extra butter and the pancakes made wafer thin.

3 lumps sugar	1 oz (25 g) caster sugar
1 orange or 2 tangerines	1 tablespoon curaçao
1½ oz (37 g) butter	3 tablespoons rum

Rub the lumps of sugar over the orange or tangerine rind until well impregnated with the oil. Crush the lumps and cream them into the butter then add the caster sugar, 1 tablespoon of the juice of the orange and the curaçao. Cook all the pancakes and keep them hot before spreading each with orange butter, rolling them up and laying in a hot dish. Warm the rum in a spoon over a flame, set it alight and pour over the crêpes. *Serves 4.*

Croquettes de Fruit

12 oz (325 g) soft fruit	cinnamon
4 oz (100 g) sugar	1 egg
1½ lbs (675 g) cake or biscuit	breadcrumbs
crumbs	frying fat
lemon rind	

Stew the fruit with the sugar and a little water until soft. Strain, remove stones, if any, and mix with the cake or biscuit crumbs, a little grated lemon rind and cinnamon and enough of the strained fruit juice to make a moist, thick mixture. Spread on a plate to cool then form into small croquettes, roll in beaten egg and breadcrumbs and fry in hot fat until brown. *Serves 6.*

Dried Fruit Fritters

Another Greek recipe – *Tiganites me stafides*.

6 oz (150 g) flour	vanilla essence
2 teaspoons baking powder	¼ pint (1.5 dl) milk and water
pinch of salt	frying fat
2 oz (50 g) sugar	icing sugar
2 oz (50 g) mixed dried fruit	cinnamon
1 egg	

Sift the flour, baking powder and salt together and add the sugar and dried fruit. Make a well in the centre and stir in the beaten egg and a little vanilla essence. Add the milk and water gradually, beating well. Drop spoonsful into hot fat and fry until golden on both sides. Drain and serve hot sprinkled with icing sugar and cinnamon. *Serves 6.*

Fillings for Pancakes

Apple – as a change from the Apple Pancakes (p. 144) you can mix sliced apples into the batter and they become Jacques – as eaten in the Périgord.

Banana – 4 bananas, 2 tablespoons brown sugar, 1 lemon. Peel the bananas and slice them thinly. Mix with the sugar and the juice and grated rind of the lemon.

Jam and Whipped Cream – the Dutch way. Spread each pancake with jam and whipped cream, pile on top of each other and serve.

Mincemeat – makes an excellent filling.

Pears – dice some ripe pears into the batter and fry.

Pineapple – 1 small tin pineapple, 2 tablespoons strawberry jam, rind ½ lemon. Chop the pineapple finely and mix with the jam and grated lemon rind. Heat through.

Praline Butter – Praline powder is made by heating together 3 oz (75 g) almonds and 3 oz (75 g) caster sugar until nut brown. It is then turned out on to an oiled plate, left to harden and crushed. For Praline Butter cream 2 oz (50 g) butter with 1½ oz (37 g) caster sugar and stir in 2 tablespoons praline powder and a little rum.

Flower Fritters

These may seem strange to us but are not uncommon in some countries. Orange and lemon flowers are used as well as acacia, lily, elder and the male vegetable marrow flowers. We can at least experiment with the last two.

flowers   coating batter (p. 146)
sugar   frying fat
brandy

Rinse the flowers briefly, sprinkle with sugar and a little brandy and leave to macerate for about 30 minutes then dip in batter, fry in hot fat, drain and serve.

Fritto Misto

A mixture of fruit fritters. The fruit is usually macerated in a mixture of sugar and brandy, kirsch, rum or curaçao – but the liqueur may, of course, be omitted.

Gooseberry Fritters

For really large, ripe gooseberries.

2 oz (50 g) flour
pinch of salt
2 egg yolks
2 tablespoons milk
2 tablespoons water
1 egg white
1 lb (450 g) gooseberries
frying fat

Sift the flour and salt into a bowl and stir in the egg yolks, milk and water gradually to form a smooth batter. Let it stand for 1 hour then stir in the stiffly whisked egg white, drop in the rinsed gooseberries, pick them out with a tablespoon three or four at a time and lower into the hot fat without separating them. Fry until golden brown, drain and dredge with sugar. *Serves 4 to 5.*

Indian Fritters

Rather like hot doughnuts.

3 oz (75 g) flour
4 egg yolks
2 egg whites
jam
frying fat

Sift the flour and stir in enough boiling water to form a stiff paste. Let it cool then beat in the egg yolks and whites. Fill a dessertspoon with the mixture, form a cavity in it and fill with jam then cover with the mixture. Drop into hot fat, fry until golden, drain well and serve sprinkled with sugar. *Serves 4 to 5.*

Kaiserschmarren

Also useful for leftover pancakes.

pancake batter (p. 147)
3 oz (75 g) sultanas
⅛ pint (0.75 dl) apple juice,
  cider or white wine

sugar
butter for frying

Make the pancakes and keep them hot. Simmer the sultanas in the liquid until plump. Tear the pancakes into strips and put them in a frying pan with the melted butter. Sprinkle with sugar and shake the pan over moderate heat. Pour in the sultanas and toss over the heat for a few minutes then serve. *Serves 4.*

Loucoumathes

The name is, apparently, a Turkish term of endearment.

8 oz (225 g) flour
¼ pint (1.5 dl) milk
¼ oz (6 g) yeast
½ teaspoon sugar

3 egg yolks
frying fat
honey
cinnamon

Warm the flour and the milk separately. Put the flour into a bowl and make a well in the middle of it. Mix the yeast and sugar together, add the milk and pour into the flour. Mix well, beat in the egg yolks and leave for 1 hour. Knead well and leave for another 10 minutes then drop in tablespoonsful into hot fat and cook until golden. Serve with warm honey and cinnamon. *Serves 6.*

Pain Perdu

A family pudding which used to be extremely popular in France. Do use butter to fry them in. If the bread is soaked in coffee instead of flavoured milk you have Coffee Fritters.

4 slices stale bread
½ pint (3 dl) milk
1 oz (25 g) sugar
1 teaspoon vanilla essence

2 egg yolks
butter to fry
icing or caster sugar

Cut the bread into neat slices and remove the crusts. Bring the milk to the boil with the sugar and vanilla essence and leave to get quite cold before dampening the bread with it (do not let it get too sodden or it will break). Dip the slices of bread in the beaten egg yolks coating them evenly on both sides and fry to a golden brown. Drain and serve hot sprinkled with sugar. *Serves 4.*

Pancake Meringue

A surprise pudding with a pleasant contrast in textures.

6 pancakes
jam or lemon curd
3 egg whites

6 oz (150 g) caster sugar
almonds

Sandwich the pancakes together with the jam or lemon curd and build into a pile. Whisk the egg whites very stiffly, fold in the sugar and enclose the pancakes in the meringue. Scatter with chopped or flaked almonds and bake at Gas Mark 8 (450 °F, 230 °C) for a few minutes until the meringue is lightly browned. Serve immediately by cutting into wedges. *Serves 6.*

Redcurrant Fritters

2 eggs
2 oz (50 g) flour
½ pint (3 dl) milk
3 oz (75 g) redcurrants

3 oz (75 g) boiled rice
nutmeg
sugar to taste
frying fat

Mix the egg yolks with the flour and add the milk gradually. Whisk the egg whites stiffly, stir them in lightly and add the currants, rice, nutmeg and sugar to taste. Drop in spoonsful into the hot fat and fry until crisp and gold. Drain well and serve hot dredged with caster sugar. *Serves 4 to 5.*

Rice Fritters

3 oz (75 g) rice	3 oz (75 g) marmalade
1½ pints (9 dl) milk	2 eggs
1½ oz (38 g) sugar	coating batter (p. 146)
½ oz (12 g) butter	frying fat

Wash the rice and simmer gently in the milk until all the milk has been absorbed then add the sugar, butter, marmalade and eggs and stir over low heat for a few minutes. Spread in ½ inch layer on a plate to get cold and then cut into strips or squares, dip in batter and fry in hot fat until crisp. Drain and serve. *Serves 4 to 6.*

Suet Scones

A useful quick pudding – a Monday special when I was a child.

8 oz (225 g) self-raising flour	3 oz (75 g) suet
pinch of salt	milk to mix
1 teaspoon sugar	

Mix the dry ingredients and add sufficient milk to give a stiff dough. Roll out about ¼ inch thick, cut out like scones and fry in hot, shallow fat until crisp and golden. Serve hot with golden syrup. *Serves 4.*

Sweet Fritters

A Greek dish called *Avgokalamara*.

12 oz (325 g) semolina	honey
pinch of salt	chopped walnuts
3 eggs	cinnamon
1 orange	icing sugar
frying fat	

Put the semolina into a bowl with the salt and add the eggs one at a time and the juice of the orange. Mix well and stir in enough water to make a stiff dough. Roll out thinly and cut into shapes. Drop into hot, deep fat and fry until golden. Drain and place on a hot dish. Dilute some honey with warm water and pour over then sprinkle with the nuts, cinnamon and sugar. *Serves 4.*

Ices &
Iced Puddings

We are living in privileged times. Almost every home now boasts a refrigerator so home-made ices and iced puddings have become a practical reality. They are not difficult to make and need not be extravagant. There is a recipe on page 159 for an economical Any-Time Cream Ice and many of the water ices are extremely inexpensive and make an elegant ending to a substantial meal.

Previously ices made at home were made with an ice machine. This was usually a wooden bucket with an inner metal container and between the two the freezing mixture was placed. A churner or some sort of spaddles were attached to move the ice cream around and these used to be hand operated. It is possible now to buy electrically operated ice machines. The only trouble about making ices in the domestic refrigerator is that the mixture remains static and so does not expand and there is a tendency for crystals to form. This is why many recipes suggest stirring or re-whisking the mixture from time to time during the freezing process. The refrigerator should always be pre-set to its maximum freezing power and all the utensils should be really cold. The time of freezing depends very much on your particular refrigerator. Usually the mixture is firm enough after about half an hour for a first beating and the whole process takes, on average, about 2 hours.

Cream ices do not necessarily contain cream but are always founded on either a custard or a mousse base. The latter gives a finer, more velvety texture. Remember that freezing diminishes the flavour, sweetness and colour of a mixture to some extent so the pre-frozen mixture must be rich.

Water ices always contain a sugar syrup. Egg white is sometimes introduced to give a foamier texture. A sorbet is basically a water ice which is correctly served less than hard-frozen. In the good old days sorbets contained a little liqueur. When I was a child itinerant vendors on man-sized tricycles sold delicious water ices for a penny packed in a triangular cardboard casing. The lime version still lingers in my mind.

Almond Cream Ice – Burnt

A tablespoon of kirsch is a happy addition to this sophisticated ice.

2 oz (50 g) almonds
2 oz (50 g) sugar
¼ pint (1.5 dl) double cream

1½ pints (9 dl) basic custard
  (p. 164)

Blanch, peel, shred and bake the almonds until brown. Put the sugar and a few drops of water into a small saucepan and boil until it acquires a deep golden brown colour. Cool a little then stir in the cream. Boil up again and stir into the prepared custard. Leave to cool, stir in the almonds (and the kirsch, if used) and freeze. *Serves 6 to 8.*

Almond Cream Ice

6 oz (150 g) ground almonds
1 teaspoon orange flower water
¼ pint (1.5 dl) milk
½ pint (3 dl) custard (p. 164)

¼ pint (1.5 dl) double cream
almond essence
sugar to taste

Mix the almonds with the orange flower water and add the warmed milk. Cover and leave to cool then mix with the cooled custard. Partially freeze then stir in the whipped cream, a few drops of almond essence, the sugar and complete the freezing. *Serves 4 to 6.*

Any-Time Cream Ice

Knock up some meringues with the leftover egg whites to nibble with this.

1 pint (6 dl) milk	1 oz (25 g) flour
4 egg yolks	1 teaspoon vanilla essence
2 oz (50 g) caster sugar	

Bring the milk to the boil then stir in the egg yolks beaten up with the sugar and flour. Heat gently, stirring, until thick. Allow to cool then pour into the freezing tray, cover with foil and freeze for half an hour. Remove and stir well then finish freezing. *Serves 4.*

Apple Water Ice

The substitution of 1 pint of cider for the water turns this into Cider Ice.

1½ lbs (675 g) apples	1 pint (6 dl) water
1 lb (450 g) sugar	2 tablespoons lemon juice

Stew the apples with a very little water and no sugar and sieve them while still hot. Make a syrup by dissolving the sugar in the water and then boiling until syrupy. Stir into the apple, add the lemon juice and freeze. *Serves 6.*

Apricot Ice

May be made with fresh or with stewed, dried apricots.

1 lb (450 g) apricots	lemon juice
2 oz (50 g) sugar	¼ pint (1.5 dl) double cream
½ pint (3 dl) custard (p. 164)	

Stew the apricots with the sugar and a little water. Remove the stones, sieve the fruit and mix the purée with the custard. Add a squeeze of lemon juice and stir in the lightly whipped cream. Pour into the freezer tray, cover with foil and freeze, stirring from time to time. *Serves 6.*

Banana and Lemon Sorbet

4 bananas
2 tablespoons honey
1 lemon

1 tablespoon rum
½ pint (3 dl) plain yogurt

Peel and mash the bananas then mix in the honey, the juice of the lemon, the rum and the yogurt. Stir until smooth. Whisk the egg whites stiffly and fold in. Place in the freezer until half frozen then remove and whisk again mixing in the grated rind of the lemon. Return to freezer until frozen. *Serves 4.*

Banana Cream Ice

Simply a frozen banana fool.

6 bananas
1 pint (6 dl) custard (p. 164)

¼ pint (1.5 dl) double cream
1 tablespoon lemon juice

Sieve the bananas and mix into the cooled custard. Add the lightly whipped cream and the lemon juice and freeze. *Serves 6.*

Biscuit Glacé Grand Marnier

4 oz (100 g) sweet biscuits
3 tablespoons orange juice
4 tablespoons Grand Marnier
2 egg whites

½ pint (3 dl) double cream
4 oz (100 g) icing sugar
4 oz (100 g) flaked almonds

Crumble the biscuits and let them soak in the orange juice and Grand Marnier. Whip the egg whites fairly stiffly and beat in the icing sugar gradually. Stir in the almonds lightly then add the biscuit mixture and, finally, the whipped cream. Cover and freeze. *Serves 6.*

Blackberry Water Ice

One of the simplest ways of using blackberries – and one of the most popular in this family. The addition of sweet-scented geranium leaves is important and imparts an exquisite flavour.

4 oz (100 g) sugar	3 sweet-scented geranium leaves
¼ pint (1.5 dl) water	1 lb (450 g) blackberries

Boil the sugar and water with two geranium leaves for 5 minutes then leave to cool. Rinse the blackberries and sieve them (uncooked). Remove the geranium leaves and stir the syrup into the blackberry purée. Place a fresh geranium leaf on top, cover with foil and freeze. *Serves 6.*

Blackcurrant Leaf Ice

Makes a delicious filling for a chilled melon.

6 oz (150 g) sugar	3 lemons
1 pint (6 dl) water	green colouring
3 handfuls blackcurrant leaves	

Dissolve the sugar in the water with the pared rind of the two lemons over gentle heat then boil rapidly for about 5 minutes. Add the washed leaves, remove from the heat and cover the pan. Leave to infuse for about 30 minutes then drain, squeezing the leaves well to extract all the syrup. Add the juice of the lemons and a few drops of colouring, cover and freeze. *Serves 4.*

Brown Bread Cream Ice

The browned crumbs give a crunchy texture and nutty taste.

3 oz (75 g) brown bread	¼ pint (1.5 dl) double cream
1 tablespoon caster sugar	vanilla essence
1 pint (6 dl) custard (p. 164)	

Crumble the bread finely, spread on a baking sheet and sprinkle with the sugar. Bake at Gas Mark 2 (300 °F, 150 °C) until thoroughly crisp and brown. Turn on to a plate to cool then stir into the custard with the lightly whipped cream and a few drops of vanilla essence. Cover and freeze. *Serves 6.*

Butterscotch Parfait

Unsweetened evaporated milk may be used in place of the cream.

1 oz (25 g) butter
3 oz (75 g) demerara sugar
¼ pint (1.5 dl) water
4 egg yolks

½ pint (3 dl) double cream
vanilla essence
nuts

Melt the butter and the sugar together in a saucepan and boil for 1 minute. Add the water and heat until the butterscotch has dissolved. Whisk the egg yolks well and add gradually to the butterscotch. Cook lightly for about 5 minutes then cool, fold in the whipped cream and a few drops of vanilla essence and freeze. Scatter with nuts before serving. *Serves 4.*

Caramel Cream Ice

2 oz (50 g) sugar
¼ pint (1.5 dl) double cream
1½ pints (9 dl) custard (p. 164)

Put the sugar into a small saucepan with a few drops of water and boil until a rich golden brown. Add the cream and bring to the boil then stir into the custard and freeze. *Serves 4.*

Cassata

A positive cornucopia of colours and flavours.

2 oz (50 g) currants
2 oz (50 g) sultanas
1 oz (25 g) chopped orange peel
1 oz (25 g) chopped glacé
  cherries

1 oz (25 g) flaked almonds
1 tablespoon brandy
1 tablespoon orange juice
½ pint (3 dl) double cream
1 oz (25 g) icing sugar

Soak the fruit and nuts in the brandy and orange juice in a screw top jar overnight, shaking occasionally. Whip the cream and sugar until fairly stiff, fold in and freeze. *Serves 6.*

Opposite Pancakes (*pages 144–52*)

Cherry Cream Ice

A useful recipe since it avoids the chore of stoning the cherries.

¾ lb (325 g) cherries
2 oz (50 g) sugar
juice 1 lemon

1 tablespoon cherry brandy
1 pint (6 dl) custard (p. 164)

Put the cherries in a saucepan with the sugar, lemon juice and cherry brandy and let them stand for about 30 minutes. Add ½ pint (3 dl) water and cook gently until the cherries are soft, then sieve. Stir into the custard, cover and freeze. *Serves 6.*

Cherry Water Ice

Enlist the services of a strong-arm member of the family to smash some cherry stones up with a hammer for you.

1½ lbs (675 g) cooking cherries
1½ lbs (675 g) sugar
1 pint (6 dl) water

1 tablespoon kirsch (optional)
1 tablespoon lemon juice

Stone the cherries and from about a quarter of the stones remove the kernels. Dissolve the sugar in the water and boil rapidly for about 5 minutes then pour over the cherries and kernels. Cover and leave until cold then add the kirsch and the lemon juice and freeze. *Serves 6.*

Chestnut Cream Ice

A can of chestnut purée will serve very well.

1 lb (450 g) chestnuts
milk
vanilla pod
7 oz (175 g) sugar

½ pint (3 dl) water
2 tablespoons rum
¾ pint (4.5 dl) double cream

Skin the chestnuts (p. 30) then cook them in a saucepan with a little milk and the vanilla pod until soft. Sieve. Dissolve the sugar in the water over low heat then stir into the chestnut purée together with the rum. Allow to cool and fold in the whipped cream. Cover and freeze. *Serves 6.*

Opposite Cassata (*page 162*)

Chocolate Cream Ice

Add a tablespoon of rum if you have it handy.

3 oz (75 g) bitter chocolate   coffee essence
1 pint (6 dl) custard (p. 164)   ¼ pint (1.5 dl) double cream
vanilla essence

Melt the chocolate in a bowl over a pan of hot water and stir into the custard with a few drops of vanilla essence and a few drops of coffee essence to bring out the flavour. Freeze for an hour then beat well, fold in the whipped cream and re-freeze. *Serves 6.*

Coffee Cream Ice

Really does have the genuine flavour of coffee.

2 oz (50 g) coffee beans   ¼ pint (1.5 dl) water
¾ pint (4.5 dl) single cream   4 egg yolks
4 oz (100 g) sugar   ½ pint (3 dl) double cream

Crack the coffee beans – which should be of a light roast – in a pestle and mortar then infuse them in the single cream over very gentle heat for at least 30 minutes. Leave to cool. Boil the sugar and water together rapidly then pour on to the beaten egg yolks and whisk until thick. Add the strained coffee-cream and, when the mixture is cold, the partially whipped cream. Cover and freeze. *Serves 6.*

Custard Base for Ices

Flavoured with vanilla (or coffee, orange rind, etc.) this makes a perfectly acceptable cream ice as it is and is also the base for many other cream ices.

2 eggs   1 pint (6 dl) milk
4 oz (100 g) caster sugar   ¼ pint (1.5 dl) double cream
½ oz (12 g) cornflour

Whisk the eggs and the sugar well together and then add the cornflour mixed with a little of the milk. Heat the rest of the milk and add. Return to the saucepan, bring to the boil and boil for 3 minutes stirring all the time. Pour into a bowl and leave to cool whisking occasionally to prevent a skin forming. When cold add the cream, slightly whipped.

Double Currant Ice

An unusual and refreshing iced pudding.

8 oz (225 g) redcurrant jelly
2 tablespoons lemon juice
6 oz (150 g) dried currants

1 pint (6 dl) plain yogurt (p. 142)

Melt the redcurrant jelly over low heat and stir in the lemon juice and currants. Simmer for 3 minutes, cool, then stir into the yogurt. Pour into the freezing tray and freeze for 1 hour then re-mix and freeze again. *Serves 4.*

Fig Cream Ice

1 oz (25 g) cornflour
1 pint (6 dl) milk
2 eggs
2 oz (50 g) caster sugar

½ oz (12 g) gelatine
½ pint (3 dl) cream
vanilla essence
2 oz (50 g) dried figs

Mix the cornflour smoothly with a little of the milk then boil the remainder, add the cornflour and stir until boiling. Beat the eggs and sugar together, stir them into the milk and add the gelatine dissolved in a little hot water. Leave to cool then add the cream, a few drops of vanilla essence and the finely chopped figs. Cover and freeze. *Serves 6.*

Ginger Cream Ice

Ginger and ice cream are one of the most delicious combinations.

4 oz (100 g) preserved ginger
½ pint (3 dl) syrup

juice 1 lemon
1 pint (6 dl) double cream

Chop the ginger very finely and mix it with the syrup (which may be ginger syrup or sugar syrup or a mixture of the two). Add the lemon juice and cream and freeze. *Serves 6.*

Ginger Water Ice

4 oz (100 g) preserved ginger
ginger syrup
4 lumps sugar
1 orange

1 pint (6 dl) sugar syrup (p. 17)
juice 2 lemons
1 egg white

Chop the ginger very finely and mix in a little of its syrup. Rub the sugar lumps on to the orange rind to absorb the oil then add to the ginger together with the sugar syrup, the juice of the orange and the lemons and 3 tablespoons cold water. Boil up once and leave to cool. Freeze and fold in the stiffly whisked egg white after about 1 hour. *Serves 6.*

Gooseberry Sorbet

1 lb (450 g) gooseberries
½ pint (3 dl) water
6 oz (150 g) sugar

juice 2 lemons
green colouring
⅛ pint (0.75 dl) maraschino

Wash the gooseberries and stew them with the water and sugar, then sieve. Add the lemon juice and a little colouring. When cold stir in the maraschino and freeze.
Serves 4.

Grape Cream Ice

2 lbs (900 g) white grapes
juice 1 lemon

2 oz (50 g) sugar
¾ pint (4.5 dl) double cream

Rinse the grapes and sieve them. You should have about ¾ pint (4.5 dl) of very liquid pulp. Add the juice of the lemon and the sugar and heat enough to melt the sugar. Cool and freeze. Whip the cream stiffly with a little sugar to taste. Turn the grape ice into a bowl, whisk well then fold in the cream and return to freezer. *Serves 6.*

Grape Water Ice

2 lbs (900 g) sugar
1 pint (6 dl) water
4 lemons

¾ lb (325 g) white grapes
1 tablespoon orange flower
  water

Dissolve the sugar in the water with the pared rind of two lemons over gentle heat. Bring to the boil and boil gently for 10 minutes then skim, strain and re-boil, discarding the lemon rind. Sieve the grapes and add the syrup and the juice of the lemons. Cool then stir in the orange flower water and freeze. *Serves 4.*

Lemon and Orange Sorbet

Very good as it is, but even better with a spoonful of white rum poured over just before serving.

4 oranges	¼ pint (1.5 dl) water
1 lemon	3 egg whites
4 oz (100 g) sugar	¼ pint (1.5 dl) double cream

Grate the rind of one orange and the lemon into the sugar and water then boil to a thin syrup. Strain when cool and mix with the juice of the fruit. Cover and freeze then turn out into a bowl, break up into a snow and fold in the stiffly whisked egg whites and the cream. Return to the ice box and re-freeze for about 1 hour. *Serves 4.*

Lemon Cream Ice

1 lemon	3 egg yolks
¾ pint (4.5 dl) single cream	3 oz (75 g) sugar

Grate the rind of the lemon into the cream in a small saucepan. Stir in the beaten egg yolks and the sugar and cook gently until beginning to thicken then remove and continue stirring until cool. Add the juice of half the lemon, pour into the ice tray, cover and freeze, stirring now and then. *Serves 4.*

Lemon Refrigerator Cake

8 oz (225 g) trifle sponges	4 eggs
4 oz (100 g) butter	1 lemon
6 oz (150 g) caster sugar	cream to decorate

Cut up the sponges and line a buttered, loose-bottomed cake tin with some of them. Cream together the butter and sugar, beat in the egg yolks, the grated rind and juice of the lemon and the stiffly beaten egg whites. Fill the tin with alternate layers of this mixture and sponge, finishing with a layer of sponge. Cover and chill for 12 hours then turn out and serve masked in whipped cream. *Serves 6.*

Lemon Water Ice

The most refreshing ice imaginable.

3 lemons
6 oz (150 g) sugar
1 pint (6 dl) water

Peel the lemons and put the rind in a saucepan with the sugar and water. Dissolve the sugar over gentle heat then boil rapidly for 5 minutes. Leave to cool before stirring in the juice of the lemons then cover and freeze. *Serves 4.*

Marsala Cream Ice

½ pint (3 dl) marsala
½ pint (3 dl) water
2 oz (50 g) caster sugar

4 egg yolks
6 oz (2 dl) double cream

Put the marsala and water together into a saucepan and put to warm while you whip together the sugar and egg yolks into a foamy batter. Pour into a saucepan and whip over fast heat for about 2 minutes then stand the pan in a bowl of ice and carry on whipping slowly until down to blood heat. Stir in the stiffly whipped cream and freeze.
Serves 6.

Melon and Ginger Sorbet

1 medium melon
5 oz (125 g) soft brown sugar
1 oz (25 g) ground ginger

juice 1 lemon
2 egg whites
mint

Halve the melon and scoop out the seeds and fibres. Scoop out twelve balls of the flesh with a melon-baller and refrigerate (covered). Cut out the rest of the flesh and put in a saucepan with the sugar, 4 tablespoons water, the ginger and the lemon juice. Cook over low heat for 10 minutes then sieve or liquidize. Refrigerate. Beat the egg whites stiffly, fold into the melon purée and chill again. Serve piled into the melon shell, decorated with the melon balls and a few sprigs of mint. *Serves 4.*

Melon Cream Ice

A richer and even more fragrant concoction than the preceding one.

1 large melon	wineglass kirsch
4 oz (100 g) sugar	juice ½ lemon
4 egg yolks	½ pint (3 dl) double cream

Cut a sliver off the base of the melon so that it will stand firmly then slice off the top, remove the seeds and fibres and scoop out the flesh. Place this in a saucepan with the sugar and cook gently for a few minutes then sieve. Beat the egg yolks thoroughly, stir in and cook gently until beginning to thicken. Leave to cool then stir in the kirsch, lemon juice and finally the whipped cream. Cover and freeze, stirring occasionally, and serve piled into the chilled melon shell. *Serves 6.*

Melon Water Ice

1 medium melon	juice 2 oranges
2 pints (12 dl) water	juice 2 lemons
4 oz (100 g) sugar	

Peel and slice the melon and simmer for 10 minutes with the water and sugar, then sieve. When cool add the juice of the oranges and lemons, cover and freeze. *Serves 6.*

Nesselrode Pudding

36 chestnuts	1 pint (6 dl) double cream
½ pint (3 dl) milk	2 oz (50 g) glacé cherries
4 egg yolks	

Shell the chestnuts (p. 30) and simmer them in ¼ pint (1.5 dl) of the milk until tender, then sieve. Bring the rest of the milk almost to boiling point, add the beaten egg yolks and stir over very low heat until thickening. Stir into the chestnut purée and leave to cool then add half the cream and freeze until nearly set before stirring in the chopped cherries and the remainder of the cream stiffly whipped. Freeze until set, stirring frequently. *Serves 8.*

Nut Cream Ice

2 eggs
2 oz (50 g) sugar
3 oz (75 g) toasted almonds or
  filberts
½ pint (3 dl) double cream

Whisk the eggs and sugar in a bowl over a pan of hot water until warm then remove and continue whisking until cool. Fold in the ground-up nuts and the whipped cream, cover and freeze. *Serves 4.*

Omelette Glacée en Surprise

1 pint (6 dl) Vanilla Cream Ice
  (p. 174)
4 oz (100 g) strawberries or
  raspberries
sugar syrup (p. 17)

2 eggs
1 egg white
1 oz (25 g) caster sugar
1 tablespoon liqueur or cream

Pack the ice cream into a chilled soufflé dish, spread the fruit on top, sprinkle with the sugar syrup and place in the refrigerator while you make the omelette soufflé. Beat the yolks of the eggs with the sugar and liqueur or cream. Beat the whites stiffly and fold them in lightly. Pile on top of the ice cream and fruit and bake at Gas Mark 7 (425 °F, 220 °C) for about 5 minutes until well browned and risen. Serve immediately. *Serves 6.*

Orange Cream Ice

2 oz (50 g) lump sugar
3 oranges
1 pint (6 dl) custard (p. 164)

Rub the sugar lumps over the rind of the orange then dissolve them in 1 tablespoon of hot water. Mix with the juice of the oranges, stir into the custard, cover and freeze. *Serves 4.*

Orange Mousse – Frozen

¼ pint (1.5 dl) orange juice
4 oz (100 g) caster sugar
pinch of salt

3 egg yolks
¼ pint (1.5 dl) double cream

Heat the orange juice, sugar and salt together over a low flame. Beat the egg yolks until pale and creamy and stir in, cooking until they thicken while you stir. Cool then fold in the lightly whipped cream and freeze. *Serves 4.*

Orange Sherbet

An unusual recipe from Sweden. A dash of curaçao added just before serving is good.

2 cups water
4 oz (100 g) sugar
1 orange
3 tablespoons lemon juice

for the meringue
½ cup water
2 oz (50 g) sugar
cream of tartar
1 egg white

Gently boil the water with the sugar for 10 minutes then add the grated rind of the orange and leave to cool before stirring in the juice of the orange and the lemon juice. Strain into the refrigerator tray and freeze until firm – about 1 hour. Break into pieces in a chilled mixing bowl and beat with an electric or rotary mixer until smooth. Make the meringue by boiling the water, sugar and a pinch of cream of tartar together until thick. Whip the egg white stiffly and beat the syrup in gradually. Continue to beat until cool then stir into the orange mixture. Stir well and freeze again, stirring occasionally, until it begins to set in small crystals. Spoon into chilled glasses and serve. *Serves 4.*

Pineapple Cream Ice

This recipe may be used with any fruit – fresh, stewed or canned.

8 oz (225 g) pineapple
⅛ pint (0.75 dl) pineapple syrup

1 teaspoon lemon juice
1 pint (6 dl) custard (p. 164)

Sieve the pineapple and mix it with the syrup and lemon juice. Stir into the cooled custard and freeze. *Serves 6.*

Pineapple Water Ice

1 lb (450 g) pineapple, fresh or canned

1 pint (6 dl) sugar syrup (p. 17)
juice 1 lemon

Sieve the pineapple, mix with the syrup and lemon juice and freeze. *Serves 6.*

Poires Hélène

Ripe William or Comice pears are best for this classic dish.

6 pears
vanilla-flavoured sugar syrup (p. 17)

Vanilla Cream Ice (p. 174)
2 oz (50 g) almonds
Chocolate Sauce (p. 207)

Peel, core and halve the pears then poach them gently in the syrup and leave to cool in it. Put the Vanilla Cream Ice in a chilled dish, arrange the drained pears around it and scatter with the toasted almonds. Serve with Chocolate Sauce. *Serves 6.*

Praline Ice

3 egg yolks
2½ oz (62 g) caster sugar
⅓ pint (2 dl) milk
vanilla pod or essence

⅓ pint (2 dl) double cream
2 oz (50 g) praline powder
  (p. 152)

Cream the egg yolks and sugar together until white. Scald the milk with the vanilla pod and add. Return to the pan and cook gently until the mixture coats the back of the spoon. Leave to cool then fold in the lightly whipped cream and freeze. Stir in the praline powder at the last minute or it will dissolve. *Serves 4.*

Raspberry Mallow Cream Ice

8 oz (225 g) marshmallows
3 tablespoons orange juice

8 oz (225 g) raspberries
½ pint (3 dl) double cream

Put the marshmallows and orange juice together in a bowl over a pan of boiling water and stir until dissolved. Remove and leave to cool. Crush the raspberries with a fork and stir in together with the whipped cream. Freeze. *Serves 4.*

Raspberry Water Ice

The redcurrants somehow heighten the flavour of the raspberries in this delicious ice. Reverse the quantities of fruit to make Redcurrant Water Ice.

1 lb (450 g) raspberries
4 oz (100 g) redcurrants
4 oz (100 g) sugar

$\frac{1}{4}$ pint (1.5 dl) water
juice $\frac{1}{2}$ lemon

Sieve the fruit. Boil the sugar with the water for 5 minutes, leave to cool then stir into the purée with the lemon juice. Cover and freeze. *Serves 4.*

Rum Sorbet

A dish to remember when lemons are cheap and there is a drop of leftover rum.

6 lemons
$\frac{3}{4}$ pint (4.5 dl) water

6 oz (150 g) sugar
$\frac{1}{4}$ pint (1.5 dl) rum

Peel the lemons thinly and pour the boiling water over the rinds in a large bowl, then stir in the sugar. Allow to cool to blood heat before adding the juice of the lemons and the rum. Cover and freeze then tip back into the bowl, whisk and re-freeze. *Serves 6.*

Strawberry Granita

A granita – as the name implies – should have a slightly grainy texture and be no more than barely frozen. The same recipe may be used for raspberries.

8 oz (225 g) sugar
$\frac{1}{4}$ pint (1.5 dl) water
2 lbs (900 g) strawberries

juice $\frac{1}{2}$ lemon
juice $\frac{1}{2}$ orange

Boil the sugar and water together for about 7 minutes to make a thin syrup. Leave to cool. Sieve the strawberries, stir in the lemon and orange juice, add to the cooled syrup, cover and freeze. *Serves 6.*

Tangerine Water Ice

Try this on jaded palates at Christmas time.

2 oz (50 g) lump sugar
6 tangerines
1 orange

2 lemons
¼ pint (1.5 dl) water
1 pint (6 dl) sugar syrup (p. 17)

Rub the sugar lumps on the tangerine skin to extract some of the flavour, then place the sugar in a saucepan with the thinly pared rind of the orange and of 1 lemon and the water. Boil for 10 minutes then add the juice of the tangerines, the orange and the lemons and the sugar syrup and boil up again. Strain, cool, cover and freeze. *Serves 6.*

Tea Cream Ice

There are various recipes for this but here is a Swiss one which is highly recommended.

1 pint (6 dl) milky tea
1 pint (6 dl) double cream
pinch of salt

4 eggs
8 oz (225 g) sugar

Mix everything together and freeze. May be decorated with whipped cream and glacé fruits. *Serves 8.*

Vanilla Cream Ice

This is a cream ice with a mousse base. It has a fine and velvety texture. These quantities make 1 pint (6 dl). A teaspoon of vanilla essence may be substituted for the vanilla pod in which case stir it into the egg yolks.

2½ oz (62 g) sugar
¼ pint (1.5 dl) water
vanilla

¾ pint (4.5 dl) cream
3 egg yolks

Put the sugar and water into a small saucepan and dissolve over gentle heat. Infuse the vanilla pod with the cream in another saucepan over very low heat until well flavoured, then strain and leave to cool. Cream the egg yolks. When the sugar is quite dissolved bring the syrup to the boil and boil rapidly until thickening slightly. Remove from the heat, leave to cool a little then whisk into the egg yolks. Keep whisking until thick and mousse-like then cool before adding the cream. Cool and freeze. *Serves 4.*

Wine Soufflé with Glacé Fruits

1 egg yolk
2 oz (50 g) sugar
juice ½ lemon
⅛ pint (0.75 dl) white wine

½ pint (3 dl) double cream
2 oz (50 g) mixed glacé fruits
grapes to decorate

Place the egg yolk, sugar and lemon juice in a bowl over a pan of hot water and whisk lightly, adding the wine gradually. When thick, remove from the heat and whisk until cool. Fold in the whipped cream and chopped glacé fruit, cover and freeze. Decorate with a few stoned grapes. *Serves 4.*

Baked, Steamed
& Boiled Puddings

These form the backbone of British puddings much beloved by children and menfolk alike and acceptable to anyone throughout the winter months. They are both economical and sustaining. All they need is time to cook – and not much of that for those with pressure cookers. Breadcrumbs are often included to make a lighter pudding.

Nowadays few of us use the old-fashioned pudding cloths in which to boil puddings and the alternative of putting the mixture into some sort of buttered pudding bowl, covering with greased paper and then foil or a cloth and steaming in a covered pan with about 1½ inches (4 cm) water simmering in the bottom seems to work perfectly well. If you are using the oven at the same time for a longish period puddings can quite successfully be steamed in the oven in a deep casserole covered with a lid. Simply stand the covered pudding basin in the casserole in about 1 inch (2½ cm) boiling water and leave for the required time in a low oven.

To line a pudding basin with suet crust roll out the pastry into a round large enough to fill the bowl then cut out one quarter of the round and reserve it for a lid fitting the remainder into the bowl and sealing the edges well together.

Alma Pudding

I never knew what 'alma' meant until I met this pudding and looked it up. It means, of course, 'nourishing and kind' so the pudding is well named being good to eat and kind to the budget. It is one of the simplest steamed puddings and contains no suet.

4 oz (100 g) butter or margarine   8 oz (225 g) plain flour
6 oz (150 g) caster sugar   4 oz (100 g) dried fruit
2 eggs   1 teaspoon baking powder
grated rind 1 lemon

Cream the butter or margarine, add the sugar and beat until thick and white. Beat in the eggs then add the rest of the ingredients. Pour into a well buttered basin, cover and steam for about 2 hours. Serve with Custard (p. 209), Lemon (p. 212) or Syrup (p. 214) Sauce. *Serves 4 to 5.*

Almond Pudding

A light and tasty pudding which can be steamed or baked either in a pudding bowl or in individual moulds or cups.

2 oz (50 g) butter or margarine   4 oz (100 g) ground almonds
1 oz (25 g) caster sugar   2 tablespoons milk
2 eggs

Cream the butter or margarine until white then add the sugar. Stir in the yolks of the eggs, the almonds and the milk. Whisk the egg whites to a stiff froth and add them lightly to the rest of the ingredients. A dash of almond essence will heighten the flavour. Pour into a buttered bowl or mould and steam or bake (at Gas Mark 4, 350 °F, 180 °C) for about 30 minutes. Serve with Custard (p. 209) or White (p. 215) Sauce. *Serves 4 to 5.*

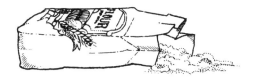

Apple Amber

A classic British pudding and one to remember for that leftover pastry. Keep the pastry in the refrigerator in a polythene bag and when you have some apples or soft fruit try this pudding.

1 lb (450 g) apples	pastry trimmings
2 oz (50 g) demerara sugar	1 oz (25 g) butter or margarine
2 tablespoons water	2 eggs
rind ½ lemon	3 oz (75 g) caster sugar

Wash the apples, cut up roughly and stew them gently with the demerara sugar, water and thinly peeled lemon rind. (There is no point in peeling and coring the apples as they are sieved anyway.) Sieve. Line the sides of a 1 pint (6 dl) pie dish with the pastry. Stir the butter or margarine and the yolks of the eggs into the apple purée and turn the mixture into the prepared pie dish. Bake at Gas Mark 4 (350 °F, 180 °C) until set – about 20 minutes. Remove and make the meringue topping by whipping up the egg whites as stiffly as possible, folding in the caster sugar lightly and piling on to the pudding. Dredge with a little more sugar and bake in a very slow oven – Gas Mark 1 (275 °F, 140 °C) until the meringue is firm and lightly browned – about 45 minutes. *Serves 4.*

Apple Hat

The apples used should be the sort that melt when cooked, e.g. Bramleys. Plums, damsons, rhubarb, cranberries, blackberries, currants, gooseberries – practically any fruit – can be substituted for apples.

6 oz (150 g) self-raising flour	cold water or milk
pinch of salt	1 lb (450 g) cooking apples
2 oz (50 g) fresh white breadcrumbs	2 oz (50 g) brown sugar
	strip of lemon rind
4 oz (100 g) suet	cup of cold water

Sift the flour and salt into a bowl. Add the crumbs and suet and rub lightly together. Mix to a spongy dough with the cold water or milk. Cut off one quarter and line a buttered pudding basin with the rest. Fill with the sliced apples layered with sugar. Add the lemon rind and the cup of cold water. Roll out the remaining dough to a round to form a lid. Cover with greased paper and then loosely with foil pressing the foil firmly around the rim of the basin. Steam or boil for 3 hours. Lift out and let it stand for a few moments before inverting on to a hot dish. Serve with brown sugar and cream. *Serves 4 to 5.*

Baked Apple Pudding

Children love this toffee version of apple pie. Serve it with custard or cream.

8 oz (225 g) suet crust (p. 56)
1 lb (450 g) cooking apples
2 oz (50 g) granulated sugar

orange juice
2 tablespoons syrup
2 oz (50 g) brown sugar

Divide the suet crust into two portions, roll out thinly and use one portion to line a pie dish or baking tin. Fill with the peeled, cored and chopped apples sprinkling them with the granulated sugar and the orange juice. Cover with the second portion of suet crust sealing the edges well and raising them slightly. Warm the syrup gently and pour it on to the crust then spread the brown sugar over. Bake at Gas Mark 4 (350 °F, 180 °C) for about 30 minutes until the apples are tender and the top is brown and toffee-like. *Serves 4 to 5.*

Apple Spiced Roll

The justly famous Jam or Syrup Roly Poly is made the same way as this simply by substituting jam or syrup for the fruit. Dried fruit alone can also be used but the amount should then be increased to about 8 oz (225 g).

6 oz (150 g) suet crust (p. 56)
8 oz (225 g) cooking apples
2 oz (50 g) demerara sugar

3 oz (75 g) mixed dried fruit
½ teaspoon mixed spice

Roll the pastry into a rectangle about 12 by 9 inches (30 by 22 cm). Mix the chopped apples, sugar, dried fruit and spice together and spread on to the pastry leaving a margin uncovered all round. Brush the edges with water. Roll up, sealing the edges together. Wrap in foil or a pudding cloth and boil for 2 hours. Turn out on to a hot dish and dredge with caster sugar. *Serves 4 to 5.*

Apple Torte

A cross between a Clafoutis and a spongy fruit pudding. The addition of walnuts makes an important difference.

4 oz (100 g) butter	8 oz (225 g) cooking apples
4 oz (100 g) caster sugar	4 oz (100 g) walnuts
2 eggs	½ teaspoon powdered mace
6 oz (150 g) self-raising flour	1 tablespoon brandy or cider

Cream the butter and sugar together until light then mix in the beaten eggs and flour alternately. Peel, core and slice the apples and add together with the chopped walnuts, the mace and the brandy or cider. Mix well together and turn into a well-buttered square baking tin. Bake at Gas Mark 4 (350 °F, 180 °C) for about 45 minutes and serve with Custard (p. 209) or a little cream laced with brandy. *Serves 4.*

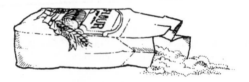

Batter Pudding

When all else failed plain Batter Pudding was sometimes served to us as children either with syrup or jam or sometimes containing dried or fresh fruit. It fills up the gaps but here is an altogether superior version which most people will enjoy.

8 fl. oz (about 2 dl) milk	2 oz (50 g) blanched, shredded
3 oz (75 g) butter or margarine	almonds
4 oz (100 g) flour	3–4 tablespoons apricot jam
3 eggs	juice ½ lemon

Put the milk and butter together into a pan and bring to the boil. Remove from the heat and add the flour, beating until smooth. Cool then beat in the eggs one at a time, reserving one white. Whip this stiffly and fold in lightly. Pour into a buttered pie or soufflé dish and scatter with the almonds. Dust with caster sugar and bake in a moderately hot oven (Gas Mark 5, 375 °F, 190 °C) for about 45 minutes. Warm the jam with the juice of the lemon and pour it over the pudding just before serving. *Serves 4 to 5.*

Betsy Pudding

I don't know who this Betsy – or Betty – was that she should have so many puddings called after her. The common denominator seems to be breadcrumbs so perhaps it was originally Bready Pudding? Here, anyway, is one version.

1 pint (6 dl) milk	1 egg
8 oz (225 g) stale bread	4 tablespoons jam or stewed
1 oz (25 g) suet	fruit
1 oz (25 g) sugar	

Bring the milk to the boil and pour on to the bread. Cover and let it stand for 30 minutes then beat out any lumps with a fork. Stir in the suet, sugar and egg. Place a layer of this in the bottom of a buttered fireproof dish, cover with a layer of jam or stewed fruit and continue in layers ending with a layer of the mixture. Bake at Gas Mark 2 (300°F, 150°C) for about 1 hour and serve hot. *Serves 4.*

Blackberry and Apple Pudding

In the last few years blackberries seem to grow in ever greater profusion in the hedgerows so here is a pudding to make the most of what you can gather.

8 oz (225 g) suet crust enriched	2 large apples
with an egg yolk (p. 56)	3 oz (75 g) sugar
12 oz (325 g) blackberries	3 leaves fresh mint

Line a pudding basin with the suet crust reserving enough for a lid. Mix the washed blackberries with the peeled, cored and sliced apples, the sugar and the mint leaves finely chopped. Pile into the basin and cover with a lid of suet crust, sealing it well. Cover with a greased paper and then loosely with foil and simmer for 2 hours in a lidded saucepan. Turn out on to a hot dish and serve with clotted cream. *Serves 4 to 5.*

Blackberry Roly Poly

More of a spongy than a suety roll. Light and lemony.

8 oz (225 g) plain flour
1 level teaspoon baking powder
½ level teaspoon salt
2 oz (50 g) margarine
1 oz (25 g) caster sugar
grated rind 1 lemon
5–6 tablespoons milk

12 oz (325 g) blackberries
2–3 oz (50–75 g) granulated
  sugar
beaten egg or milk
caster sugar
1 oz (25 g) butter

Sift the flour, baking powder and salt into a bowl and rub in the margarine. Stir in the sugar and lemon rind and mix to a soft dough with the milk. Roll out into a rectangle about 12 by 10 inches (30 by 25 cm). Cover with 10 oz (275 g) of the blackberries to within 1 inch of the edges. Moisten the edges with water, sprinkle the fruit with sugar then roll up, sealing the joins well. Place in a fireproof dish. Make three slits slantwise across the top, brush with egg or milk and sprinkle with granulated sugar. Dot small pieces of butter on top, pour 3 tablespoons of water into the dish and add the remaining blackberries. Bake at Gas Mark 7 (425 °F, 230 °C) for 15 minutes then reduce to Gas Mark 4 (350 °F, 180 °C) for a further 25 minutes. Serve hot with cream or Custard (p. 209). *Serves 4 to 5.*

Blackcurrant Layer Pudding

The same recipe may be used with apples, rhubarb, other soft fruit or even jam.

1 lb (450 g) blackcurrants
5 oz (125 g) sugar
8 oz (225 g) plain flour
1 teaspoon baking powder

½ teaspoon salt
4 oz (100 g) suet
cold water

Gently cook the fruit for 5 minutes with the sugar and a little water. Leave to cool. Sieve the flour with the baking powder and salt and add the suet. Mix with the water to a soft dough and knead lightly. Place in a greased pudding basin a layer of fruit then a layer of rolled pastry and repeat until the basin is full. Cover and steam for 2 hours. Turn on to a hot dish and serve with cream or Custard (p. 209). *Serves 4 to 5.*

Blackcurrant Streusel

A crumbly sandwich concoction.

6 oz (150 g) plain flour
7 oz (175 g) butter or margarine
2 oz (50 g) caster sugar
1 lb (450 g) blackcurrants

4 oz (100 g) granulated sugar
3 oz (75 g) brown flour
5 oz (125 g) brown sugar

Make the base by sifting together the flour and caster sugar then rubbing in 4 oz (100 g) of the butter or margarine. Knead until the mixture forms a dough then press into an 8 by 10 inch (20 by 25 cm) tin. Mix the blackcurrants with the granulated sugar and strew them over the base. Rub the rest of the butter or margarine into the brown flour and brown sugar until crumbly and spread over the blackcurrants. Cook at Gas Mark 5 (375 °F, 190 °C) for about 1 hour until golden brown. Cut into squares to serve and eat hot or cold topped with clotted cream. *Serves 4 to 5.*

Bread and Butter Pudding

Don't wait until you have leftover bread and butter in order to make this pudding. It is excellent in its own right so long as you avoid getting it too 'bready'. Coconut may be added for variety.

2 rounds thin bread and butter
2 oz (50 g) mixed dried fruit
½ pint (3 dl) milk

1 egg
1 oz (25 g) caster sugar
grated nutmeg

Arrange the buttered bread and fruit in layers in a buttered fireproof dish. Warm the milk and pour it on to the beaten egg and sugar. Strain into the side of the dish and let the pudding stand for an hour or so. Grate a little nutmeg on top, sprinkle with caster sugar and bake either standing on a baking sheet or in a tin of hot water at Gas Mark 4 (350 °F, 180 °C) for about 30 minutes until the custard is set and the top well browned and crisp. Serve hot. *Serves 4.*

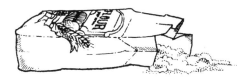

Bread Pudding – Baked

Poor man's Christmas pudding. The addition of a few nuts is good.
The pudding can also be cooked by boiling for 2 hours.

6 oz (150 g) stale bread
2 oz (50 g) suet
3 oz (75 g) mixed dried fruit
1 oz (25 g) sugar
¼ teaspoon mixed spice

¼ teaspoon ground ginger
large pinch bicarbonate of soda
1 tablespoon syrup
1 oz (25 g) chopped nuts

Cover the bread with cold water and leave to soak for 1 hour. Squeeze
out and beat with a fork. Mix in all the other ingredients except the
nuts and turn into a buttered pie dish. Sprinkle with the nuts and bake
at Gas Mark 5 (375 °F, 190 °C) for 1 hour. Dredge with sugar and serve
with Custard (p. 209). *Serves 4 to 5.*

Brown Bread and Chestnut Pudding

8 oz (225 g) chestnuts
½ pint (3 dl) milk
2 oz (50 g) butter or margarine
4 oz (100 g) brown sugar

8 oz (225 g) brown bread
4 oz (100 g) sultanas
1 tablespoon almonds
2 eggs

Simmer the peeled chestnuts (p. 30) in the milk until tender. Beat
well and add the butter or margarine and sugar. Crumble the bread
and mix with the chestnut purée, the sultanas and the almonds. Stir in
the beaten eggs, pour into a buttered basin, cover and steam for about
2½ hours. Turn out on to a hot dish and serve with a suitable sauce.
Serves 5 to 6.

Burbidge Pudding

The ingredients are similar to those in Betsy Pudding but the method
and end-product differ considerably.

6 oz (150 g) breadcrumbs
6 oz (150 g) suet
4 oz (100 g) brown sugar
pinch of salt

3 tablespoons red jam
1 level teaspoon bicarbonate of
 soda
1 egg

Mix the dry ingredients together then add the jam and the egg beaten up with the bicarbonate of soda. Turn into a well-buttered basin, cover and steam for 3 hours. Turn on to a hot dish and serve with Jam (p. 211) or Custard (p. 209) Sauce. *Serves 4 to 5.*

Cabinet Pudding 1

The everyday version as found in canteens and clubs across the country. It is really a steamed Bread Pudding.

6 thin slices bread	1 oz (25 g) sugar
2 oz (50 g) sultanas	1 pint (6 dl) milk
2 eggs	almond or vanilla essence

Remove the crusts from the bread and cut into 1 inch (2½ cm) strips. Line a buttered pudding basin with some strips of bread and the sultanas. Beat the eggs and add to them the sugar, milk and flavouring. Cut the remaining bread into dice, pile into the lined basin, pour the custard over, cover and steam for about 1 hour. *Serves 4 to 5.*

Cabinet Pudding 2

Cabinet Pudding *par excellence.* Many of our more old-fashioned puddings include these delicious little ratafia biscuits – bitter and crunchy. They can be found nowadays in good grocers and some supermarkets but macaroons, which are more readily available, can always be substituted. They tend, however, to be sweeter and I usually add a little almond essence if I am using macaroons.

glacé cherries and angelica	3 eggs
8 oz (225 g) sponge cake	1 oz (25 g) caster sugar
6 ratafias or 2 macaroons	⅓ pint (2 dl) milk

Butter a pudding basin and decorate the bottom of it with the glacé cherries and angelica. Break up the sponge cake and the ratafias or macaroons and pile into the basin. Beat the eggs, add the sugar and the milk and pour into the bowl. Allow to stand for 20 minutes or so then cover and steam gently for 1 hour. Turn out and serve with Jam (p. 211) or Custard Sauce (p. 209). *Serves 4 to 5.*

Canary Pudding

A basic sponge pudding with the addition of lemon. It lends itself to innumerable variations: chopped glacé cherries transform it into a Cherry Pudding; cooked in individual moulds or cups it is usually known as Castle Puddings; and with 2 tablespoons marmalade stirred in you can call it Marmalade Pudding.

2 eggs *and their weight in:*
margarine   milk
caster sugar   grated rind ½ lemon
self-raising flour

Beat the margarine until quite soft. Add the sugar and cream thoroughly then add the grated lemon rind. Beat the eggs and add them a little at a time to the creamed mixture. Stir in the sieved flour lightly and add enough milk to make a dropping consistency. Turn into a well-buttered basin, cover and steam for 2 hours. Turn on to a hot dish and pour Jam Sauce (p. 211) around the pudding.
Serves 4.

Cannelle Pudding

'Cannelle' is a French word for cinnamon, whose flavour should permeate this pleasantly light pudding.

½ pint (3 dl) milk   2 eggs
cinnamon stick   4 oz (100 g) ground almonds
3 oz (75 g) stale sponge   nutmeg
1½ oz (37 g) butter or margarine   1 oz (25 g) flour
4 oz (100 g) caster sugar   breadcrumbs

Bring the milk to the boil and let the cinnamon stick infuse in it off the heat for about 20 minutes then strain over the sponge cake. Beat the butter or margarine and sugar together until creamy, add the yolks of the eggs and stir in the ground almonds and a good pinch of freshly grated nutmeg. Whip the whites of the eggs stiffly and stir them in lightly sprinkling in the flour at the same time. Butter a pudding dish, sprinkle it lightly with breadcrumbs and pour in the mixture. Bake at Gas Mark 4 (350 °F, 180 °C) for about 45 minutes. Serve with a fruit sauce or Custard (p. 209). *Serves 4 to 5.*

Caramel Pudding

A welcome change from the now common Crème Caramel.

3 oz (75 g) lump sugar
1 tablespoon water
1 pint (6 dl) milk
2 oz (50 g) sponge cake

2 oz (50 g) breadcrumbs
1 oz (25 g) caster sugar
1 teaspoon vanilla essence
2 eggs

Heat the lump sugar and water together very carefully shaking the pan – to prevent burning and to move the contents – but not stirring. Cook until coffee-coloured then add the milk and continue to warm gently. Pour over the crumbled sponge cake and the breadcrumbs and add the caster sugar, vanilla essence and yolks of the eggs. Lastly stir in the whites of eggs whipped to a stiff froth, pour into a buttered basin, cover and steam for about 1 hour. Turn out and serve with a bland sauce. *Serves 4 to 5.*

Carrot Pudding

Carrots are bulky and rich in sugar. We used to make several versions of this pudding during the war and even, I remember, a carrot cake.

8 oz (225 g) young carrots
8 oz (225 g) margarine
4 oz (100 g) caster sugar
2 eggs

8 oz (225 g) breadcrumbs
1 teaspoon cinnamon
4 oz (100 g) glacé cherries

Scrub the carrots and boil in lightly salted water until tender then sieve. Cream the margarine and sugar together, add the yolks of the eggs then mix in the breadcrumbs, cinnamon, cherries cut in quarters and the carrot purée. Whisk the whites of eggs to a stiff froth and stir in lightly. Pour into a well-buttered basin, cover and steam for about 2½ hours. Try a Lemon Sauce (p. 212) with it. *Serves 5 to 6.*

Cherry Pudding

A genuinely old pudding rarely met with today yet, once the cherries are stoned, it is simple and very good.

1 lb (450 g) ripe cherries
4 oz (100 g) plain flour
3 eggs

½ pint (3 dl) milk
caster sugar

Butter a 1½ pint (9 dl) pudding basin generously and fill with the washed, stoned cherries. Make a batter by sifting the flour into a bowl and gradually beating in the eggs and the milk. Pour this on to the cherries, cover and boil for 1 hour. Turn on to a hot dish and sprinkle liberally with caster sugar. *Serves 4 to 5.*

Chocolate Pudding

Anything flavoured with chocolate is always a nursery favourite. This is the simplest sort of steamed chocolate pudding.

4 oz (100 g) plain flour
½ teaspoon baking powder
2 oz (50 g) margarine
2 teaspoons cocoa or 2 oz (50 g)
  grated chocolate

2 oz (50 g) caster sugar
1 egg
¼ pint (1.5 dl) milk

Sieve the flour and baking powder together and rub in the margarine. Stir in the cocoa or grated chocolate and the sugar. Beat up the egg with the milk and pour into the other ingredients. Mix well and turn into a buttered pudding basin. Cover and steam for 2 hours. Turn out on to a hot dish and serve with Chocolate (p. 207) or Vanilla (p. 215) Sauce. *Serves 4.*

Chocolate Fudge Pudding

This seems unorthodox and may look a mess before you bake it but it emerges a lovely rich, gooey pudding.

4 oz (100 g) self-raising flour
4 oz (100 g) sugar
pinch of salt
2 oz (50 g) cocoa
½ cup milk

1 teaspoon vanilla essence
2 oz (50 g) melted butter or
  margarine
4 oz (100 g) brown sugar
2 oz (50 g) cocoa

Simply mix all the ingredients except the last two and pile into a fireproof dish. Top with the brown sugar mixed with the cocoa and pour 1¾ cups of hot water over the lot. Bake at Gas Mark 4 (350 °F, 180 °C) for 50 minutes. This pudding does not need a sauce. *Serves 4.*

Chocolate Soufflé Pudding

1½ oz (37 g) butter
1½ oz (37 g) flour
½ pint (3 dl) milk
3 oz (75 g) chocolate

1½ oz (37 g) caster sugar
2 eggs
sugar

Melt the butter. Remove from the heat and stir in the flour. Heat the milk with 2 oz (50 g) of the chocolate and pour on to the butter and flour. Return to the heat and stir until boiling. Beat in the sugar with 1 whole egg and 1 egg yolk. Lastly add the remaining egg white stiffly beaten. Pour into a buttered pudding basin, cover and steam for 45 minutes. Turn out on to a hot dish and make a sauce by melting the remaining ounce of chocolate in about ¼ pint (1.5 dl) water sweetened to taste. Simmer until thick. *Serves 4.*

Christmas Pudding

Recipes for Christmas pudding are legion. This is the one I use and have never had any complaints yet. These quantities make 4 puddings. They will keep for a year in a cool place and, in fact, improve with keeping so it is worth making a large amount while you are about it. With good-quality ingredients you just cannot go wrong, and all you need is muscle power and a big mixing bowl.

1 lb (450 g) currants
1 lb (450 g) sultanas
1 lb (450 g) stoned raisins
4 oz (100 g) chopped candied
  peel
2 oz (50 g) chopped almonds
1 chopped apple
1 teaspoon mixed spice
1 teaspoon salt

8 oz (225 g) self-raising flour
12 oz (325 g) fresh breadcrumbs
12 oz (325 g) suet
6 eggs
1 lb (450 g) brown sugar
juice and grated rind 1 orange
½ nutmeg grated
¼ pint (1.5 dl) milk or brown ale

Boil for 6 to 8 hours in greased and covered basins. After this time remove and re-cover before cooling and storing. Before use re-boil for 3 hours. Serve with Hard Sauce (p. 206), Brandy Sauce (p. 205), Brandy Butter (p. 205) or cream. *Each pudding serves 6.*

Coconut Pudding

If you like coconut there are many puddings which are improved with it. It gives you something to bite on. Desiccated coconut is a useful commodity because, as nuts go, it is not expensive and goes a long way.

8 oz (225 g) plain flour
1 teaspoon baking powder
pinch of salt
2 oz (50 g) margarine
2 oz (50 g) lard

3 oz (75 g) sugar
2 oz (50 g) desiccated coconut
1 egg
¼–½ pint (1.5–3 dl) milk

Sieve the flour, baking powder and salt together and rub in the fat. Stir in the sugar and coconut and mix in the egg and sufficient milk to make a fairly stiff mixture. Turn into a fireproof dish and sprinkle with a little more coconut. Place on a baking sheet and bake at Gas Mark 5 (375 °F, 190 °C) for 45 minutes to 1 hour. Test with a skewer as for cakes and serve dredged with caster sugar handing Jam Sauce (p. 211) separately. *Serves 4 to 5.*

Coffee and Walnut Pudding

Children's tastes are getting increasingly sophisticated and I found this pudding was popular even when mine were quite young.

4 oz (100 g) plain flour
½ teaspoon baking powder
2 oz (50 g) margarine
2 oz (50 g) sugar

1 egg
⅛ pint (0.75 dl) coffee syrup
 (p. 90)
2 oz (50 g) chopped walnuts

Sieve the flour and baking powder into a bowl and rub in the fat. Add the sugar. Beat up the egg and add it with the coffee and mix well together. Butter a pudding basin and strew the chopped walnuts in the bottom before turning the mixture into it. Cover and steam for 2 hours. Turn out on to a hot dish and pour Custard (p. 209) around it. *Serves 4.*

Curate's Pudding

Good, rib-sticking stuff this, useful for filling hungry tummies (and using up leftover potato).

2 oz (50 g) margarine	1 lemon
4 oz (100 g) sugar	pinch of salt
2 eggs	a little milk
6 tablespoons mashed potato	

Cream the margarine and sugar together and beat in the eggs. Stir in the potato, the juice and grated rind of the lemon, salt and a little milk. Turn into a buttered pie dish and bake at Gas Mark 4 (350 °F, 180 °C) for about 30 minutes. Try a Lemon (p. 212) or Jam (p. 211) Sauce with it. *Serves 4.*

Date Pudding

Dates are an agreeable change from our usual mixed dried fruits.

4 oz (100 g) plain flour	4 oz (100 g) chopped dates
½ teaspoon baking powder	½ teaspoon grated lemon rind
2 oz (50 g) margarine	1 egg
2 oz (50 g) caster sugar	⅛ pint (0.75 dl) milk

Sieve the flour and baking powder together and rub in the margarine. Stir in the sugar, dates, lemon rind and mix together with the egg and milk. Turn into a buttered pudding basin, cover and steam for 2 hours. Turn on to a hot dish and serve with Custard (p. 209) or Lemon (p. 212) Sauce. *Serves 4 to 5.*

Dutch Apple Cake

The only dish my son remembers with pleasure from his secondary school days.

4 oz (100 g) plain flour	a little milk
2 level teaspoons baking powder	1 lb (450 g) apples
pinch of salt	4 oz (100 g) brown sugar
1 oz (25 g) sugar	2 teaspoons cinnamon
1 oz (25 g) margarine	

Make a dough by mixing together the flour, baking powder, salt and sugar, rubbing in the margarine and adding enough milk to moisten. Spread this about $\frac{3}{4}$ inch (2 cm) thick in a buttered fireproof dish. Peel and core the apples and cut them into wedge-shaped pieces. Arrange these in rows with the thin end of the wedges sunk into the dough. Sprinkle with the brown sugar mixed with the cinnamon and bake at Gas Mark 4 (350 °F, 180 °C) for about 30 minutes. *Serves 4.*

Exeter Pudding

Macaroons may again be substituted for ratafias.

5 oz (125 g) breadcrumbs	2–3 tablespoons milk
$3\frac{1}{2}$ oz (90 g) suet	$\frac{1}{2}$ teaspoon grated lemon rind
2 oz (50 g) sago	1 oz (25 g) ratafias
3 oz (75 g) moist sugar	4 oz (100 g) sponge cake
3 eggs	jam

Mix together all the ingredients except the ratafias, sponge cake and jam. Butter a pie dish and cover the bottom with ratafias. Add a layer of the mixture, cover with slices of sponge cake spread thickly with jam and on the top place a few ratafias. Repeat until all the materials are used up finishing with a layer of the mixture. Bake at Gas Mark 2 (300 °F, 150 °C) for 1 hour and serve with some sort of fruit sauce. *Serves 4 to 5.*

Fig and Ginger Pudding

3 oz (75 g) stoned raisins	4 oz (100 g) breadcrumbs
6 oz (150 g) stoned dates	4 oz (100 g) suet
6 oz (150 g) figs	3–4 tablespoons preserved
brandy or rum	ginger syrup
4 oz (100 g) plain flour	juice 1 lemon
$\frac{1}{2}$ teaspoon salt	2 eggs
$1\frac{1}{2}$ teaspoons baking powder	

Chop the fruit and let it stand for 1 hour covered with a little brandy or rum. Sift the flour and salt with the baking powder and mix in the breadcrumbs, suet, soaked fruit, chopped ginger, ginger syrup and lemon juice. Beat the eggs into the mixture and turn into a large (3 pint, 1.8 l) buttered pudding basin. Cover and boil or steam for 4 hours. Serve with Sabayon Sauce (p. 214). *Serves 8.*

Fig Pudding

4 oz (100 g) plain flour	2 oz (50 g) figs
½ teaspoon baking powder	1 teaspoon grated lemon rind
2 oz (50 g) margarine	1 egg
2 oz (50 g) caster sugar	⅛ pint (0.75 dl) milk

Sift the flour and baking powder into a bowl and rub in the margarine. Add the sugar, chopped figs and lemon rind and mix with the egg and milk. Turn into a buttered pudding basin, cover and steam for 2 hours. Serve with Custard (p. 209) or Lemon (p. 212) Sauce. *Serves 4.*

Ginger Pudding

Basic and useful. Some dried fruit, chopped ginger or nuts can be added for variety.

6 oz (150 g) suet	1 teaspoon ground ginger
6 oz (150 g) breadcrumbs	2 eggs
2 oz (50 g) plain flour	7 oz (175 g) golden syrup
1 level teaspoon bicarbonate of soda	

Mix all the dry ingredients together then add the eggs beaten up with the syrup. Turn into a buttered pudding basin, cover and steam for 3 hours. Turn on to a hot dish and serve with Custard (p. 209) or additional warmed syrup. *Serves 4 to 5.*

Hasty Pudding

A sort of boiled dumpling – useful when you come in late on a cold day and everybody is starving.

Simply mix together flour and water to make a thick batter and drop spoonsful into a large pan of fast-boiling water (salted). They form themselves into strange shapes, are removed after a few minutes with a perforated spoon, dropped on to hot plates and eaten very hot covered in syrup.

Honey Pudding

Many of the old English recipes make use of honey – sad for us that it has become something of a luxury.

1 oz (25 g) semolina
¼ pint (1.5 dl) milk
6 oz (150 g) breadcrumbs
4 oz (100 g) honey

rind ½ lemon
½ teaspoon ground ginger
1 oz (25 g) butter
2 eggs

Cook the semolina in the milk for 10 minutes then pour over the breadcrumbs. Stir in the honey, grated lemon rind, ginger, warmed butter and the egg yolks. Beat well. Whisk the egg whites stiffly and stir lightly into the mixture. Turn into a buttered pudding basin, cover and steam for 2 hours serving with Custard (p. 209) or cream. *Serves 4 to 5.*

Hungarian Noodle Dessert

Hungarian cookery uses noodles quite widely for both sweet and savoury dishes. They provide the bulk and are an interesting change from our more usual flour, suet, rice, breadcrumbs.

8 oz (225 g) wide noodles
1½ oz (40 g) butter
2 oz (50 g) chopped nuts
3 tablespoons jam
grated rind 1 lemon

2 oz (50 g) breadcrumbs
2 oz (50 g) sugar
½ pint (3 dl) sour cream
icing sugar

Boil the noodles until just tender, drain and mix with all the other ingredients except the icing sugar. Turn into a buttered baking dish and bake at Gas Mark 4 (350 °F, 180 °C) for about 30 minutes. Dust with icing sugar before serving. *Serves 4.*

Jam Sponge Pudding

The simplest sort of steamed jam pudding – an invaluable standby.

4 oz (100 g) plain flour
½ teaspoon baking powder
2 oz (50 g) margarine
2 oz (50 g) caster sugar

1 egg
milk to mix
2 tablespoons jam

Opposite Syrup Pudding (*page 202*)

Sieve the flour and baking powder together and stir in the sugar. Rub in the margarine and mix with the egg and enough milk to form a thick, creamy mixture. Put the jam in the bottom of a buttered basin, turn in the mixture, cover and steam for 2 hours. Turn out on to a hot dish. *Serves 4.*

Lemon Pudding 1

6 oz (150 g) breadcrumbs	2 eggs
2 oz (50 g) flour	2 lemons
3 oz (75 g) suet	milk to mix
3 oz (75 g) sugar	

Mix the breadcrumbs, flour and suet together and stir in the beaten eggs, the juice and grated rind of the lemons and enough milk to make a fairly stiff mixture. Turn into a buttered basin, cover and steam for about 2½ hours. Serve with Lemon Sauce (p. 212) or Custard (p. 209). *Serves 4 to 5.*

Lemon Pudding 2

This version is something rather special. It is very light with a suggestion of lemon curd and the accompaniment, though it sounds unorthodox, provides an attractive contrast in texture. It makes extremely interesting eating.

4 oz (100 g) margarine	2 lemons
4 oz (100 g) sugar	½ teaspoon baking powder
2 eggs	3 oz (75 g) caster sugar
4 oz (100 g) breadcrumbs	1 large apple

Cream the margarine and sugar together thoroughly and add the yolks of the eggs, the breadcrumbs and the juice and grated rind of the lemons. Add the baking powder last of all. Turn into a buttered basin, cover and steam for 40 minutes. Whip the whites of eggs stiffly with the caster sugar then lightly stir in the grated or finely chopped apple. Pile this in a circle on the serving dish, dust with a little more caster sugar and set at Gas Mark 6 (400 °F, 200 °C) then turn the pudding out into the centre of it. *Serves 4.*

Opposite Charlotte Russe (*page 220*)

Light Sponge Pudding

A pudding with an airy texture, useful if you have egg whites left over.

3 oz (75 g) butter
4½ oz (112 g) caster sugar
rind ½ lemon
⅛ pint (0.75 dl) milk

8 oz (225 g) plain flour
3 level teaspoons baking powder
3 egg whites

Cream the butter and sugar together until white then stir in the grated lemon rind, the milk and the flour sifted with the baking powder. Whip the whites stiffly and fold in lightly. Turn into a buttered and floured pudding basin, cover and steam for 1 hour. Turn out on to a hot dish and serve with Chocolate (p. 207) or Lemon (p. 212) Sauce. *Serves 4 to 5.*

Madeira Pudding

In Mrs Beeton's golden days this really had madeira (or, at a pinch, sherry) in it. It is acceptable without – but better with!

4 oz (100 g) bread
2 oz (50 g) caster sugar
1 teaspoon grated lemon rind

½ pint (3 dl) milk
2 eggs
1 wineglass madeira or sherry

Cut the bread into small dice and mix with the sugar and lemon rind. Bring the milk to the boil and pour on to the beaten eggs. Stir in the madeira or sherry and pour on to the bread. Let it stand for about 20 minutes then pour into a buttered basin, cover and steam gently for 2 hours. Serve with Wine Sauce (p. 215) or Custard (p. 209). *Serves 4.*

Messina Pudding

An unusual and satisfying pudding.

6 oz (150 g) plain flour
2 oz (50 g) suet
½ teaspoon baking powder
salt
water

2 eggs
4 oz (100 g) sugar
1 lemon
1 oz (25 g) butter

Make a suet crust by mixing together the first four ingredients and binding with water. Roll it out. Line a buttered pudding basin reserving enough for a layer in the middle as well as on top. Beat the eggs, sugar, juice and grated rind of the lemon and the melted butter together. Pour half the mixture into the basin, put in the layer of suet crust, add the remainder and seal on the top layer. Cover, steam for $2\frac{1}{2}$ hours and serve with Lemon Sauce (p. 212). *Serves 4.*

Mincemeat and Cherry Layer

A surprising combination to be tried either in the summer with mincemeat left over from Christmas or in the winter with canned cherries.

8 oz (225 g) cherries	4 oz (100 g) self-raising flour
4 oz (100 g) margarine	2 oz (50 g) breadcrumbs
4 oz (100 g) caster sugar	2 tablespoons milk
2 eggs	8 oz (225 g) mincemeat

Stone the cherries and place in the bottom of a buttered, fireproof dish. (If using canned cherries, drain them and stir 2 tablespoons of the juice into the mincemeat.) Cream the margarine and sugar and beat in the eggs. Fold in the flour and breadcrumbs and mix to a dropping consistency with the milk. Spread alternate layers of the sponge mixture and the mincemeat on top of the cherries ending with a sponge layer. Bake at Gas Mark 4 (350 °F, 180 °C) for 45 minutes. Turn on to a hot dish and serve with cream or Custard (p. 209). *Serves 4 to 5.*

Mountain Pudding

White sauce sandwiched between lemony ratafias and a crisp meringue topping.

4 oz (100 g) ratafias	1 pint (6 dl) milk
1 lemon	2 eggs
1 oz (25 g) butter	1 oz (25 g) granulated sugar
1¼ oz (30 g) flour	2 oz (50 g) caster sugar
pinch of salt	

Butter a pie dish copiously, place the broken ratafias in the bottom of it and grate the lemon rind over them. Make a white sauce by melting the butter, stirring in the flour with a pinch of salt and the ounce of granulated sugar and gradually adding the milk and the yolks of the 2 eggs. Bring to the boil, stirring, and pour over the ratafias. Make a meringue from the stiffly beaten egg whites and the caster sugar and pile on top of the pudding, spreading it to the edges. Bake for 1½ hours at Gas Mark 1 (275 °F, 140 °C) and serve hot or cold. *Serves 6.*

Nell Gwynne Pudding

A hot orange pudding is quite unusual and very welcome in the depths of winter.

2 oranges	1 egg
2 oz (50 g) brown sugar	5 oz (125 g) plain flour
1 lemon	1 oz (25 g) cornflour
4 oz (100 g) margarine	2 level teaspoons baking powder
4 oz (100 g) caster sugar	3 tablespoons milk

Peel the oranges and divide into segments removing any pith and pips. Arrange in the bottom of a buttered pie dish and sprinkle with the brown sugar and the juice of the lemon. Cream the margarine with the sugar and the grated rind of the lemon and beat in the egg. Sift in the flour, cornflour and baking powder and fold carefully into the creamed mixture adding enough milk to make a dropping consistency. Turn into the dish and smooth over. Bake at Gas Mark 5 (375 °F, 190 °C) for 40 minutes and serve sprinkled with sugar. *Serves 4 to 5.*

Oatmeal Pudding

Now that we are more health-food conscious oatmeal is again widely available and a useful thing to keep in the store cupboard.

3 oz (75 g) medium oatmeal	2 oz (50 g) mixed dried fruit
3 oz (75 g) self-raising flour	1 lemon
½ teaspoon bicarbonate of soda	1 egg
2 oz (50 g) margarine	¼ pint (1.5 dl) milk
1½ oz (37 g) demerara sugar	2 tablespoons golden syrup

Mix together the oatmeal, flour, bicarbonate of soda and rub in the margarine. Stir in the sugar, dried fruit, grated lemon rind and bind together with the egg, the warmed milk and the syrup. Turn into a buttered ring mould or pudding basin, cover and steam for 2½ hours. Turn out and serve with cream or Lemon Sauce (p. 212). *Serves 4 to 5.*

Orange Pudding

4 oz (100 g) short crust pastry (p. 55)	3 oz (75 g) caster sugar
4 oranges	pinch of salt
½ pint (3 dl) milk	nutmeg
3 oz (75 g) cake crumbs	2 eggs

Line the sides of a pie dish with the pastry. Remove the rind of 1 orange in very thin strips, place them in a saucepan with the milk, bring to the boil then turn off the heat and leave to infuse for 20 minutes. Strain over the cake crumbs and stir in the sugar, salt, a sprinkling of grated nutmeg, the beaten eggs and the juice of the oranges. Pour into the pie dish and bake at Gas Mark 4 (350°F, 180°C) for about 30 minutes. Dredge with caster sugar and serve hot or cold. *Serves 4 to 5.*

Pear Gingerbread Upside-Down Pudding

Decorated with a few glacé cherries and whorls of cream this both looks exciting and tastes good. Pineapple or peaches can be used in the same way.

3 pears	3 oz (75 g) suet
6 oz (150 g) syrup	1 teaspoon ground ginger
rind 1 lemon	1 teaspoon baking powder
6 oz (150 g) plain flour	¾ pint (4.5 dl) milk

Peel, core and halve the pears. Butter a fireproof dish and put a little of the syrup and the grated lemon rind in the base. Arrange the pears on this. Mix together the flour, suet, ginger, baking powder and stir in the remaining syrup and the milk. Pour over the pears, cover and steam for 2 hours. Turn out on to a hot dish. *Serves 4 to 5.*

Queen of Puddings

A triumph of our gastronomic heritage.

rind 1 lemon	2 oz (50 g) fresh breadcrumbs
½ pint (3 dl) milk	2 eggs
½ oz (13 g) butter	2–3 tablespoons jam
1 oz (25 g) granulated sugar	4 oz (100 g) caster sugar

The lemon rind should be pared very thinly off the lemon and infused in the milk over gentle heat for about 15 minutes. Strain into a bowl and stir in the butter and the granulated sugar. When these have dissolved mix in the breadcrumbs and leave to cool. Now add the egg yolks, mix well and turn into a buttered pie dish. Let it stand for 30 minutes then bake at Gas Mark 4 (350 °F, 180 °C) for a further 30 minutes. Remove and let it cool slightly before spreading the jam on the surface. Whisk the egg whites stiffly, fold in the sugar and pile on top sealing the meringue to the edges. Dust with a little more caster sugar and let stand for 5 minutes before returning to a very slow oven (Gas Mark ¼, 225 °F, 110 °C) until the meringue is crisp and beige. This may take an hour or so. Delicious hot or cold, and chocolate or coffee may be stirred into the main mixture as a change from jam. *Serves 4 to 5.*

Rhubarb Caramel Pudding

Equally good made with apples, cherries, plums, damsons, gooseberries or any soft fruit.

2 oz (50 g) soft brown sugar	1 lb (450 g) rhubarb
1 oz (25 g) butter	2 oz (50 g) granulated sugar
suet crust (p. 56)	

Cream the brown sugar and butter together and spread in the bottom of a buttered fireproof dish. Now line the dish with the suet crust (on top of the sugar mixture) reserving enough for a lid. Fill with the chopped rhubarb mixed with the sugar and seal the lid at the edges. Bake at Gas Mark 3 (325 °F, 170 °C) for 1½ hours then turn on to a hot dish. Serve with Custard (p. 209) or cream. *Serves 4.*

Roly Poly Baked

Many people prefer this crisper version to the boiled one (see Apple Spiced Roll, p. 179) which I *have* heard dubbed 'Dead Man's Leg'!

8 oz (225 g) suet crust (p. 56)
jam

Roll the suet crust out into a rectangle and spread liberally with warmed jam keeping the edges clear. Roll up, press the edges together and bake at Gas Mark 4 (350 °F, 180 °C) for about 30 minutes. Serve with Custard (p. 209). *Serves 4.*

Six Cup Pudding

Like an everyday version of Christmas Pudding – extremely heart-warming.

4 oz (100 g) plain flour	1 teaspoon mixed spice
4 oz (100 g) fresh breadcrumbs	$\frac{3}{4}$ cup milk
4 oz (100 g) brown sugar	1 teaspoon bicarbonate of soda
4 oz (100 g) mixed dried fruit	1 egg
4 oz (100 g) suet	

Mix the first six ingredients together. Warm the milk and dissolve the soda in it. Stir this into the pudding together with the egg and turn into a well buttered pudding basin. Cover and steam for 3 hours. Turn into a hot dish and serve with Rum Butter (p. 214) or Custard (p. 209). *Serves 6.*

Spicy Betty

Quick to make and deliciously crunchy.

1½ lbs (675 g) rhubarb	3 oz (75 g) demerara sugar
1 teaspoon ground ginger	4 oz (100 g) fresh breadcrumbs
1 oz (25 g) caster sugar	2 oz (50 g) suet
1 tablespoon water	½ oz (13 g) butter

Chop the rhubarb and mix it with the ground ginger, caster sugar and water. Mix together the demerara sugar, breadcrumbs and suet. Fill a buttered pie dish with alternate layers of the mixtures finishing with the breadcrumb mixture. Dot with butter and bake at Gas Mark 4 (350°F, 180°C) for about 1 hour. Serve with cream or Custard (p. 209). *Serves 4 to 5.*

Spotted Dick

4 oz (100 g) flour
4 oz (100 g) suet
4 oz (100 g) dried fruit

1 egg
milk to mix

Simply mix all the ingredients together, turn into a buttered basin, cover and steam for 2 hours. Can be served with any sweet sauce or with butter and sugar or sugar and lemon. *Serves 4.*

Syrup Pudding

This pudding with the golden syrup running down its sides epitomizes the warmth of home on cold winter days and loving, caring family cooking.

6 oz (150 g) plain flour
½ teaspoon bicarbonate of soda
2 oz (50 g) breadcrumbs
4 oz (100 g) suet
pinch of salt

2 oz (50 g) sugar
1 lemon
2 tablespoons golden syrup
2 eggs

Mix together the flour, bicarbonate of soda, suet, salt, sugar and the grated rind of the lemon. Stir in the syrup and the eggs beaten up with the juice of the lemon. Turn into a buttered basin, cover and steam for 2½ hours. Serve with more syrup or Lemon Sauce (p. 212).
Serves 4 to 6.

Syrup Sponge

A lighter sort of syrup pudding.

6 oz (150 g) margarine
6 oz (150 g) caster sugar
3 eggs

6 oz (150 g) plain flour
2 level teaspoons baking powder
2 tablespoons golden syrup

Cream the margarine and sugar together and add the beaten eggs a little at a time. Sift the flour and baking powder together and fold gradually into the creamed mixture. Add the milk and mix well. Butter a basin and pour the syrup into the bottom then turn the mixture on top of it. Cover and steam for 2 hours. Turn on to a hot dish and serve with more syrup or with Custard (p. 209). *Serves 4 to 6.*

Toffee Pudding

3 oz (75 g) butter
3 oz (75 g) sugar
3 eggs

4 oz (100 g) plain flour
$\frac{1}{8}$ pint (0.75 dl) milk

Cream the butter and sugar and beat in the eggs one at a time. Sift in the flour and stir in enough milk to make a runny consistency. Butter three sandwich tins and share out the mixture between them. Bake at Gas Mark 6 (400 °F, 200 °C) for about 15 minutes. Turn out and place one in serving dish, pour some Toffee Sauce (p. 214) over it, then put the second one on top, pour more sauce, and repeat with the third. Serve hot. *Serves 4 to 5.*

Treacle Layer Pudding

A little more trouble than the previous Syrup Pudding – but well worth it.

4 oz (100 g) suet
12 oz (325 g) plain flour
pinch of salt
2 rounded teaspoons baking
   powder

2 oz (50 g) breadcrumbs
1 lemon
8 oz (225 g) golden syrup

Make a suet crust by mixing together the flour, suet and baking powder and adding enough water to form a fairly stiff dough. Divide the dough into two and roll out one half to line a buttered pudding basin. Now mix together the breadcrumbs, grated rind of the lemon and the warmed syrup and put a layer of this into the basin. Sprinkle with breadcrumbs and cover with a thin layer of the suet crust, moistening the edges and sealing it to the sides. Repeat (the more layers the better) until all is used up finishing with a layer of suet crust. Cover and steam for $2\frac{1}{2}$ hours. Turn on to a hot dish and pour a little hot syrup over it. *Serves 4 to 6.*

Sauces

Quite a lot of puddings – particularly some of the baked, steamed and boiled puddings and some ices – really need to be served with a sauce so I am including some of the more useful sauces.

Sauces will not form an unattractive crust on top if you cover them while still hot with a fitting piece of greaseproof paper wetted on both sides with cold water.

Christmas pudding is pretty pedestrian without one of the brandy or rum sauces, and home-made cream ices with hot chocolate or fruit sauces are a gastronomic treat.

Apricot Sauce

8 oz (225 g) apricot jam
1 orange

juice $\frac{1}{2}$ lemon
1 tablespoon brandy

Melt the jam very slowly with the juice of the orange and lemon and a little grated orange rind. Add the brandy at the last minute.

Banana Sauce

2 oz (50 g) butter   1 egg white
4 oz (100 g) icing sugar   lemon juice
1 banana

Cream the butter and gradually beat in the icing sugar then the mashed banana, the well-beaten egg white and a good squeeze of lemon juice.

Brandy Butter

Otherwise known as Senior Wrangler Sauce. It is meltingly good with almost any baked, steamed or boiled pudding (or pancakes) and traditional with Christmas Pudding and mince pies. With the addition of 1½ oz (37 g) ground almonds it becomes Hard Sauce.

3 oz (75 g) unsalted butter
3 oz (75 g) icing sugar
2–3 tablespoons brandy

Cream the butter until white then beat in the sugar gradually. Beat in the brandy a few drops at a time until well flavoured. Pile up in a glass dish and leave to harden or spread ½ inch thick on a dish and cut into cubes when firm.

Brandy Sauce

1 oz (25 g) arrowroot or   1 oz (25 g) caster sugar
  cornflour   1 wineglass brandy
½ pint (3 dl) milk   1 egg yolk

Mix the arrowroot or cornflour smoothly with a little milk then add to the rest of the milk in a small saucepan and stir until boiling. Add the sugar and cool slightly before stirring in the brandy mixed with the egg. Re-heat and stir until thick.

Brown Sugar Hard Sauce

In our house this is what Christmas Pudding is all about. We usually have a fairly small pudding and mountains of this sauce.

3 oz (75 g) butter
2 oz (50 g) brown sugar
3 dessertspoons double cream

2 tablespoons sherry
2 tablespoons brandy

Cream the butter with the sugar and add the cream drop by drop beating thoroughly. Now add the sherry and the brandy also by slow degrees until completely absorbed. Chill before serving.

Butterscotch Sauce

3 oz (75 g) brown sugar
3 oz (75 g) white sugar
2 tablespoons golden syrup
$\frac{1}{2}$ cup cold water

$1\frac{1}{2}$ oz (37 g) butter
$\frac{1}{4}$ cup hot water
$\frac{1}{2}$ teaspoon vanilla essence

Cook together the sugars, syrup and cold water until a little when dropped into a cup of cold water becomes brittle. Remove from the heat and beat in the butter, hot water and vanilla essence.

Chantilly Cream

$\frac{1}{4}$ pint (1.5 dl) double cream
1 egg white
icing sugar to taste

apricot or peach brandy
(optional)

Whip the cream until thick but not stiff. Add the icing sugar a little at a time stirring gently, and then the liqueur, if used, drop by drop. Whip the egg white stiffly and fold it in smoothly.

Cherry Sauce

$\frac{1}{2}$ lemon
2 tablespoons sherry
1 heaped teaspoon arrowroot

1 tablespoon red jam
$\frac{1}{2}$ oz (13 g) sugar
1 oz (25 g) glacé cherries

Mix together the juice of the lemon, the sherry and enough water to make up to $\frac{1}{3}$ pint (2 dl). Mix the arrowroot smoothly with a little of this mixture and heat up the remainder with the jam, sugar and the pared rind of the lemon. Stir in the prepared arrowroot and boil until the sauce is clear, stirring continuously. Strain, add the chopped cherries and re-heat.

Chocolate Sauce

Recipes for this are numerous and, in fact, you can make a perfectly acceptable sauce just by melting a block of chocolate in a little water or coffee and beating in a knob of butter. Here, however, is one that is rather better but not too elaborate.

5 oz (125 g) cooking chocolate
2 oz (50 g) soft brown sugar
2 tablespoons sugar syrup
  (p. 17)

2 oz (50 g) unsalted butter
$\frac{1}{2}$ orange
1 dessertspoon Tia Maria or
  Crème de Cacao (optional)

Melt the chocolate with the sugar and syrup over low heat then beat in the butter. When smoothly mixed add the juice of the orange and the finely grated rind then stir in the liqueur, if used.

Chocolate and Coffee Sauce

2 oz (50 g) demerara sugar
2 teaspoons coffee syrup (p. 90)
3 tablespoons water

knob of butter
4 oz (100 g) cooking chocolate

Put the sugar, coffee syrup and water into a saucepan and bring slowly to the boil. Add the chocolate off the heat and stir until melted and smoothly mixed.

Chocolate and Honey Sauce

1 tablespoon clear honey
2 tablespoons water
4 oz (100 g) cooking chocolate

Place the honey and water together in a small saucepan and bring to the boil. Remove from the heat and stir in the chocolate mixing well until thoroughly dissolved.

Chocolate Marshmallow Sauce

4 oz (100 g) marshmallows
3 tablespoons milk
4 oz (100 g) cooking chocolate

Put the marshmallows and milk together in a saucepan and stir over low heat until the marshmallows have melted. Remove from the heat and add the chocolate, stirring until smooth.

Chocolate Orange Sauce

4 oz (100 g) cooking chocolate
3 tablespoons water

2 heaped tablespoons orange
  marmalade

Heat the chocolate and water together slowly until the chocolate has melted and the mixture is smooth. Remove from the heat and stir in the marmalade.

Citron Sauce

2 egg yolks
½ oz (13 g) cornflour
1 oz (25 g) caster sugar

rind ½ lemon
½ pint (3 dl) milk

Blend the yolks and cornflour together, add the sugar, finely chopped lemon rind and the boiling milk. Whisk over moderate heat until the mixture becomes creamy.

Coffee Cream Sauce

There is a surprising dearth of coffee sauce recipes but here is one I find good.

3 egg yolks
3 oz (75 g) sugar
pinch of salt

½ pint (3 dl) strong black coffee
  or ¼ pint (1.5 dl) coffee syrup
  (p. 90)
½ cup double cream

Beat the egg yolks slightly with the sugar and salt then add the coffee by slow degrees stirring in a bowl over a pan of hot water until thick. Allow to cool slightly before folding in the stiffly whipped cream.

Custard

Traditionally flavoured with vanilla (and therefore more correctly called Vanilla Sauce) but lends itself to almost any flavouring – almond, chocolate, coffee, orange, rum, sherry, etc.

2 egg yolks
1 oz (25 g) sugar

½ pint (3 dl) milk
½ vanilla pod

Beat the egg yolks with a fork. Put the sugar, milk and vanilla pod together in a saucepan and bring slowly to the boil. Remove the vanilla pod and pour the milk mixture on to the egg yolks while stirring. Stir over moderate heat (without boiling) until it will coat the back of the spoon.

Fresh Fruit Sauce

You can make this with almost any fruit although the soft fruits are probably the best. Very good with Rice Pudding (p. 139).

7 oz (175 g) fresh fruit
2 oz (50 g) sugar
¼ pint (1.5 dl) water

1 oz (25 g) cornflour or
arrowroot
2 tablespoons cold water

Cook the fruit with the water and sugar until soft. Mix the cornflour or arrowroot with the 2 tablespoons cold water and stir in. Stir and cook for 3 to 4 minutes until clear and shiny. Strain and serve.

Frothy Sauce

Also known as German Egg Sauce.

¼ pint (1.5 dl) milk
1 oz (25 g) caster sugar

1 egg
1 wineglass sherry or white wine

Bring the milk to the boil and pour it on to the sugar. Cool slightly before mixing in the egg and the sherry or wine. Stand the basin over a pan of boiling water and whisk vigorously until the sauce is thick and frothy. Serve at once.

Fruit Syrup Sauce

A useful sauce to make from the leftover juice of stewed and canned fruit. It is excellent with Petits Suisses, milk puddings, pancakes, etc.

½ pint (3 dl) fruit syrup
½ pint (3 dl) water
2 teaspoons lemon juice

1 oz (25 g) cornflour or
 arrowroot
2 tablespoons water

Bring the syrup and ½ pint of water to the boil and add the lemon juice. Mix the cornflour or arrowroot with the 2 tablespoons water and stir in. Bring to the boil again stirring constantly then reduce the heat and cook for 3 to 4 minutes, stirring occasionally. Can be used hot or cold.

Fudge Sauce

3 oz (75 g) brown sugar
2 level tablespoons golden syrup

1 oz (25 g) margarine
4 tablespoons evaporated milk

Place all the ingredients in a small saucepan and heat gently for about 5 minutes. Do not boil.

Ginger Sauce

1 teaspoon ground ginger
4 oz (100 g) caster sugar
½ lemon

½ pint (3 dl) water
2 tablespoons brandy or wine

Put the ginger, sugar, the pared rind of the lemon and the water into a saucepan and simmer gently for 15 minutes. Strain, return to the pan and add the juice of the lemon and the brandy or wine. Re-heat and serve.

Golden Almond Sauce

½ oz (13 g) butter
1½ oz (37 g) almonds

2 tablespoons golden syrup
juice ½ lemon

Melt the butter and fry the blanched, peeled and split almonds in it until golden. Stir in the syrup and lemon juice, heat through and serve hot.

Honey Sauce

1 level teaspoon arrowroot
⅛ pint (0.75 dl) water

1 orange
2 tablespoons clear honey

Blend the arrowroot with the water, add the grated rind of the orange and bring to the boil, stirring. Boil gently for 2 minutes then remove from the heat and mix in the juice of the orange and the honey.

Honeyed Pineapple Sauce

2 tablespoons clear honey
1 teaspoon lemon juice
8 oz (225 g) pineapple

Heat the ingredients together in a small, strong saucepan until the honey begins to caramelize. Serve at once.

Jam Sauce

Useful with all the plainer boiled puddings, pancakes, etc.

2 tablespoons jam
½ pint (3 dl) water

sugar to taste
1 teaspoon lemon juice

Put the jam, water and sugar into a saucepan and heat thoroughly. Add the lemon juice and a few drops of colouring, if desired, strain and serve.

Jamaican Sauce

3 tablespoons golden syrup
½ pint (3 dl) water
1 oz (25 g) arrowroot
1 oz (25 g) nuts

1 oz (25 g) glacé cherries
1–2 tablespoons rum
lemon juice

Heat the syrup in a small, strong saucepan until lightly caramelized. Remove from the heat and carefully add half the water. Blend the arrowroot with the remaining water and add to the caramel liquid. Stir until boiling and boil for several minutes then stir in the other ingredients. Serve hot.

Lemon Sauce

1 oz (25 g) lump sugar
1 lemon

½ pint (3 dl) water
1 oz (25 g) arrowroot

Rub the sugar lumps over the lemon until the oils and juices have been removed and absorbed. Bring the water to the boil and put in the sugar lumps. Mix the arrowroot smoothly with a little cold water, pour into the saucepan and stir until boiling then stir in the juice of the lemon and serve.

Melba Sauce

1 lb (450 g) raspberries
4 oz (100 g) icing sugar

Sieve the raspberries and the sugar into a small saucepan and stir and cook gently for about 5 minutes. Use hot or cold.

Mincemeat Sauce

Mincemeat made with suet does not make a very good sauce, so try this fresh mincemeat. It is good with plain ices.

½ oz (12 g) butter
4 oz (100 g) white grapes
1 dessert apple
1 banana
1 oz (25 g) glacé cherries

1½ oz (37 g) almonds
1 lemon
sugar to taste
rum or brandy

Melt the butter, add the peeled and pipped grapes, the diced apple and banana, the sliced cherries and the shredded almonds. Fry for 3 to 4 minutes then stir in the juice of the lemon, a little of the grated rind, sugar to taste, the rum or brandy and simmer for a few minutes. Serve hot.

Mousseline Sauce

3 oz (75 g) lump sugar
⅛ pint (0.75 dl) water
vanilla pod
3 egg yolks

1 tablespoon brandy
1 tablespoon maraschino
1 egg white
⅛ pint (0.75 dl) double cream

Place the sugar, water and vanilla pod in a small saucepan over very low heat and allow it to dissolve – shaking, not stirring, from time to time. Simmer until syrupy then remove the vanilla pod, tip the mixture into a bowl standing in a bigger bowl of ice and whip in the egg yolks. When thick and creamy beat in the brandy, maraschino and stiffly whisked egg white. Finally fold in the whipped cream and leave on ice until required.

Nut Sauce

2 oz (50 g) butter	$\frac{1}{4}$ pint (1.5 dl) water
2 oz (50 g) brown sugar	2 oz (50 g) nuts
1 oz (25 g) cornflour	2 teaspoons lemon juice

Melt the butter over low heat then stir in the sugar, cornflour and water. Cook for a few minutes, stirring, until the sauce is thick then add the chopped nuts and the lemon juice. Serve hot.

Pineapple Sauce

$\frac{1}{8}$ pint (0.75 dl) pineaple juice	1 oz (25 g) sugar
$\frac{1}{8}$ pint (0.75 dl) water	$\frac{1}{2}$ oz (12 g) glacé cherries
juice $\frac{1}{2}$ lemon	1 tablespoon chopped pineapple
1 heaped teaspoon arrowroot	yellow colouring

Mix the pineapple juice, water and lemon juice together and blend the arrowroot with a little of the liquid. Heat the remaining liquid, add the prepared arrowroot and cook until clear. Cook for 5 minutes then stir in the sugar, chopped glacé cherries, pineapple and a few drops of colouring. Serve hot.

Punch Sauce

1 oz (25 g) cornflour	2 oz (50 g) butter
2 lemons	sugar to taste
$\frac{1}{2}$ pint (3 dl) white wine	rum to taste
cinnamon stick	

Mix the cornflour smoothly with the juice of the lemons. Warm the wine with the grated rind of 1 lemon, the cinnamon and the butter and, when hot, stir in the prepared cornflour and cook, stirring, until thick and clear. Add sugar and rum to taste and serve hot.

Rum Butter

This goes down very sweetly with baked fruits and pancakes as well as the more usual boiled fruit puddings. Margarine will not serve.

3 oz (75 g) butter
3 oz (75 g) soft brown sugar

½ lemon
rum to taste

Cream the butter well and beat in the sugar gradually. Add the grated rind and the juice of the lemon, enough rum to flavour it well and chill before serving.

Sabayon Sauce

2 oz (50 g) caster sugar
2 eggs

1 teaspoon vanilla essence or 2 tablespoons sherry
rind 1 lemon

Beat the sugar, egg yolks, vanilla essence or sherry and the grated rind of the lemon together in a bowl until smooth. Place over a pan of hot water and whisk until fluffy then fold in the stiffly whisked egg whites.

Syrup Sauce

1 oz (25 g) cornflour
juice 1 lemon

½ pint (3 dl) water
4 tablespoons golden syrup

Blend the cornflour with the juice of the lemon and then put all the ingredients into a saucepan. Stir over gentle heat until the sauce thickens and comes to the boil.

Toffee Sauce

3 oz (75 g) sugar
2 oz (50 g) golden syrup
½ oz (12 g) butter

½ lemon
¼ pint (1.5 dl) water

Cook the sugar, syrup, butter together over moderate heat stirring occasionally until a good toffee colour. Remove from the heat and stir in the grated rind and juice of the lemon and the water by degrees. Re-boil and serve.

Uncooked Vanilla Sauce

½ pint (3 dl) double cream   4 oz (100 g) caster sugar
3 egg yolks   1 teaspoon vanilla essence

Whip the cream stiffly. Beat the egg yolks gradually incorporating the sugar and vanilla then fold the two mixtures together. Chill before serving.

White Sauce

1 oz (25 g) cornflour   pinch of salt
¾ pint (4.5 dl) milk   sugar to taste
rind ½ lemon

Blend the cornflour smoothly with a little of the milk and simmer the rest with the lemon rind and salt for 15 minutes then strain over the cornflour, stirring well. Return to the saucepan, sweeten to taste and simmer for 5 minutes.

Wine Sauce

1 oz (25 g) caster sugar   1 tablespoon jam
¼ pint (1.5 dl) water   lemon juice
1 wineglass sherry

Put the sugar and water into a saucepan and simmer for 10 minutes then add the rest of the ingredients, bring to the boil, strain and serve.

Special-Occasion Puddings

These are distinguished very often by the length of their names, the long list of ingredients, the extravagance of same and the length of the instructions involved. They are obviously not dishes for Monday lunchtime or to make after a long hard day at work but we all have occasions when we want to produce something memorable and economy is a second consideration. So – here are some suggestions.

Babas – or Savarin

Really good Babas make a super sweet course which is always popular. Good ones seem practically impossible to buy in this country although available in the humblest of French pâtisseries.

4 oz (100 g) hard flour
pinch of salt
1 oz (25 g) caster sugar
¼ oz (6 g) yeast
little milk or water

2 eggs
2 oz (50 g) butter
sugar syrup (p. 17) and rum
cream or fruit to fill

Sieve the flour, salt and 1 teaspoon of the sugar together. Cream the yeast with a little warmed milk or milk and water mixed and pour into a well in the flour. Add the beaten eggs and mix with a wooden spoon gradually incorporating the flour. Beat well for 3 or 4 minutes then sprinkle the rest of the sugar on top and add the butter cut into small pieces. Cover the bowl with a damp cloth and leave to rise in a warm place for ¾ hour then beat in the sugar and butter and put into buttered and sugared baba moulds (or Savarin ring). Leave to 'prove' until the mixture rises to the top of the tin (about 15 minutes) then stand on a baking sheet and bake at Gas Mark 7 (425 °F, 220 °C) for 10 minutes thereafter reducing the heat to Mark 6 (400 °F, 200 °C) for a further 15 minutes or so. Turn out and cool before pouring over the sugar syrup and rum and filling the centre with whipped cream or fruit. *Serves 4.*

Baked Alaska

When the children were still fairly young we had a holiday in a châlet in the French Alps. Once or twice we ate out. One evening we were tucking into the least expensive of the table d'hôte menus when a large family party at the next table ordered this – or Omelette Norvégienne, as it was called. My son was only 8 at the time and couldn't take his eyes off the chef who, with great panache, flambéed the Omelette at the table. Richard abandoned whatever boring pudding we were having, stood fascinated, and was later repaid, to his sisters' disgust, by having a generous slice sent round to our table for *'le petit anglais'*.

plain sponge cake
1 pint (6 dl) ice cream

3 egg whites
6 oz (150 g) caster sugar

Fill a roasting tin with ice and place the serving dish in the centre. Place the sponge upon the dish and mould the ice cream on top of it. Whip the egg whites up very stiffly, beat in the sugar and pile on top of the ice cream, sealing it well to the edges of the dish. Dust with caster sugar and bake at Gas Mark 8 (450 °F, 230 °C) for 5 minutes. Serve at once – flambéed in rum if desired. *Serves 6.*

Biskotten Torte

Not really extravagant but takes a little time and care.

6 oz (150 g) butter	1 teaspoon instant coffee
6 oz (150 g) caster sugar	40 sponge fingers
1 egg	little sherry and milk
4 oz (100 g) minced nuts	
¼ pint (1.5 dl) thick white sauce (p. 215)	

Cream the butter, sugar and egg together and stir in the nuts. Gradually add enough white sauce to give a creamy texture then stir in the coffee. Line an 8 inch cake tin with greaseproof paper and arrange a layer of sponge fingers (sugar side down) upon it. Sprinkle with some sherry and milk mixed together and add alternate layers of the cream and sponge fingers until all are used up. Cover and chill. Unmould before serving. *Serves 6.*

Biscuit Creams

There seems to be a whole range of sweets appearing based simply on biscuits and cream. Although a boon for the busy hostess they are extravagant and not really 'cooking' – rather just putting together. However, they do offer some scope for imagination and certainly taste good.

Almost any sweet biscuits can be used but their flavour will affect what you put with them. For six people you will need two 8 oz (225 g) packets of biscuits and ½ pint (3 dl) double cream. You simply moisten the biscuits with some liquid, layer with whipped cream and chill. Ginger nuts may be soaked in ginger syrup and a little chopped ginger mixed in with the cream; chocolate biscuits can be soaked in sweet sherry and the dish garnished with grated chocolate; shortbread fingers can be moistened with orange juice or curaçao and grated orange rind mixed into the cream – and so on.

Biscuit Pudding

8 oz (225 g) dried and glacé fruits	5 oz (125 g) sugar
kirsch	3 eggs
8 oz (225 g) sweet biscuits	4 oz (100 g) butter
1 pint (6 dl) milk	2 egg whites

Put the fruits to macerate in a little kirsch. Crush the biscuits and pour on the boiling milk and sugar then add the fruits, the 3 egg yolks, the butter and lastly the 5 egg whites beaten to a stiff froth. Turn into a soufflé dish, stand it in a roasting tin of hot water and bake at Gas Mark 4 (350 °F, 180 °C) for about 30 minutes. *Serves 6.*

Brandy Pudding

Like a hot – and very superior – trifle.

2 oz (50 g) glacé cherries
8 oz (225 g) sponge cake
2 oz (50 g) ratafias
1 wineglass brandy
4 eggs
½ pint (3 dl) cream
½ pint (3 dl) milk
4 oz (100 g) sugar
lemon rind
nutmeg

Butter a soufflé dish and decorate with the halved cherries then line with thin slices of sponge cake. Half fill the dish with alternate layers of ratafias and sponge cake adding a little sugar and pour the brandy over. Mix the eggs, cream, milk, sugar, a little grated lemon rind and nutmeg together and pour on. Let it stand for 1 hour then steam gently for 1½ hours. Serve hot with Brandy Sauce (p. 205). *Serves 6.*

Caramel Chiffon Pudding

This is a Swedish recipe known in Sweden as *Nougatpudding*.

10 oz (275 g) sugar
3 oz (75 g) almonds
4 eggs
2 oz (50 g) caster sugar
¼ pint (1.5 dl) milk
1 oz (25 g) gelatine
1 teaspoon vanilla essence
rind ½ orange
3 tablespoons rum
½ pint (3 dl) double cream
grapes to decorate

First make some caramel strips by melting the sugar over very low heat then adding the chopped almonds and stirring until the mixture turns to amber. Pour on to a well-greased baking sheet and mark into strips with an oiled knife. Lift the strips off the sheet before they harden, curl them over a rolling pin and leave to set.

Now make the cream by beating the egg yolks into the sugar and pouring on the boiling milk. Return to the saucepan and cook gently, stirring all the time, until thickening. Add the gelatine dissolved in a little hot water, the vanilla essence, grated orange rind and rum. Leave to cool, stirring occasionally. Beat the egg whites stiffly with a little sugar and fold in together with the whipped cream and any leftover bits of the caramel. Turn into a buttered mould and chill until set then unmould on to a dish and decorate with alternate strips of the caramel and little clusters of grapes. *Serves 6.*

Cerito Pudding

Presumably 'cerito' means cherry – but in what language eludes me.

8 oz (225 g) ratafias
8 oz (225 g) glacé cherries
raspberry jam
¼ pint (1.5 dl) sherry

¾ pint (4.5 dl) milk
2 oz (50 g) caster sugar
1 oz (25 g) gelatine
cream to decorate

Fill a buttered soufflé dish with alternate layers of ratafias and the halved cherries putting a layer of jam between each. Pour the sherry over and leave to soak for 30 minutes before adding the hot milk mixed with the sugar and gelatine. Leave to set in a cool place then turn out and decorate with cream before serving. *Serves 6.*

Charlotte Russe

Troublesome – but spectacular. The filling may be flavoured with coffee, chocolate, liqueur, instead of vanilla. Try also the Strawberry Bavaroise (p. 102) as a filling.

¼ pint (1.5 dl) lemon jelly
glacé cherries and angelica
8 oz (225 g) sponge fingers
¼ pint (1.5 dl) milk

6 oz (150 g) caster sugar
vanilla pod
¾ pint (4.5 dl) double cream
2 egg whites

Chill a soufflé dish and pour in the jelly. Leave to set then decorate with the cherries and angelica. Square the ends of the sponge fingers and brush the sides very lightly with egg white before standing them upright, packed tightly together, around the inside of the dish. Fill in any cracks with a paste of sponge crumbs mixed with a little jelly. Now bring the milk to the boil slowly with the sugar and vanilla pod and leave to infuse until cold. Remove the pod and stir the milk into the whipped cream and add the gelatine dissolved in a little hot water. Beat in the whisked egg whites and continue beating until thickening. Turn into the prepared dish and leave to set. Unmould to serve and tie a scarlet ribbon around it. *Serves 6.*

Coffee Ice Cream Charlotte

1 tablespoon apricot jam
20 sponge fingers
4 eggs
4 oz (100 g) icing sugar

4 tablespoons coffee syrup (p. 90)
3 tablespoons rum
½ pint (3 dl) double cream

Brush the sides of a 7 inch (18 cm) cake tin with the warmed jam. Trim the sponge fingers to the depth of the tin and fit them closely on end around the inside of the tin. Whisk the whites of egg stiffly and gradually whisk in the sifted icing sugar. Whisk the egg yolks, coffee essence and rum together then whisk gradually into the egg whites. Fold in the lightly whipped cream. Turn into the prepared tin, cover with foil and chill well. To unmould – run a palette knife carefully around the inside of the tin then dip the bottom of the tin briefly into a bowl of hot water and invert quickly on to a serving dish. May be decorated with cream and toasted almond flakes. *Serves 6.*

Crème Brûlée

Justly famous – a speciality of Trinity College, Cambridge – and worth investing in a pint of cream for occasionally.

4 egg yolks
2 oz (50 g) caster sugar
1 pint (6 dl) double cream

vanilla pod
caster sugar for top

Mix the egg yolks well with the sugar and pour on the cream, which has been brought to scalding point with the vanilla pod. Remove the pod, return to the pan and thicken very carefully over low heat, stirring constantly. Strain into a pie dish and leave overnight if possible then cover with an even layer of caster sugar, slip under a very hot grill and allow the sugar to melt and colour slightly. Chill before serving. May be served with fruit. *Serves 6.*

Crème de Noël

We always have this on Christmas Day and save the traditional pudding to follow the cold turkey and salad on Boxing Day.

2 oz (50 g) glacé cherries	3 egg yolks
2 oz (50 g) angelica	4 oz (100 g) caster sugar
2 oz (50 g) glacé ginger	1 oz (25 g) flour
2 oz (50 g) crystallized pineapple	½ pint (3 dl) milk
2 oz (50 g) mixed dried fruit	½ pint (3 dl) double cream
¼ pint (1.5 dl) sweet white wine	

Chop the fruit finely and leave to soak in the wine overnight, then strain. Whip together the egg yolks, sugar and flour. Bring the milk to the boil and whip in. Pour into a bowl over a pan of hot water and stir until thick and smooth then remove and leave until cold. Whip the cream stiffly and fold into the custard with the fruit. Pour into the freezing tray, cover with foil and freeze. *Serves 6.*

Easter Pudding

An Eastern European speciality known as Paschka which I always make at Easter – but you are allowed to make it at other times.

2 egg yolks	2 oz (50 g) butter
5 oz (125 g) caster sugar	3 oz (75 g) almonds
¼ pint (1.5 dl) double cream	3 oz (75 g) sultanas
1 lb (450 g) curd cheese	cherries and angelica

Clean up a 7 inch (18 cm) flowerpot (if earthenware, soak in cold water for 24 hours) and line it with a piece of butter muslin large enough for the edges to fold over the top. Cream the egg yolks with the sugar and stir in half the cream. Put in a bowl over a pan of boiling water until it is the consistency of a thickish custard then put to cool. Sieve the curd cheese and beat in the butter then stir in the chopped almonds and the sultanas. When the egg mixture is cool stir it into the cheese mixture and turn into the flowerpot. Fold the muslin over and cover with a saucer with a weight on top. Stand on a cake rack inside a roasting tin and leave overnight for the surplus moisture to drain out through the flowerpot hole. Turn on to a serving dish and decorate with the rest of the cream and the cherries and angelica. *Serves 6.*

Flan à la Frangipan Praliné

7½ inch (19 cm) flan case
  (cooked)
¾ oz (18 g) cornflour
¾ pint (4.5 dl) milk
4 egg yolks
caster sugar

3 oz (75 g) ground almonds
vanilla essence
4 oz (100 g) white grapes
2 oranges
1 banana
2 oz (50 g) flaked almonds

Mix the cornflour with a little of the milk then stir into the rest of the milk and bring to the boil. Cook for 2 minutes then remove from the heat and beat in the egg yolks one at a time. Add 1 oz (25 g) caster sugar, the ground almonds and a little vanilla essence, cover and leave to cool. Arrange the peeled, pipped and halved grapes, the oranges cut into segments and the sliced banana in the pastry case and spread the frangipan over them. Dust thickly with caster sugar. With a red hot skewer brand the sugar to caramelize it re-heating between each branding. Sprinkle with toasted almond flakes. *Serves 6.*

Fraises à la Créole

8 oz (225 g) strawberries
8 oz (225 g) pineapple

kirsch
sugar syrup (p. 17)

Soak the strawberries and pineapple (which can be fresh or canned) in the kirsch for 1 hour then drain, arrange in a serving dish and pour over a thickish sugar syrup well flavoured with kirsch. *Serves 4.*

Fruit Meringue Basket

You can fill this with canned fruit salad but it is much better with fresh.

4 egg whites
½ teaspoon vinegar
pinch of salt
1 teaspoon vanilla essence

6 oz (150 g) caster sugar
1½ oz (37 g) oats
½ pint (3 dl) double cream
fruit salad

Beat the egg whites with the vinegar and salt until stiff. Sprinkle in the sugar and whisk for another second then fold in the oats. Cover a baking sheet with oiled paper and pipe an oval of meringue (about 9 by 5½ inches; 23 by 14 cm) on to it to form the base of the basket sides. On another baking sheet use up all the rest of the mixture by piping small rounds a little apart. Bake at Gas Mark ¼ (225 °F, 110 °C) for 1 to 2 hours until dry and crisp then leave to cool. Transfer the basket base to an oval serving dish. Whip the cream stiffly and pipe a layer over the base then arrange the small meringues about ½ inch (1 cm) apart on top of the cream between each meringue and build up the wall this way until all the meringues are used up. Just before serving pile the very well-drained fruit salad carefully in the centre. *Serves 6.*

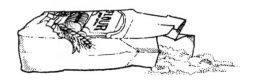

Highland Flummery

'These are two of my favourite things . . .' happily married.

½ pint (3 dl) double cream
3 oz (75 g) honey
3 tablespoons whisky

½ teaspoon lemon juice
medium oatmeal

Whip the cream until really stiff then gradually stir in the melted honey. Add the whisky and lemon juice, turn into individual glasses and sprinkle with toasted oatmeal. *Serves 4.*

Marrons à la Crème

Very rich – a little goes a long way.

2 lbs (900 g) chestnuts
8 oz (225 g) bitter chocolate
1 pint (6 dl) double cream

Nick the skin of the chestnuts and boil them for about 2 hours then skin and sieve. Just before serving mix in the grated chocolate and whipped cream. *Serves 6.*

Marrons Mont Blanc

A famous pudding. You may cheat here and use a tin of chestnut purée.

1 lb (450 g) chestnuts	1½ oz (37 g) butter
½ vanilla pod	sponge cake
milk and water	rum
2½ oz (67 g) sugar	1 egg white
¼ pint (1.5 dl) water	double cream

Peel the chestnuts (p. 30) and cook them with the vanilla pod and enough milk and water to cover them until tender. Drain very well then sieve. Boil the sugar and water to a thick syrup and beat it gradually into the chestnut purée with the butter so that a soft and pliable paste results. Break up the sponge cake and lay it in a flat glass dish. Sprinkle with rum. Fill a forcing bag with the purée and pipe round the edge of the sponge continuing round and round in layers until a low wall is formed. Add the whipped egg white to the sweetened whipped cream and spoon into the centre. May be dusted with grated chocolate before serving. *Serves 6.*

Mocha Cake

I have yet to meet anyone who doesn't positively lap this up – but few people can guess just how it is made.

3 oz (75 g) unsalted butter	¼ pint strong, sweet black coffee
3 oz (75 g) icing sugar	sponge fingers
1 egg yolk	1 oz (25 g) almonds

Warm the butter and cream it very thoroughly with the sugar beating in the egg yolk at the end. Mix in about half the coffee (cold) very gradually. Soak each sponge finger in the remains of the coffee and pack one-third of them closely side by side in a row on a serving dish. Spread with about one-third of the coffee cream then add another layer of the sponge and cream, scatter with chopped or flaked almonds and let it stand in a cool place for 24 hours. *Serves 6.*

Pavé au Chocolat

6 oz (150 g) bitter chocolate
⅛ pint (0.75 dl) strong coffee
4 egg yolks
2 oz (50 g) butter

4 tablespoons brandy
sponge fingers
double cream to decorate

Melt the chocolate in the hot coffee and stir until smooth then add the egg yolks, the butter and 2 tablespoons of the brandy. Blend well. Mix the rest of the brandy together with a little cold water. Line the base of a loose-bottom cake tin with waxed paper, dip the sponge fingers into the diluted brandy and arrange a layer of them in the bottom of the tin. Spread a layer of chocolate mixture on top and continue in layers ending with a layer of sponge fingers. Cover and chill for at least 3 hours then unmould and decorate with whipped cream before serving. *Serves 6.*

Peach Ratafias

The skin of a raw peach is like finest velvet and most fragrant, but cooked it is like wet flannel – so do take the trouble to peel them (p. 44) for this recipe.

24 ratafias
2 oz (50 g) preserved ginger
3 tablespoons white wine

3 large, ripe peaches
single cream

Place the ratafias in a bowl with the chopped ginger, cover with the wine and leave to soak for 30 minutes. Peel the peaches, halve them and remove the stones. Place each in a small glass dish, fill with the ratafia mixture and mask with single cream before serving.
Serves 6.

Pommes Castillanes

Choose hardish eating apples (e.g. Cox's) and they will remain intact and look splendid.

8 dessert apples
sugar syrup (p. 17)
4 oz (100 g) glacé fruits
rum
8 oz (225 g) plain flour

3 oz (75 g) caster sugar
6 oz (150 g) butter
1 egg
3 oz (75 g) ground almonds

Opposite Fruit Meringue Basket (*page 223*)

Core and peel the apples and poach them gently in the syrup until tender, then drain and fill with the chopped glacé fruits macerated with rum. Make an almond pastry by sifting the flour, making a well in the centre and putting in the sugar, butter, egg and ground almonds. Mix gradually into the flour until a soft paste is formed. Chill – wrapped – for at least 30 minutes then roll out, line a flan dish with it and bake blind. When cold stand the apples in it and serve coated with Sabayon Sauce (p. 214). *Serves 6 to 8.*

Raisins Ivrognes

These little pots of 'drunken grapes' covered with cream, caramelized and then chilled are out of this world.

8 oz (225 g) white grapes   ½ pint (3 dl) double cream
brandy   soft brown sugar

Peel, halve and de-pip the grapes and marinate them in the brandy. Place in individual fireproof pots and cover them with their own depth of cream. Sift some soft brown sugar on top and caramelize it under a very hot grill then ice before serving. *Serves 6.*

Raspberry Torte

5 oz (125 g) margarine   rind 1 lemon
3 oz (75 g) caster sugar   8 oz (225 g) raspberries
1 egg   sugar to taste
7 oz (175 g) plain flour   ½ oz (12 g) cornflour
2 oz (50 g) ground almonds   2 oz (50 g) sultanas

Cream the margarine and sugar together and beat in the egg. Gradually mix in the flour, ground almonds and grated lemon rind. Spread half the mixture evenly over the base of an 8 inch (20 cm) tin and add 1 to 2 teaspoons milk to the remaining mixture so that it is soft enough to use in a forcing bag. Sieve the raspberries and sweeten to taste. Blend the cornflour with a little of the cold purée then add the remaining purée. Bring to the boil, stirring continuously, and cook for 1 to 2 minutes before adding the sultanas. Spread the filling to within ½ inch (1 cm) of the edge of the torte then pipe the almond mixture around the edge and decorate with the rest. Bake at Gas Mark 6 (400°F, 200°C) for about 30 minutes. *Serves 6.*

Opposite Mincemeat Sauce (*page 212*), Fudge Sauce (*page 210*), Chocolate Sauce (*page 207*), Fresh Fruit Sauce (*page 209*)

Strawberry Shortcake

No book of puddings would be complete nowadays without a recipe for this. It can equally well be made with raspberries. Butter is a must.

6 oz (150 g) plain flour	1 lb (450 g) strawberries
6 oz (150 g) butter	icing sugar
4 oz (100 g) caster sugar	cream to decorate

Rub the butter lightly into the sieved flour, add the sugar and work together until it forms a paste. Divide into two and press each half into 7 inch (18 cm) flan tins lined with buttered and floured greaseproof paper. Smooth out with your fingertips and bake at Gas Mark 3 (325 °F, 170 °C) until only just coloured. (Don't overcook or it will be too crisp.) It only needs about 10 minutes and will still feel soft to the touch. Leave in the tins for 5 minutes before turning out. When cold cover one with whole strawberries (reserving some for decoration), sprinkle liberally with icing sugar, place the other shortcake on top. Decorate with the remaining strawberries and luscious rosettes of whipped cream. *Serves 6.*

Syllabub – Everlasting

The perfect finale to a good meal, cleansing the palate and satisfying the soul. It is beginning to be found again in really good restaurants and merits a revival. There are various recipes for it and the amounts of the different ingredients are reasonably variable. Some recipes include ratafias, some involve endless whipping. One Victorian version I read somewhere recommended milking the cow straight into the bowl to work up a good froth! Here is an altogether simpler, modern version which will, usefully, keep for a day or two without separating. To make it even more delectable substitute half a glass of brandy for the same amount of wine.

1 lemon	3 oz (75 g) caster sugar
1 wineglass white wine	½ pint (3 dl) double cream

Put the thinly pared lemon rind and the juice of the lemon into the wine and leave overnight. Next day strain the liquid into a deep bowl, stir in the sugar and whisk in the cream gradually. Whisk until the mixture stands in peaks and then pile into tall glasses. *Serves 6.*

Tipsy Cake

Trifle *par excellence* and a far cry indeed from trifle as we have come to know it nowadays. Contemporary trifle usually has fruit laid over the sponge and then liquid jelly poured over. When set it is covered in custard and, finally, cream.

8 oz (225 g) sponge cake
brandy and sherry
jam
½ pint (3 dl) rich custard (p. 209)

½ pint (3 dl) double cream
vanilla sugar to taste
almonds

Break up the sponge cake and soak it well in equal parts of brandy and sherry for an hour or two. Spread each piece with jam and arrange in a glass dish then pour over the hot custard and leave until well chilled. Whip the cream stiffly, sweeten and flavour to taste and pile it on top scattering with almonds before serving. *Serves 6.*

Zabaglione

4 egg yolks
4 oz (100 g) caster sugar
¼ pint (1.5 dl) marsala

Put all the ingredients together in a bowl over a pan of simmering water. Whisk until thick and foamy, pour into glasses and serve warm with sponge fingers. *Serves 4.*

Index of *'Any-Time' Puddings*

Time and again I seem to hear people saying, 'Oh, I can't make a pudding, there's nothing to make one of.' I challenge you to take a long, cool look at your store cupboard and refrigerator. I suspect you will almost always find there bread, milk, eggs, sugar, margarine, flour, jam, marmalade, rice, suet, dried fruit and so are able to make many of the puddings in this list. If you make a point of keeping in stock gelatine, arrowroot, brown sugar, cocoa, coffee, syrup and a lemon then you can knock up just about all of these 90 puddings at the drop of a hat.

Index for Leftovers

From time to time you will find left over in your refrigerator or pantry a cupful of egg whites or egg yolks, some pastry wrapped in polythene, stale bread and biscuits, odds and ends of sauces and juices. Waste is wicked so here are some suggestions for using them up. I am not going to pretend that you will always have the other ingredients to hand (that only applies to the Index of Any-Time Puddings) but you may think it worthwhile getting hold of a pound of apples or a bar of chocolate to create something entirely different. The French call it *'l'art de raccomoder les restes'* – and it *is* an art.

Pastry – contd.
  Empress Pudding, 134
  Lemon Pudding, 39, 195
  Orange Pudding, 199

White Sauce
  Biskotten Torte, 218
  Malvern Pudding, 40
  Mountain Pudding, 197–8

General Index of Recipes

Alma Pudding, 177
Almond
  and Date Flan, 68
  Cream, 84–5
  Cream Ice, 158
  Cream Ice – Burnt, 158
  Crisp Cherry Flan, 57
  Currant Flan, 68
  Fritters, 143–4
  Fruit Cream, 130
  Milk, to make, 87
  Pudding, 130–31, 177
  Sauce, Golden, 210
  Soufflé, 106
  Sweetmeat, 85
  to blanch, 85
Amber
Apple, 178
  Gooseberry, 34
  Jelly, 120
Angelica Tart, 57
Any-Time Cream Ice, 159
Apple
  Amber, 178
  and Blackberry Crumble, 14
  and Blackberry Pudding, 181
  and Lemon Crisp, 13
  and Orange Flan, 58
  and Rice Soufflé, 114
  Baked Pudding, 179
  Betty, 14
  Cake, Dutch, 191–2
  Cake, Modern Swedish, 15
  Caramel Pudding, 200
  Caramel Tart, 58
  Charlotte, 15
  Chausson, 16
  Cheesecake, 59
  Custard, 16–17
  Dumplings, 17
  Fritters, 144
  Hat, 178

Jelly, 120
Meringues, 17
Mousse, 85–6
Pancakes, 144
Pie, 59
Pudding – Crusty, 18
Pudding – Dutch, 18
Scotch Flan, 60
Snow, 18–19
Soufflé, 106, 116
Spiced Roll, 179
Tart – German, 60
to prevent discolouration of, 85
Torte, 180
Turnover, *see* Chausson
Water Ice, 159
Apples
  Baked, 19
  Caramelled, 19–20
  Castillanes, 226–7
  Chartreuse de Pommes, 28
  Cooked in Butter, 20
  Diana's, 20
  Gingered, 21
  in Blackcurrant Layer Pudding, 182
  in Cider, 21
  Lexington, 21–2
  Scalloped, 22
Applescotch Flan, 60
Apricot
  Cream, 86
  Fritters, 145
  Ice, 159
  Jelly, 121
  Mousse, 86
  Pancakes, 145
  Sauce, 204
  Soufflé, 106–7
  Tarte (*Bourdaloue*), 60–61
Apricots
  Baked, 22
  in Pancakes, 144